Dan Richards was born in Wales in 1982 and grew up in Bristol. He has studied at UEA and the Norwich Art School. He is the co-author of *Holloway* with Robert Macfarlane and Stanley Donwood, first published in 2012 as a limited run of 277 books – letterpress printed by Richard Lawrence in his Oxford workshop – followed by a general edition by Faber & Faber in 2013. He is also the author and editor of *The Beechwood Airship Interviews*.

Further praise for *Climbing Days*:

'A totally engaging and satisfying book on every level – as biography, memoir, travelogue and erudite meditation on the restlessness and indomitableness of the human spirit.' Andy Childs, *Caught by the River*

'Richards's image of Dorothy emerges slowly, his preconceived ideas shifting with the fragments of knowledge he gleans on his journey . . . It is these details that gradually dispel the ghost, make Dorothy tangible, present. Richards has something of Jerome K. Jerome about him.' Katharine Norbury, *Guardian*

'An affectionate portrait . . . For non-climbers, the attractions of mountaineering might seem inexplicable, but Richards conveys much of the thrill and sense of achievement.' *Sunday Times*

'Dan Richards sets out to celebrate the remarkable life of his great-gre?t ?\"   \"   In doing so,   thy

where she belongs, in the vanguard of twentieth-century trailblazers.' *World Travel Guide* 'Top Ten Holiday Reads'

'A rich and illuminating portrait of a remarkable woman.' Roger Cox, *Scotsman*

'With its roots in psychogeographical writing about landscape, this fascinating account of the life of the early twentieth-century pioneering mountaineer Dorothy Piley eschews objectivity in favour of dramatising the relationship between writer and subject, melding personal reflection and the process of historical investigation.' *TLS*

---

by the same author

HOLLOWAY
(with Robert Macfarlane and Stanley Donwood)

THE BEECHWOOD AIRSHIP INTERVIEWS

DAN RICHARDS

Climbing Days

FABER & FABER

First published in 2016
by Faber & Faber Ltd
Bloomsbury House
74–77 Great Russell Street
London WC1B 3DA
This paperback edition first published in 2017

Typeset by Faber & Faber Ltd
Printed in the UK by CPI Group (UK) Ltd, Croydon, CR0 4YY

p. 99: Excerpt from *Sombrero Fallout* by Richard Brautigan. Copyright © 1976 by
Richard Brautigan. Reprinted with the permission of the Estate of Richard
Brautigan; all rights reserved.

p. 301: 'when faces called flowers float out of the ground'. Copyright 1950, © 1978,
1991 by the Trustees for the E. E. Cummings Trust. Copyright © 1979 by George
James Firmage, from *Complete Poems: 1904–1962* by E. E. Cumming, edited by
George J. Firmage. Used by permission of Liveright Publishing Corporation.

Every effort has been made to trace or contact all copyright holders. The publishers
would be pleased to rectify any omissions or errors brought to their notice at the
earliest opportunity.

A CIP record for this book
is available from the British Library

ISBN 978-0-571-31193-4

FSC
www.fsc.org
MIX
Paper from
responsible sources
FSC® C020471

2 4 6 8 10 9 7 5 3 1

For my family and friends:
the Richards, the Pilleys and the Georges.

Contents

Hope

May 2013

I wake early and set out into the shining day with the sun still low behind Pen yr Ole Wen – Head of the White Slope – which looks a perfect pyramid from the hostel door, a child's drawing of a mountain. The peak casts a deep shadow over the western flanks of Foel-goch to the west and down Nant Ffrancon Pass ahead, but the path that I take from the Ogwen Lake climbs into the sun – a land of luminous yellows and violets – turning first to face the broken slopes of Tryfan, then sweeping round toward the Glyder massif and the bowl of Cwm Idwal.

As I walk, I pass in the shadow of huge boulders dumped by the Quaternarian glacier which scooped this valley out as it retreated down to Bangor. Monoliths stand about, silent toughs who watch me go. Charles Darwin first noted these perched rocks in 1842 on his second visit to the valley. Returning with a new perspective, having developed what he called a 'glacial eye', Darwin saw that Cwm Idwal possessed a uniquely rich testimony to the ice that had once filled it: 'a house burnt down by fire did not tell its story more plainly than did this valley.'

One hundred and seventy-one years later the rocks remain – distinct, unmoved, their ridged sides flecked with bright lichens – except now there's a well-trodden path, buffed by the thousands who pass this way each year, and the rocks are called Darwin's Boulders whereas they just *were* in the 1840s. Further on I find hawkweed and damson-coloured butterwort, sour wood sorrel growing amidst razor-haired grasses. Ogwen is also a rare southern outpost for opalescent arctic moss and alpine saxifrages.

As I reach the lakeside, the wind rises to heckle the collar of my jacket. Out on the water it swoops in bands, strafing silver ripples which track back to the shore. The landscape here is even rockier, the thin skin of plant-life barely covering the igneous alluvium beneath. The underland breaks out at my feet whilst, opposite, Y Garn soars – outworks swathed in purple scree – stone walls towering all around me, a tiny spider in a rhyolite bath.

Drizzle begins to fall as I pass through a metal gate, the warm light suddenly sucked from the day. The clouds gloom in with a startling speed, like a snap migraine. Before me, the tussocked slope steepens to form a rubble-pocked terrace, rising in irregular rucks. Above this, darker crags slide out of the white clouds which hug the ridgeline and frame the valley head; the parsley fern and mosses stalling on the sharp incline, lush greens fading through stubble to slate.

Still higher, the slopes suddenly flash up pale straw as sun breaks through the grey, the light scanning round like a compass point to settle momentarily on my destination, the Idwal Slabs or Rhiwiau Caws – 'Slopes of Cheese'. Today the slabs are a jet wedge angling down, dark grey fingers pushed into the wet earth – the rock massed and pleated, already looming massive from half a mile away.

* * * * *

I'm on the trail of my great-great-aunt, Dorothy Pilley – a prominent and pioneering mountaineer of the early twentieth century – with her 1935 memoir *Climbing Days* as my guide. The book details her time climbing in Wales, the Lakes, the Alps and North America with her husband, the literary critic and scholar Ivor Armstrong Richards ('I.A.R.'); the final chapter is an account of their celebrated first ascent of the north ridge of the Dent Blanche in 1928 – one of the last great mountaineering problems of the Alps.

'I began this book in China, being homesick for European hills,' wrote Dorothy in her *Climbing Days* preface. 'It was a substitute for climbs in Britain and the Alps. In the final stages it was only too truly a substitute; stealing away days that might have been spent high, for a low struggle with commas.'

I'd recently finished writing a book set deep in the overgrown lanes of Dorset; a collaboration with two others, inspired by Geoffrey Household's 1939 pulp thriller *Rogue Male* and the poetry of Edward Thomas. *Holloway*, as we called it, explored landscape, journeys, paths and interrelation, and left me thinking of my family tree and literary roots since the project had proved a strange and revealing way into the past. Maybe here was a means of approaching the mystery of Dorothy and I.A.R., Dorothea and Ivor; my father remembers her as 'always aunt Dorothea';* Dorothy Pilley on her book jackets; Dorothy Pilley (Mrs I. A. Richards) on the title page of *Climbing Days* – the couple whose several names had long featured in family conversation but whom nobody seemed to have known. Perhaps, in the mountains, I could meet them halfway.

---

* Although she should really have been *Great*-aunt Dorothea to my father and his brothers.

* * * * *

Without knowing it, I'd practised the close reading advocated in I.A.R.'s *Practical Criticism* throughout my secondary education, and it wasn't until I was studying English Literature at university that I began to understand his importance and contribution. At one point I had the strange experience of sitting through a lecture about him, the professor at the front dismantling Shakespearean sonnets with the semiotic toolkit I.A.R. developed at Cambridge in the 1920s.

Returning home for Christmas after my first term, I discovered other of his books: *The Meaning of Meaning* and *Mencius on the Mind: Experiments in Multiple Definition*, unread and shelved away, publishers' 'With Compliments' slips still crisp between their pages. First editions given during their stopovers and kept like talismans. Beside them sat *Climbing Days* – Dorothy Pilley, London: G. Bell & Sons Ltd, 1935 – bound in Munsell green cloth. In place of a 'With Compliments' slip I found a copy of I.A.R.'s poem 'Hope – To D.E.P. in hospital for a broken hip' folded up and tucked inside the dust jacket. By whom? I never knew, but I rescued all three books and set them on my bedroom desk and there they rested, occasionally grazed but mostly neglected. It wasn't until I had cause to make a trip to Snowdonia of my own – to visit the sculptor David Nash in Blaenau Ffestiniog – that, recalling the early pages of *Climbing Days*, I made a point of sitting down to read it through, together with Roger Deakin's *Wildwood*, in preparation for the trip.

Exploring *Climbing Days*, I began thinking that, were I not related to Dorothy – had I just stumbled upon her writing by chance – my feelings about the book might be quite different. I'd have probably just taken the writing at face value and enjoyed the escapades, but the fact Dorothy was a peripheral and mysterious presence coloured her words. I.A.R., for instance, turns up early on and is described as lean, athletic and logical in his approach, calm and agile: often seeming to choose footholds 'up round his ears'. Dorothy is factual rather than fervent in her descriptions of him and whilst there's definite admiration there are few hints of a relationship developing. Friends, comrades, the sort to use last names and punch each other on the arm, although, after they've scaled Hope together, she writes that 'all through the winter' I.A.R. sent her drawings of the cliffs above with new suggestions for attempts. A correspondence had been established away from Wales: Pilley in London, Richards in Cambridge.

But exultant language is reserved for the mountains, and events beyond their border are touched upon rarely; as if Dorothy enters a state of suspended animation at Bangor railway station, resigning herself to a sepia spell, truly living only during 'odd weekends whenever I could fit them in, framed between night journeys in which the endless serried lights of Crewe shunting-yards seemed the great gateway to the hills'.

So I resolved to visit Snowdonia early in 2013 but had to postpone several trips in the face of high winds and snow. The bad weather wore on over Easter, when temperatures on the high ground fell to minus twenty degrees Celsius and thirty-foot drifts shrouded Snowdon, smothering the valleys below for many weeks – the worst winter for sixty years.

It was May before I reached North Wales, and dark when I got to the Idwal Cottage hostel, but I awoke next morning to a clear sky and the dubbin smell of boots. I spoke to the hostel manager over breakfast and explained my expedition. He was enthusiastic and knew the names of many climbs founded by the pair; climbs with names like Lazarus, Holly Tree Wall and Hope – and that was good to hear because it was Hope, 'Hope – To D.E.P. in hospital for a broken hip', which had drawn me to Idwal. Having helped establish the route with Mrs E. H. Daniell in 1915, both Dorothy and Ivor wrote of it, first in *Climbing Days* and then, much later, in 'Hope'.

I see an aged I.A.R. working on 'Hope', reaching back to the sure-footed agility of years past, his lines nimble, the poem flowing with an assured fluency – deft tribute to a cherished place and partner.

Hope

My dear: Wales has a slab
Named Hope – a tall, buff, tilting thing.
It listens, these late centuries,
To querulous, lost, impatient lambs
And the ambiguous sheep
Conversing through the mist.
There, leading, one cool Spring,
Rope out, the holds glare ice,
You found your pocket scissors:
                stab by stab
Picked enough clear, floated on up.
                     I keep
A memory of that for other jams:
You immaterialist,
Who know when to persist.

Recall the Epicoun:
Night, welling up so soon,

Near sank us in soft snow.
At the stiff-frozen dawn,
When Time has ceased to flow,
– The glacier ledge our unmade bed –
I hear you through your yawn:
'Leaping crevasses in the dark,
That's how to live!' you said.
No room in that to hedge:
A razor's edge of a remark.[1]

* * * * *

At close quarters the slabs are splashed with zebra quartz striation, daubed like a gannet stack, its slashed diagonals misleading the eye like the dazzle camouflage of battleships,

Llyn Ogwen,
May 2013
(Dan Richards)

an analogy which holds truer the nearer I get as the cliffs hove up gigantic. Above me on the polished scarp, two figures hug the rock, bright beetles in red helmets, blue rope trailing. The leader, apparently impervious to the downpour, edges up a flake; pale hands searching for holds ahead, radiating concentration as he tries to decipher the slab. Below him, his partner, a younger girl, watches on, paying out the line as fat raindrops din on the crag and my coat.

Slowly ascending, body taut, the leader disappears from my view – lost inside a sloping cleft, the blue trail the only clue he's there until, with a shout, the rope grows tight and the pitch is set. The girl begins to follow, gingerly ascending, shifting her weight from hand to foot, jamming an elbow to pivot on a knee, stealing higher in the skiddy cracks until she too vanishes, slack rope snaking after her, and I'm left alone in the white noise of the rain.

* * * * *

Dorothy doesn't describe her walk to the foot of every climb. For her, such journeys are a proem to an object, a prelude. But she often sketches her immediate view, the feelings inspired and the climbing available, with brilliant alacrity: 'When I got out of the car from Bangor – for the first of how many times? – the mountain seemed to hang over our heads . . . Tryfan, the grim guardian of the upper Nant Ffrancon, the rockiest peak south of the Tweed and the only Welsh mountain that cannot be climbed without using the hands.'

Dorothy's landscapes are always rooted and contextualised by the attendant ascent, shaped by her enthusiasm for that challenge, the path a precursor to the pitch. As a walker, for the time being at least, I am in the same position as the young Pilley. 'The climber', she writes, 'speaks generally of "going up Snowdon" when he follows the zigzags of the path, and "climbs" only when he uses his hands as well as his feet.' Touch-paper lit, passion kindled, she's atop Tryfan leaping from Adam to Eve by page four – '"Mountain madness" has me now for ever in its grasp' – hungry for thrills, giddy for the camaraderie of those few who shared her newly discovered passion, the peaks and cliffs taking on 'something of the place that a university might hold for others'.

The first chapter of *Climbing Days*, 'Initiation', reveals an ardent young woman at a loss, seeking definition, determined to escape a cycle of social expectation. Climbing was to be her saviour, both a revelation and revolution, and *Climbing Days* is a record of discovery and a concerted effort to secure a foothold in this new domain – written in thrall to the possibilities Snowdonia afforded. Post-Tryfan she was charged and changed for ever. So it is here that I have come, with *Climbing Days* as guide, visiting Snowdonia much as Nan Shepherd – Dorothy's great contemporary and fellow mountaineer – describes visiting the Cairngorms 'as one visits a friend, with no intention but to be with him'. I am here to visit Dorothy and I.A.R., following them up this track at a distance of ninety years with no intention other than to be here, as they were.

* * * * *

Climbing Days and 'Hope' painted a very different portrait of the couple from the vague stories I'd been told, growing up. I was born too late to know my great-great-aunt and uncle. They existed in published books of letters and poetry that nobody seemed to have read and occasional anecdotes when my father recalled them as elderly, contained and otherworldly;

the pair arriving at his already crowded childhood home bearing exotic gifts from far-flung places, expecting to be entertained and driven to appointments, apparently oblivious that 'other people had to work'. Pressed further he admitted to finding Dorothea 'terrifying', recollecting that she and I.A.R. always pitched up with a vast amount of hats and sticks, after which the children would be presented, 'like a Royal visit'.

He remembers standing in the garden as the car arrives. My father is seven years old, lined up with his brothers. Great-aunt Dorothea emerges from the house with I.A.R. – mysterious and striking, dark hair in winding plaits about her ears. The three boys know that these are important visitors, academics. Famous, although they're not sure why. There's been talk of books and climbing but it all seems so incredible in light of these two impossibly elderly people, advancing now with their sticks. My father tries to picture them climbing the stairs in the house and his mind skips to an image of an impossible staircase, big as a mountain, an Everest of stairs like he's seen in *A Matter of Life and Death* ... but he blinks and smiles to shake their papery hands and waits with the shy confidence of a child who knows there will be presents because he's seen the packages behind Great-uncle Ivor's back.

Recently returned from America, another impossible idea, the pair talk quietly with the children in an atmosphere of reverence. The sense of formal occasion is such that, when the act of gift giving takes place, it resembles nothing so much as the presentation of prizes at a fête or Victores Ludorum at a sports day.

After Dorothea and Ivor disappear back into the house, the boys still stand in line, stunned, turning the presents – a cap gun with its red leather cartridge belt, the Davy Crockett hat with real raccoon tail, and the bow and quiver of sharp

Dorothy Pilley,
c.1922 (RCM)

arrows – over in their hands. Impossible trophies: the sort of dangerous and exciting presents given by people who don't have children of their own.

The first picture I ever saw of Dorothy was a posed shot which seemed to give little away, a face amongst other Edwardian faces. Timeless, serious and distant. Old. But old in a very different way from my father's memories; old in the way that pictures of football teams from that era, despite being composed of young men, show faces that are older than you'll ever be. Hewn landscapes at the age of thirty. She's glamorous, certainly, with ivory skin, her gaze seeming to glide left beyond the camera and out of shot. Hair a tad dishevelled, a deep fur collar. The gown she wears has an academic air, the thin V of the neckline diving down to a silver brooch. All so buttoned up at first glance; an airless picture. The caption reads: 'Dorothy Pilley, Secretary of the British Women's Patriotic League, c.1922'. She was twenty-eight years old. My great-great-aunt, two years younger than I am now.

But looking again at the photograph, having read *Climbing Days* – I do often, the shot now pinned up beside where I write – I see that her head is held proud and she smoulders, amorous and challenging, her lips slightly parted on the cusp of a smile, her eyes playful but steely. Transplanted onto a mountain, or to a bar or running for a train, freed from the silver nitrate square, she possesses great possibilities of fun and explosive energy. The picture leads me on to imagine the several seconds either side of this frozen moment, the laughter which had to be stifled so the shot could be taken, the itchiness of that collar, the restless hands in her lap. I sense the desperation to get out of the stuffy studio and back out into the fresh air, or anywhere else for that matter – the same desperation that, years later, led my teenage father and his brothers to play the Who VERY LOUDLY at another family gathering in an attempt to jolt an elderly Dorothea and I.A.R. into 'some sort of emotional response'.

How had this happened? Had she mellowed with age and become the very thing she'd so rebelled against? I saw that I had no idea who Dorothy really was. She remained beyond reach, ambiguous, a divided personality, her life split into two distinct acts, the young elemental 'Pilley' who wrote *Climbing Days*, and the elderly lady who appeared sporadically in my father's childhood, dispensing lethal gifts, amalgamate of I.A.R. But that line recurred:

'Leaping crevasses in the dark,
That's how to live!' you said.

Even in later years, in hospital with a broken hip, D.E.P. was still one who left no room to hedge: still recognisably the author of that razor's edge remark.

I couldn't help but read *Climbing Days* with a forensic eye, looking for the writer in the writing – which should have been easy enough; it was, after all an autobiography – but Dorothy kept shifting, avoiding my eye, the narrative constantly switching tenses, viewpoints and locales; soaring, alighting, dwelling, darting elsewhere. I couldn't make her out. There seemed so much unsaid or, perhaps, I wanted something more than the text could give.

I couldn't just enjoy the book like a civilian, it threw up too many questions. But here, again, I found that 'Hope', the more I read it, felt like a way into the pair's relationship and work – a Richards/Pilley Rosetta Stone; an isthmus between the two apparently disparate figures. Here was Dorothy as I.A.R. saw her, revelling in the wildness of her element: freed to be herself in the mountains which were to be the fulcrum to their partnership – a watershed for Dorothy and a healing force for the pulmonary tuberculosis which cast a shadow over I.A.R.'s early life. Here they delighted in the harsh topography which tested and matched their vastly different temperaments – Dorothy's frenetic energy counterpoint to I.A.R.'s logic and precision – specifically the Ogwen Valley, the place where they first met, the situation which drew them together.

As some walk or swim to think – the act fulfilling as much a cerebral as physical role – so climbing, for Pilley, keyed into her soul. She was a climber, first and foremost, an amazing thing to be at that time.

'Dorothea was an immensely strong-willed woman, determined to get her own way,' writes Dr Richard Luckett in the introduction to *Selected Letters of I. A. Richards*. 'Her inclination to be a great lady went with an equal and opposite desire to be off with the raggle-taggle gypsies.'

The mountains were her true domain, anathema to London, egalitarian and feral; satisfying needs untouched by her family, work and social life: 'How the contrast shook one!' she writes at the end of Chapter 2.

To go back to gloves and high heeled shoes, pavements and taxicabs. Walking with an umbrella in Piccadilly one felt as though, with a little more strain, one could become a divided personality. This time yesterday! One lay munching a dry sandwich on a rocky ledge, plucking at a patch of lichen and listening to the distant roar of the white Ogwen Falls . . . Kind, firm friends would say, 'All good things come to an end', or 'You can't expect all life to be a holiday'. But to me, and to climbers before and after me, this was no question of holidays. It went down into the very form and fabric of myself.

Of her childhood and the period between the end of *Climbing Days* and the beginning of my father's remembrance I knew nothing. Her life seemed strangely front-loaded – *Climbing Days* emerging as a lone work of disclosure amidst intriguing fragments such as the succinct biography which prefaces *Selected Letters*:

RICHARDS, DOROTHY ELEANOR (1894–1986)

The daughter of a strict father (a science teacher at Alleyn's College, Dulwich), Dorothy achieved her independence by climbing mountains, writing for newspapers, and working as a secretary for the proto-feminist British Women's

Patriotic League. Her looks and vivacity ensured her the many suitors she periodically repulsed as threats to her hard-won liberty. Ivor Richards (whom she met in Wales in 1917 and married in Honolulu on 31 Dec. 1926), though a special case, had not only her disinclination to overcome, but her family's as well. The Pilleys were well-to-do part-owners of a firm manufacturing baby food, and did not believe that a young don could support their daughter. The marriage was an exceptionally happy one.

Dorothy Richards's account of their climbing days together up to 1928 (*Climbing Days* – London, 1935; 2nd edition, London, 1965) is a classic of its kind, and her significance as a pioneer of women's climbing is well recognised.

She merits a biography.

I didn't want to write a biography.

So there, again, I let it rest, relieved.

But I did want to understand her, and her need for the mountains, and the broader question of how we are formed by certain strong landscapes. And the character of 'Hope' still loitered and my mind continued wandering for the next few years . . . and it was during this time that I began reading mountain literature – not for any particular reason, I told myself – but the pile of books beside my bed began to spiral: *I Chose to Climb* by Chris Bonington, *The Living Mountain* by Nan Shepherd, *Into Thin Air* by Jon Krakauer, *Coronation Everest* by Jan Morris, *The Hard Years* by Joe Brown, *Climbing with Joseph Georges* by Dorothy E. Thompson[2] . . . and then, one day, I began rereading *Climbing Days* whilst making pencil notes in the margins, a map of Snowdonia unfolded on the table beside me.

I would go to the mountains.

Cambridge

June and July 2013

But first I went to Rye on the South Coast marshes – a town
set in a remarkably flat part of Sussex – to meet Dr Richard
Luckett, former Pepys Librarian of Magdalene College,
Cambridge, and a great friend of the Richardses in their later
years, a friendship he sketches in the introduction to *Selected
Letters of I. A. Richards*.[1] After retiring from Magdalene he
moved down to Rye and now he welcomes me to his home
with great zest and cordiality.

It turns out we have a friend in common in Robert
Macfarlane – travel writer, mountaineer, Emmanuel fellow and my *Holloway* co-author. 'Yes, I lent him the letters
found on Mallory's body,' explains Richard in a tone which
implies this is quite normal Cambridge interaction. 'He
asked me about getting copies of the letters and I said,
look, it would be much easier to lend him the letters
themselves.'

Were they in a good state? I ask, intrigued.

'Oh yes! marvellous. If you wanted to make the best
library in the world you would build it on top of Everest;
humidity down to nothing, absolutely optimum – yes,
they could have been written yesterday. And he'd just
put them in the pocket of his tweed jacket, with his pipe,
and other things – which actually Magdalene ought to

have but we don't, unfortunately.'*

I tell him how much I enjoyed his *Selected Letters* introduction and he seems pleased, if slightly embarrassed. 'Well,
of course, I was trying to account for a very odd thing; why
a musical historian should be diverted into something . . . I
mean, it was ten years out of my life, really. Not wasted, no;
just different!' He laughs.

Sat next to a harpsichord which fills most of the room, he
describes how he first met Dorothea and Ivor in April 1976
whilst researching for a PhD at St Catharine's College,
Cambridge. Ivor had been invited to give a lecture to the college's Shirley Society, the oldest literary society in the university, but opted to read his poetry instead. After the reading he
and Dorothea attended drinks in Richard's attic lodgings, at
the top of seventy-two steps. It was the climb that attracted
them, more than the offer of whisky, reckons Richard. Once
there, the company were held spellbound by Dorothea's stories of screes, dysentery and Sherpas on an abortive expedition to explore the flanks of K2, after which I.A.R. spoke, *to
the vast astonishment of most of those present*, about Swinburne.

The introduction was the first time he'd written about
his relationship with the pair, he explains, an attempt to
frame them on a domestic level rather than as an intellectual
whole. He appears apologetic about this but I reassure him
that it's precisely this approach which I like about it, the
personal insights and interactions.

---

* Richard went on to say that the missing items are currently in New York
with the chap, Simonson, who led the expedition: 'He did return the letters
but he didn't grasp that the rest of the things were not his property but the
Mallory family's so, unfortunately, we haven't been able to get them back;
though they're technically Mallory property and the Mallorys have given
them to Magdalene. It's a sorry story . . .'

That's exactly what I'm after, I tell him.

'Oh right!' he says, all enthusiasm. 'I didn't know. I hadn't grasped the angle at all.'[2]

I tell Richard the story of the brothers attempting to jolt and shock Ivor and Dorothea by playing them 'Baba O'Riley' by the Who, and Richard laughs and laughs.

'Oh dear!' he says, wiping his eyes. 'Oh dear, well, first of all, you see, Ivor was tone-deaf. I've never understood that but it's absolutely true and, actually, also true of Yeats! It wasn't true of Eliot, who was very keen on music, but Yeats: music meant nothing to him and yet, when you read his poetry, the music within that is absolutely truthful.

'Now, one of the points on which Ivor and Dorothea would never have agreed was music. Dorothea even tried to play the violin . . . God knows . . . Sorry, ha ha! But music to Ivor meant nothing. I mean it was quite literally a case of it being "God Save the Queen" because other people stood up! That was the way he could tell. In a funny sort of way Ivor was completely ahistorical; though he was completely up to date with the contemporaneous in poetry, he wasn't really interested in what was contemporaneous generally. The fact that the Who was modern music wouldn't actually have meant anything to him at all . . . it wasn't where he lived, *mentally*, I mean.'

It's amazing to think that Ivor wrote books about aesthetic perception whilst music remained a mystery: like writing an RAC manual whilst unable to drive, I told him. Richard agreed: Ivor wrote books about communications, television and its effects but never possessed a television in his life. He never possessed a radio: 'It was just that he wasn't interested. Not interested *at all*. In fact it's quite remarkable. I think he barely gave a radio talk in his life.'

Ivor was interested in the mechanics below the bonnet of aesthetics, said Richard, the workings of literature, art and theatre but not the performative aspects. He didn't need to see it raced, but Dorothea was always dragging him to art exhibitions despite this, he remembers. 'She even, with gratuitous cruelty, dragged him to concerts.'

A protesting Ivor being dragged to see culture by Dorothea is a fun image to mull, dragged reluctantly for fifty years – characters in a play that Ivor would never have gone to see. What excited and engaged Ivor, instead, was experience of the natural world; 'standing on a lesser Rocky looking at a higher Rocky,' as Richard put it; 'or Shakespearian tragedy; but there wasn't any way that he could *do* Shakespearian tragedy by proxy.'

I ask Richard what the pair's dynamic together was like when he knew them, towards the end of their lives, and mention my father's view that whilst they seemed inseparable, they were not like any married couple he'd ever known – more like devoted companions.

'That is an extraordinarily perceptive comment, absolutely dead on. That's how I would put it, yes. Totally devoted.' But he queries the idea of social awkwardness, rolling the idea around a while, repeating the phrase to himself. 'Social awkwardness. Well, was it a sort of social awkwardness? I think Ivor always felt, however much it might not have seemed so to your father, quietly at home with the family. I think we might put any atmosphere down to, well . . . I think he might possibly have been slightly on edge as to what Dorothea might do next.'

She had form in that area?

'Well, she had . . . Yes, I don't know anybody who encountered her who wasn't alarmed in some way. But it's difficult to put your finger on it. Not socially but, as I say, you never quite knew what she might do next."*

She could make people uneasy?

'Yes.'

Her raggle-taggle gypsy nature?

'Yes, or, having had a drink or two, "Hallelujah, I'm a bum!"' He laughs. 'She was capable of outrageous behaviour . . . but I should say, and this is important: whilst she was aware of what she could do, she was quite incapable of using it for manipulative or controlling effect. In other words, she was perfectly aware that she might shock and surprise people but she never used it . . . by which I mean, she wasn't one of these wretched people who would do something fully aware of the effect and then attempt to draw back and say, "Oh dear, what did I do that for?"'

So Ivor was very steady in that respect.

'Ivor was totally steady, yes. He put up with a great deal – I mean, to read the account of the dance that she led him across America, to the Rockies, finally to marriage in Honolulu . . . amazing story.

'Janet Adam Smith once said to me, "Of course, Ivor was a saint." And Janet didn't use religious terms lightly. I remember her saying that to me after Ivor died.

'One absurdly agonising thing was that Ivor was agnostic, I don't think he was an atheist but an agnostic – he may

---

* A couple of months after this chapter was written my father remembered an incident when Dorothea threw several pieces of toast out of a window one breakfast-time. Her objection was that my grandmother made such shatteringly brittle Aga toast that she found it inedible but, rather than flag the issue, Dorothea began to surreptitiously fling it out a nearby window, giggling to herself. Problem solved. 'To be fair to Dorothea, it was awful,' confirmed my mother. 'As soon as you approached it with a buttered knife, it shattered into splinters.'

have felt a moral obligation to go to plays with Dorothea but he would draw certain lines. He would never set foot in Magdalene chapel – and therefore getting him buried was difficult because the order of service had to be devised but the word "God" could not appear. I remember going down to London for Dorothea and trying to find Rationalist burial services – which of course are absolutely dreadful . . . Dorothea was a litmus paper for what was bad, you know? She could tell you at once. She couldn't tell you what was good or how it could be improved; but she'd say, "No, this wouldn't go, it simply would not do." Eventually I devised a series of readings and poems about death which didn't mention God and stuck these together so they made a kind of service; something you could read in the crematorium. And it seemed to work but Dorothea was absolutely superb at digging in her heels and saying, "No, it wouldn't do."'

Without offering any alternative, I suggest, and he laughs.

'Exactly. Yes.'

Richard has diaries of his own which cover that period, he tells me.

'The way I thought of it was that Dorothea was quite literally my nearest neighbour. I lived in the Pepys building and she lived at the bottom of the garden. As I used to say, "There are furies at the bottom of my garden!"'

* * * * *

My bridge into the lives of Dorothea and Ivor is formed of their writings and the remembrance of people who knew them. When I mentioned that I was writing this book a lot of people responded, 'Oh, right!? *Practical Criticism* in the

mountains?' and I would smile and think, 'Oh dear, that
sounds like a terrible idea . . .' and then worry what I was to
do – because, bluntly, a lot of people have heard of I. A.
Richards and few have heard of Dorothy Pilley.

I needed to confront this obstacle, clear the academic bar-
ricade which 'I. A. Richards' seemed to represent.

There seemed very little point in approaching Ivor and
Dorothea from an academic slant because that wasn't their
world. It was Ivor's world. Dorothea wasn't an academic
and my focus on *Climbing Days* pointed towards the climbing overlap in their interests; a climbing *angle*, to use Dr
Luckett's word.

The key thing was for me to be present in the story and
go forward rather than forever looking back. It had to be a
journey. Ivor famously disliked autobiographical writing
and agreed to a biography only on the proviso that it examined his life through the prism of his work. Describing himself as 'fundamentally an inventor', he saw the story of his
life as supplemental to his inventions – even to the extent
that he expressed regret in later years for having spent so
much time climbing mountains. So, strange as it may sound,
in writing about such a man, the last thing I wished to do
was get too involved with academia, because that part of
Ivor's life had already been written about at length by better
attuned, more studious minds than mine.*

I had a fairly solid grounding in *Practical Criticism* from
my university days and my memories of the book centred
on the excitement and insight afforded by redaction.

---

* Frank Kermode has written that Ivor 'liked best to start a book and then,
writing with great speed, find out what the book wanted to be'. When I
discovered that, I determined to do likewise, albeit slower. Frank Kermode,
'Educating the Planet', *London Review of Books*, vol. 2, no. 5 (20 March 1980).

Remove the names, the dates, the clues, mine down to the words on the page, the raw impersonal materials, afresh and unaffected. Wasn't the deployment of anonymity I.A.R.'s primary feat?

Ivor's official biographer, John Paul Russo, succinctly explains this quandary:

> In 1912 Richards told his history supervisor Frank Salter, that he 'didn't think history ought to have happened.' In 1974 in the Clark Lectures he told his audience the same thing. Another time, privately, he said that he 'hated the past' for its suffering and cruelty and always looked ahead, 'even now' (1972). So Richards 'turned by accident to philosophy' because he 'couldn't bear history.' This deep conviction left its imprint on his criticism, with its rejection of the heavy backgrounding of works of art in historical periods and his antipathy to personal memoir and biography.[3]

Russo's *I. A. Richards: His Life and Work*, where this passage appears, is not the sort of book which invites casual investigation from a layman.[4] The trouble really started when my copy arrived and was twice as thick as the letterbox. It weighed 1.4 kg, the weight of the average adult brain. I'd like to think my brain was average but several months with Russo's book made me question that. As an intellectual biography it succeeded on two fronts, revealing Ivor's intellectual brilliance whilst making me feel fairly thick.

Early on there are some brilliant passages – stories of school and Ivor's boyhood – but then the book hits Cambridge and, shortly after, Cambridge rather hits the book. Ivor is there but submerged beneath scholarship, the narrative so cerebrally loaded at times that it reminded me of a floating head in a vitrine – as if the man went out the window once the heavy lifting of academia began. The world reduced in scope to university life.

It's clear that Russo's aim is to elucidate the work: celebrate its genus, evolution, form and function. That's where his interest lies, and that may have been what Ivor wanted from the book, but the result is that the domestic is often squeezed – Ivor's meeting and early relationship with Dorothea is covered on two thirds of page 48, for example, along with the First World War – and whilst the writing flows when discussing 'the work', the life in between is sometimes delivered in a brusque tone, like a harassed teacher thrashing out a school report the night before a parents' evening:

> In the Welsh mountains, in 1917, Richards was introduced to his future wife, Dorothy Eleanor Pilley[5] ... A vivacious, strong-minded and competent individual of liberal sympathies, she had decided upon a career in journalism when she met Richards. She had also taken up rock climbing. It is fitting that their long partnership began in the rugged hills, because mountaineering was their lifelong enthusiasm. Pilley became one of the great sportswomen in the history of British mountaineering.[6]

Throughout *I. A. Richards: His Life and Work* I was acutely aware that Russo was going to great lengths to clarify and contextualise Ivor's thought but, I'm afraid, by page 100 and a labyrinthine section on Synaesthesis, my arms and brain were aching from the book's weight. I began to think, 'Blimey, how long was he alive?' And 'I wonder if

Dorothea ever read this all the way through . . .' because I'm not sure even Dorothea would have been so fascinated by Ivor that she'd have read 850 pages of tightly set print about him, perhaps even less so Ivor himself.*

I knew I was in danger of getting overawed and completely lost in an epistemological maze for want of a plan. I wanted to know what Ivor was like but this book made that seem a somewhat lightweight quest. So, thoroughly intimidated, tired and worried, I was relieved to discover K. E. Garay's review of *I. A. Richards: His Life and Work*, which revealed that I was not alone in these thoughts. Whilst she praises Russo for a 'substantial, skillful and scholarly example of intellectual biography' which explores the contours of Richards' mind and deftly 'places his ideas within their intellectual framework', Garay suggests that 'for all its brilliance and richness this work does not fully succeed as a life': 'Richards the Welsh Wizard, at once the skilled practitioner and implacable foe of "word magic"; Richards the

---

* I was later to discover exactly what Dorothy thought of it when I listened to a tape-recorded conversation she had with her nephew, Anthony, in Cambridge in 1985: 'I'm having a terrible amount of correspondence with people who want to come and visit Magdalene and see the manuscripts about Ivor and then his student, Jean-Paul [*sic*] Russo, who's written an autobiography, which is now going to be published by Kegan Paul; he's worked on it for five years and it's been very hard work . . . And he's done the thing that I think one should never do, as an old journalist, and that's give them much more material than they can use, so that's the question, should they cut it, or should he cut it? And he wrote and told me he's sending 750 pages, seven hundred and fifty! And he thinks there's going to be about a thousand, which is a ridiculous length – a sort of whole history of English. Ivor didn't want him to put in mountaineering and all of that and I'm sorry now that I stopped Ivor doing a most amusing thing on adventures. He wrote about three chapters. He was always against it and I sort of agreed. But I'm very sorry now he didn't, because all those adventures you know, as I get older they get more and more like faded photographs.'

intrepid mountaineer, scaler of heights and obstacles, physical and emotional as well as intellectual; Richards the teacher, friend and husband; Richards the man, has escaped the searching gaze of his biographer and one cannot but imagine him smiling.'[7]

But here, again, was a way into my book. I should attempt to explore those areas mentioned only in passing, details fallen through the cracks. Everything flagged by Garay as missing, I would seek to find: *Ivor the intrepid mountaineer, scaler of heights and obstacles, dynamic, physical and emotional; Ivor the teacher, raconteur, friend and husband; Ivor the man that Dorothea knew and loved. The man in* Climbing Days.

My hope was to find him in diaries, letters, scrapbooks, papers and articles housed in the Pepys Library at Cambridge. I would go in with an open mind and look at his life, intertwined with Dorothea's, from the holistic stance of a relative climber. I planned to circumvent academia, literally climb outside it.

Things improved once I got on to the roof of Magdalene College.

* * * * *

Ivor first arrived at Magdalene from Clifton in 1911, aged eighteen, to study History. A photograph of him from the time shows a gentle owlish youth with a generous mouth and distant eyes. As with so many posed pictures of the type, he sits in front of darkness, emerging from the void as if riding a singularly uneventful ghost train. There he sits, looking a little awkward, brimful of self-belief and doubt, oscillating potential – a boy new to Cambridge, idealistic, dreamy and fired, who writes perfervid letters home full of plans to found a new society; utopian treatises addressed to his mother, 'Little Owlie'.

A. C. Benson, Master of Magdalene, notes in his diary of 9 November 1911:

The point is that Richards, an able fellow and exhibition freshman, declares himself an Anarchist. He says he won't take up any profession, or accept any payment by Government. He means to till a plot of land and teach non-resistance. He's a silly boy with a mixture of Shelley and Carpenter. Meanwhile he makes no sacrifices, uses the ordinary comforts and securities, and holds these doctrines. He wants to change his Tripos: he can't bear History because it is the record of Government. And that is all immoral.

Shortly after this existential skirmish, Ivor moved over to Moral Sciences, suffered a serious attack of pulmonary tuberculosis and was taken away by his mother to convalesce on Dartmoor's sweeping warm-wet uplands. He did not return to Cambridge until the autumn of 1913, having spent the interim reading anything and everything he could find and, whenever possible, climbing. Later he'd say that his years of remote recuperation were central to the formation of his character and career, claiming he'd emerged 'out of books, any old books'.

A picture I have from 1915 finds him taller, stood on a chair, second back left of a Cambridge Moral Science Club group shot. Hands clasped behind his back, shoulders slack, suit front rumpled – he seems to have graduated from owl to awkward heron, grown into a diffident, faintly wry fellow, dark-orbed, gaunt, not yet a man. Traces of illness still attend his whey face. There's something of John Le Mesurier in his posture. He meets the camera's eye soft-faced; a slightly smiling, even gaze where others in the three rows challenge, squint or look away. The picture may turn about Bertrand Russell sat sunny and jovial in the centre row, but Ivor hovers – sleepy face topped with frazzled hair, mussed, anglepoise, peripheral but present amongst the philosophers, teachers and student thinkers – a world away from the war.

By this point, Russo writes, Ivor had already made several successful night climbs of the chimneys and towers of Magdalene as well as other colleges. 'In his last year he moved into rooms on the top floor over the main gate, making the roofs of Magdalene easy for access. In a photograph journal, *Magdalene College Roofs and Climbs*, he captured the mood of the suspenseful nights of 1915: "lights out everywhere in expectation of a Zeppelin raid."'[8]

It's one of very few references to the First World War that I've found in relation to Ivor. A memory recalled and transcribed sixty years later, in Ivor's final decade, for a book that would be published ten years after he died.

In Rye I ask Richard if Ivor wrote about the war in his diaries of the time.

'Oh, there is a huge confusion about this,' he tells me, leaning forward in his seat and suddenly reminding me of Desmond Llewelyn's Q.* 'Now, this is terribly important because it's a major confusion regarding I.A.R. Everything I could find in Wentworth House – where they retired to in Cambridge – every scrap of paper that was complete is preserved at Magdalene. There's a room in the Old Library which has their archive in it and it's almost all catalogued, so

* Desmond Wilkinson Llewelyn (1914–99) was a Welsh actor who played Q in seventeen James Bond films between 1963 and 1999.

that is all safely there, but I.A.R.'s diaries . . . there *are* I.A.R. diaries but they are Cambridge pocket diaries, just notes and engagements, and they're completely unrevealing unless you really know the circumstances.

'Dorothea's diaries predate her acquaintance with Ivor, they start in 1912 and they go on right until a couple of weeks before she died. They are also at Magdalene and they are a full record but some of them are in Ivor's handwriting. This is because, when she couldn't keep them, she asked him to keep them for her but they're not his diaries; but John Haffenden in his *Life of William Empson*[9] – it's very important, you must read it – mentioned "Ivor's diaries", which has led to huge confusion.'

He sits back, exasperated and crestfallen that it should be so. In the moment of silence which follows I review this unexpected news: *Ivor kept no diaries of his own but sometimes wrote Dorothea's for her, from her point of view* – an anomalous quirk in his slash-and-burn approach to biography.

'But you asked about the war, the first war,' Richard breaks back in. 'It's very strange but it always used to remind me of *To the Lighthouse*. Do you know it? If you remember, the whole of the war is put in parentheses, literally so, so you've got just those thirty pages in which nothing actually happens but there are descriptions of nothing happening and that's the war for the Ramsay family. That always struck me as being very much the same as the Richardses.'

* * * * *

Magdalene College Roofs and Climbs was one of the first arte-facts I requested to see the morning I arrived at the college, together with the pair's collected passports because I knew

Passport photographs, *c.*1931 (Pilley Family archive)

they'd be a graphic record of their travels. I suspected the diaries would take time to assimilate, to develop an eye for the handwriting – at first glance both hands looked similar, Dorothea's a spindly knotted script, Ivor's slightly more scratchy. Dr Luckett's revelation that they'd shared diary duties identified a possible future problem. I'd need to familiarise myself with their chirography, so I asked for a couple of diaries too, almost at random; an early one, a later one, 1928 – 'The Great Year' as Dorothy described it in *Climbing Days* . . .

I began to read, sat alone in the Old Library. It was quite hard going and I stumbled through a few months, tripping on the closely-packed script. As I read, I felt the world outside retreat in the vacuum of the books tiered ten high about me. Drawing the unseen ceiling up, the weight of the room bearing down.

I read several months of one, then put it aside and began

to look at another, aware that I didn't have a plan. The pages did not smell old, as I'd expected, and something about the uniformity of the diaries, each bound in black leather with the year on the front, gave them an ageless quality. The pages turned crisply; touching them, I felt the line-braille emboss of Dorothea's pen. Her day-to-day thoughts caught up, set down.

But eventually, conscious that the diary wasn't of this place – out of context here, neither written for this room nor for me to read piecemeal but a private journal of Dorothea's everyday – I closed the books and slid the pile of passports over, a thick stack tied with black ribbon.

One in Dorothea's name was dated '31. Dec 26 HONOLULU' – the day of her marriage to Ivor. Royal blue, gold crest, dog-eared, buffed and worn with wanderlust. The photograph inside shows her washed out in bright light with pageboy hair and a white dress accentuating her neckline. 'CANCELLED' is written in red ink across the previous page, four purple stamps, and then on into page upon page of foreign stamps, franks, signatures, coral papers, parchment, 'H.B.M. Consulate Peking', 'LIETUVA', 'SUISSE', 'IMPERIAL JAPANESE LEGATION PEKING'; gummed emerald and burgundy tickets showing George V, debossed horses and coats of arms on fine-mesh watermarks, a red octagonal Chinese seal, impressed wax and ribbons. They had four passports each. One was renewed in 1955: 'BRITISH CONSULATE GENERAL NEW YORK'. Another, Dorothea's earliest, 1924, has a posed photograph, hand on her cheek, above a velvet cuff and sleeve of fabric-covered buttons. Her clothes are reminiscent of a naval rig, the picture debossed 'FOREIGN OFFICE' – a proud lion and unicorn covering her signature: 'D. E. Pilley'. Set for travel. Egypt,

Republiky Československá, vertical shupai and tategaki.

Ivor's final picture shows him squashed in a photo booth somewhere – the blinds the same colour and texture as his tie. How handsome he was in 1931. The most handsome I've seen him – Clark Kent-esque:

Profession: Lecturer

Place and date of birth: Sandbach, Cheshire / 26th February, 1893

Domicile: England

Height: 5 ft. 9 ¾ in.

Colour of eyes: Brown

Colour of hair: Brown

Special peculiarities: –

Dorothea's last passport lists her profession as 'housewife' in a hand not her own – the sepia picture to the right of this makes it clear she is not impressed. Even her steely cinnamon-bun hair bristles. 'Swashbuckler' clearly wasn't an available option.

Corners cut off, the passports act as light-speed flip-books of Dorothy and Ivor's travelling lives. How they zoom back and forth across the globe but always forward in time, weathered and crumpling in twenty-year increments, faces flashing older, lived-in, corners worn.

I'd stuttered through the diaries as the room's edges flaked and fell away, the light of the large courtyard window frosting until all that existed were the desk and the delicate spidery pages before me. In the silence I'd become aware of myself, leant forward in a leather chair, peering gloomily, out of place. Time setting from sap to amber, my vision tunnelling down – a few dim blue-black words with

Gs like Ss, Ts with their crosses flung ahead along the word
. . . had there been a clock upon the wall the second hand
would have creaked to a halt.

The passports had let the life back in, they were portals
out; gateways to mountains.

The first chapter of this book ended with the promise of
peaks but instead I'd gone to the flats and fens of Rye and
Cambridge to discover more about the lives Dorothea and
Ivor lived outside the sphere of *Climbing Days*. But, of course,
I was finding it difficult to relate the fragments I was finding
back to the mountain world. Everything felt rather flat.

Writing a previous book, I'd spent time speaking with
Judi Dench about acting and then visited the Old Vic theatre without her. There I felt a similar sense of anticlimax –
none of which was the fault of the Old Vic, it was just I felt
her absence keenly; the playhouse lacked a player. So it was
here in Magdalene after the lively doings of *Climbing Days*.
I felt marooned in a world shorn of verbs, and remembered
with a smile how Dorothy wrote that Ivor used to post her
sketch-maps of climbing routes and stratagems he'd dreamt
up whilst marking essays or invigilating examinations – his
mind similarly drawn back to exploits in Snowdonia, Skye
and the Lakes.

* * * * *

This is not to say I disliked Cambridge. I was delighted to
be working at Magdalene, staying in a corner room above
and along from the Porter's Lodge, overlooking the First
Court's four wide striped lawns surrounded by sixteenth-
century monastic brick, whose modulating tones, differing
styles and size of windows relate how the buildings have

grown and been renewed since Magdalene's inception as a modest Benedictine hostel. If I leant out of my window, I could see the formal hall, beyond, behind which stands the neoclassical, warm stone-fronted Pepys Library. Above the door of the formal hall is a tiered clock tower, indigo face set in the first of three square boxes which rise to be topped with a sharp lead spire.

Outside the Old Library, stood in the court, sun on my face, I looked at the flower borders and thought of the 1912 diary I'd just left back inside, in which the eighteen-year-old Dorothea wrote of her struggle to convince her father to allow her to study horticulture instead of housewifery: 'Rather dreading ride with Father for fear of interview about future career. It is so hard to decide definitely for the gardening with everybody against you.'[10]

Hard to decide what you want to be when you're young in an old world. Strange to think of Dorothea's life archived in such a cloistered place, but wonderful that it was so preserved and cared for; wound up with Ivor in death as she was in life, although she never seems to have felt totally comfortable here.

'Dorothea's attitude to Cambridge was complex,' writes Dr Luckett in his introduction to the *Selected Letters*: 'a community where her husband was a lion was good but a community where she was a non-entity was bad; she enjoyed university ceremonial but loathed giving tea parties for dons' wives; she was capable of interest in undergraduates but suspected that she bored them. On the whole she disliked the place.'[11]

Above me the spindly college weathervane shivered on its ash lead witch's hat.

The windows in the belfry taper up – arched sets of glass in wooden frames.

Imp recovery, Magdalene
College, February 1915
(RCM)

Along the roof, atop the ridge, are two Heath Robinson-style chimneys made of flue pipe crowned with busby turbines. Hulking, turning, creaking on the roof.

The clock reads 10:45.

Ivor stands on the topmost pitch, leaning lightly on the spire; slightly slouched, looking down, a rope looped over his shoulder and down to a coil at his feet. The other end drops down the belfry tiers to a man frozen mid-dash, flailing to climb the clock house, coat tails swirling blurred. Running bow-legged, straddling the ridge to fling himself upon the lowest box. A mad crux of genuine urgency; an exposed point of real exertion, the very antithesis to Ivor's relaxed stance above.

Above both flies a bat-like puppet, strung up as a prank.

The imp billows at the top of the shot, hung on the letter

E. The lower man flaps and scrambles and between them, at the heart of the picture, the calm figure of Ivor draws the eye – fascinating for his stillness.

'[Richards] has been complained of by a policeman for climbing a chimney stack the other day,' writes the Master of Magdalene, A. C. Benson, in his diary of 28 February 1915. 'Dickens, Roxburgh,[12] and Richards, three intellectuals, have signalised themselves by suspending a sort of dummy from the weathercock . . . It is a silly and impertinent thing for men, whose scholarships have been expressly prolonged, to do just now.'* Nearly a fortnight later he's still rumbling: 'B. Dickens to lunch, gave him a piece of my mind about the Richards episode. I maintained that the men whom the College paid were not the men to rag.'

All this is mentioned in *I. A. Richards: His Life and Work* – 'lights out everywhere in expectation of a Zeppelin raid' – but there Russo stops. He doesn't mention that, having strung the cloth dummy up under cover of night, the guilty party returned in daylight hours to take it down – an exercise recorded in *Magdalene College Roofs and Climbs*.

The whole show looks deadly in daylight. In blackout it must have been ridiculous – by which I mean scary: clambering out of a skylight or round the frame and gutter of a top-floor dormer onto the tiled roof, crawling up to sit on the ridge and then along, bent double, tensed to make no noise. The calendar for 1915 tells me there was a waning gibbous moon not far off full – lights out below, lights out everywhere, moonlight on the chilly tiles, a slight breeze,

* Ivor's £20 exhibition had been extended a year on account of his absence from Cambridge in 1912–13.

Imp recovery, Magdalene College, February 1915 (RCM)

the courtyard yawning four floors below, hands pricked by cold sweat. Had they a rope? They must have had; the plan being 'If I begin to slide off this side you jump over the other.' Amazing how loud your heart becomes, the skitter of a stone dislodged by gym shoes or socks perhaps, the silent night sprung waiting like a trap.

So then, up the boxes of the belfry, lead-covered box on box, first you then him – the third must have been keeping watch, leant out of the dormer to hiss warning. White-faced in the silver night. Everything illuminated strangely flat, rendered dreamlike, one dimension short but the drop is real enough. And then the spire, breath steaming. How very tall it is when stood beneath: twelve foot high, crimped lead sheet on a conical peak, the weathervane trembling, everything grey-white in the moon, the rope no help here.

The imp, Magdalene College, February 1915 (RCM)

No, you have to hug the steeple. I'll hug it and go . . . Right. So. Just stay there. Now. Up. Are you all right?

Foot in stirrup palms, foot on a shoulder – the black cloth imp about his neck, riding up to its perch. Clinging to the spire, digging his insteps into the lead, 'greatly venturing', as Dorothea would later write of a similar initiation.

And all around him Cambridge, the first of two, spread out luminescent, mild and unsettled below the silver sky.

A moment of absolute stillness as his fingers fight, fight to tie it. Holding his breath. The boy below's face facing in, inches from the steeple, feeling the taut boot on his shoulder tremble as the one above ties the imp fast about the E of East.

Then down, done; the spindle like a slide. Fast movements after the drawn-out tension. A surge of relief but celebration can wait. Now to retreat back down and off, scrabbling towards the third face. Bright as a landing light in the dark.

* * * * *

Ghosts. Not just in my imagination either; the ghosts are there in *Magdalene College Roofs and Climbs*, where several of the photographs are double exposures – posed shots taken after the imp's recovery, meshed with earlier scenes. Ivor is still stood high atop the spire, imp held aloft, but turn the picture ninety degrees left and there is A. C. Benson formally robed and white-moustached, standing with Ivor on his left and Roxburgh on his right. Clearly the master was not so apoplectic that he wouldn't have his photograph taken the next day. Clearly not so appalled by the risks of the venture that he wouldn't send the boys back up to get the thing down!

As well as being in two places at once, Ivor is wearing a black beret, that most revolutionary of hats. It is a prelude to a later shot taken with Dorothea in the American Rockies in 1926, although that beret is grey;[13] a cousin of this earlier beret perhaps, but it sets the pattern of hats and glasses that would follow for both him and Dorothea the rest of their climbing lives.

I have a photograph of Ivor in Snowdonia titled 'North Wales, 1917'. Pipe in mouth beneath a soft sunhat, edging along a ledge towards the camera wearing what appears to be a cream linen suit; dressed up as if for extreme beekeeping – the Man from Del Monte standing in for the Milk Tray Man. The suit and hat are so bizarre they distract from the issue that tissue-paper-lunged Ivor is climbing *whilst smoking a pipe*.

And then there's a later picture of Dorothea and Ivor having breakfast in the garden of one of the several houses around Bath which my father's parents had. This one, the Ridge, was sat up on a hill. Boiled eggs on plates give a clue to the meal, the woolly lawn looks parched yet frosty.* It's clearly an unusual event because there aren't enough chairs – the dining room has been moved outside for the guests. The chair nearest the camera is empty because my grand-father, Derek, is behind the camera taking the shot. Around a table on the lawn sit my father, his brothers and their mother in the sun, with Ivor and Dorothea, who are wearing hats. The feeling is one of leave-taking. The hats are restless. The hats want to go. The hats make Ivor and Dorothea *other* in that they make them transitory, both *of another time* and, shortly, *of another place*. They are not staying. They are visi-tors in hats and at this point in their photographed lives the same hats begin to recur. It is no longer the case of *a beret like another beret*, the hats have fixed themselves as if both have been looking for the right hat all their lives and now, having found that hat, they're going to wear it.

First they found each other, then they found their hats.

Ivor's lends him an American air, as if he's stepped out of a John Cheever novel. Dorothea's looks like she cadged it off an angler, a scuffed wax bonnet that crops up in Switzerland, Skye, Massachusetts – wherever she went, it went too: an unapologetically mad hat with a story. A hat which begs a question, the answer to which was probably 'I beg your pardon?' followed by a stony glare. We'll meet it again later on in this book.†

---

* My father has covered the photograph's reverse in scribbled notes:
  Photo taken in the garden of The Ridge, Ashton Hill, Corston. Taken by Derek Armstrong Richards. Mum with her back to us.
  Uncle Ivor & Aunt Dorothea about 1962.
  The day after this I jumped in the water butt bush which hurt a lot. The thorns did not come out for ages.
  Me on the right. Michael behind mum and Simon David looking at I.A.R.
† My mother's Scottish grandmother, Margret Greenland, was also famous

Young Simon David, sat to the left of Dorothea, sporting a haircut which looks like it involved sheep clippers and a mixing bowl, stares at the pair, caught mid-munch; the stare is unabashed; the open incredulity of '*What* is going on?' My father, similarly occupied with toast, perched up on a side table in lieu of a chair, regards the scene with the wise sad face of one who knows that something ineffably peculiar is afoot.

Looking at my father with the toast, I see that he still makes the same motion when eating and thinking, that slight pause as he changes mental gear from thought to fork . . . just as he tends to keep his coat on indoors until my mother tells him to take it off; and just as my gestures are mirrors of his and he his father, the way we hold our hands; which brings me back to ghosts, of course; ghosts and apparitions.

Another palimpsest picture in the 1915 Magdalene imp series shows three boys emerging from the velveteen body of the button-eyed imp. Ivor appears cradling the lolling bugbear which takes his place as a mirrored image. Ghosting there and there.[14]

In a final picture, two sets of brothers; my father, Simon David and Michael stand in front of Ivor, Kenneth and George. A smiling line of thick wool suits in various earthy hues behind a beaming row of shirts under jumpers and high-waisted shorts.

Ivor's white hair blends into the pale sky. Kenneth stands in the centre, a country doctor who served in a field hospital at the front before starting a practice near Westbury, and next to him, George, a Royal Engineer who fought in the

for wearing a hat but she wore hers whilst she did the housework so that, should anyone come to the door, she could claim that she was 'just on her way out' and so not have to invite them in. She was a great exponent of 'You'll have had your tea' as well, I'm told, from earliest afternoon onwards.

Two sets of three brothers. The Ridge, Ashton Hill, Corston *c*.1962 (Derek Richards)

trenches, was awarded the Military Cross and mentioned in dispatches before returning home to become a horticultur-alist and celebrated nurseryman:

> Sec. Lt. (temp. Capt.) George Eustace Armstrong RICHARDS, R.E.
> For conspicuous gallantry during operations. He carried out several reconnaissances under heavy fire, and, with a party of sappers, put a newly-captured position into a state of defence under heavy fire.[15]

My father remembers George, lost in thought at the end of his life, talking of 'a Highlander trapped in the wire'. Always that same image. Over and over.

Unimaginable things. Horrors unspoken which disfig-ured a generation, within and without. Ivor spared by fluke of illness. Did they talk about it? I don't know. I can't find anything directly related in the Magdalene archives.

'I didn't probe at all,' Dr Luckett told me when I asked. 'Ivor was a friend of great interest to me but . . . whilst I might have asked about Cambridge English I'd never have probed about the war.'

Looking at the pictures in *Magdalene College Roofs and Climbs* again, I find Benson's appearance particularly affecting. As well as tutoring Ivor in literature and essay-writing he seems to have taken a fatherly interest and his diaries show him warming to the young man, full of praise and encouragement.* Now here he stands in a Cambridge emptied out – overseeing the dismantling of a weathercock rag doll, a childish stunt by one of his 'ablest men', exempted by twist of fate. There's a bittersweetness to the scene, a pathos – an element of benediction to good-humoured disobedience – but the spectre of France looms over all.[16]

* * * * *

The same spire, eight years later. 19 November 1923. Ivor is again out on a limb, on the cusp of something dangerous and revolutionary, although he hardly suspects. He sits in Magdalene Hall, below the belfry weathercock – 'that gold and brown place with stairs going out of it, with coats of arms in the windows, and banners hanging from the roof'

---

* As opposed to the rather dim view he took of Ivor's fellow undergraduate George Leigh Mallory: 'Mallory and Richards to lunch – it was curious to see Richards who is very able, well-read, thoughtful and a delightful creature too, full of modesty, showing up so feebly as regarded conversation etc. by the side of the shallow-minded, pretentious, self-assured and yet entirely pleasant and nice Mallory.' A. C. Benson, Diary, 17 March 1914, Magdalene College, Cambridge. See also Russo, *I. A. Richards*, p. 19.

– writing Dorothea a letter whilst invigilating an exam: 'Beneath at the table are the victims. Beginning to show signs of desperation. Some of them horribly haggard. Some writing like nuisances, what a lot of rot. I shall have to read through this. Oh Alack! Woe's me.'

'The victims' were occupied with the College's Davidson Prize, an annual award for 'an essay on a literary subject'. A month earlier, A. C. Benson noted in his diary that, over dinner, Ivor had suggested a good examination for English students would be 'to print five extracts of poetry and prose, with no clue as to author and date, and containing one really *worthless* piece – and ask for comments and opinion'.[17]

The Davidson Prize provided the first chance to try the experiment out. John Constable notes in his introduction to the recent Routledge reissue of *Practical Criticism* that, although not yet a college Fellow, Ivor was already responsible for the setting and marking of the prize.[18] So on that November afternoon he sits supervising the candidates in the first Practical Criticism exam, the great invention that would go so far to make his name and reputation, writing to Dorothea.

He is depressed, he tells her. Magdalene is nearly too much. He looks down at a baker's dozen of candidates and wonders whether, had such an exam been mooted or placed before him in his time, he'd have engaged or have refused.

Some of 'em must by now hate me. Most of them I've never seen before. They have seen me of course. What exactly they think I am and what doing now I don't know. Such sighs resounding in the chamber! (I *couldn't* make up my mind about anything *ever* in this place or such a place. It smells of dead thoughts, a hellish stink.)

'What am I doing here?' he asks her. 'It's an educational institution: one of the best in the land no doubt. But I don't touch it and it doesn't touch me.'

In essence he's going to tell Magdalene to stuff it and pack himself off to a place he can think and work, but first he has to invigilate this prize exam.

'Oh poor people before me, you don't know how I pity you!' he tells Dorothea and the room at large. 'Still they scribble down below. Mountains and reams of crabbed writing to read over. How I'm to decide, I don't know.'[19]

It's an extraordinary letter. A sketch plan drawn on the original shows Ivor as a scribble, sat alone at the front of the hall whilst ten other scribbles wrestle with the problem he's set, which, doubtful and disparaging as he sounds, would change the course of his life; comparable to the night in 1919 when, without a job and on his uppers, he went to see Mansfield Forbes of Clare College with the intention of quitting Cambridge to become a mountain guide in Scotland. On both occasions his luck was in.

Arriving at Forbes' rooms with 'a sheaf of letters and applications' in hope that the latter's Hebridean connections might help secure him a post on Skye, 'the conversation turned from the mountains of the Lake District to Wordsworth's *Prelude*. After two hours, Forbes put all his notes and Richards' letters in the fire and offered him a job teaching English as a "freelance" or "recognised lecturer".'[20]

The series of lectures on the contemporary novel which followed made a tremendous impact, not just on undergraduates of the time but on Cambridge English as a whole, Dr Luckett told me in Rye. They featured works by Lawrence,

Hardy, Joyce and Conrad* – although, of these, he thought Conrad was really the nearest to Ivor's own interest:

'You see, he was very aware on the contemporary [literary] scene, as well as being alert to the work of Eliot, Pound and people like F. S. Flint; he was very much involved but then he shifted – because his marriage involved a tremendous shift to America – you could almost think of it as comparable to the way the Auden anthologies have come out; *The English Auden* then *The Later Auden*, in other words *The American Auden*. I think you can almost make a division like that with Richards. The wonderful *Collected Edition* of Richards by John Constable, which I can't praise too much, that's all *The English Richards*.[21]

---

* Ivor famously deployed a line of Conrad's to close a footnote to his article 'A Background for Contemporary Poetry' – 'In the destructive element immerse.' 'To those familiar with Mr Eliot's *The Waste Land*, my indebtedness to it at this point will be evident. He seems to me by this poem, to have performed two considerable services for this generation. He has given a perfect emotive description of a state of mind which is probably inevitable for a while to all those who most matter. Secondly, by effecting a complete severance between his poetry and all beliefs, and this without any weakening of the poetry, he has realised what might otherwise have remained largely a speculative possibility, and has shown the way to the only solution of these difficulties. "In the destructive element immerse. That is the way."' I. A. Richards, 'A Background for Contemporary Poetry', *Criterion*, vol. 3, no. 12 (July 1925).

The fame of the footnote is such that I first discovered it during my A levels whilst studying *The Waste Land* – was taught it, in fact – then again at university. It was by means of this footnote that I discovered both the disparate heart of Eliot's poem, the first steps on a path through the shattered world, and the work of Joseph Conrad, specifically *Lord Jim*. It was the first time I had come across I.A.R. in the classroom and the line has stayed with me ever since – *In the destructive element immerse* – a web of associations; I. A. Richards and T. S. Eliot, Conrad and Richards; Richards and school/ university life, his life touching mine across time. And now, in this chapter, that quote again seems apt since it describes the connection of Richards and Pilley, their audacious lives in and outside Cambridge, in the destructive element immersed. That was their world, arena, common ground.

'But, as I say, I think the shift probably happened with his marriage because, after all, he chased Dorothea. She went to Canada and he followed, and that's the most extraordinary story, not for nothing was Ivor in later life obsessed with Don Quixote. It was the most Quixotian thing and in Magdalene there are what are called in the catalogue the *sixty-page letter*: from Dorothea to Ivor explaining why she couldn't marry him, and *forty-page letter*: a later letter saying exactly the same thing . . . and then they married.'[22]

John Constable's introductions to the different books of *I. A. Richards: Selected Works 1919–1938* are superbly engaging, perhaps because he spent so much time reading and editing Ivor's letters into book form before turning his attention to his work.

His prologue to *Practical Criticism* (volume four of the ten which make up *Selected Works 1919–1938*) begins with the letter quoted above – the first time Ivor had experimented with 'unsigned' pieces, as he called it then – *Practical Criticism* as it would become known.

The results of the test were dramatic. The day after Ivor wrote to Dorothea again:

'Oh Strange, beyond report, thought or belief', all the candidates for my prize with only one exception prefer Mrs Wilcox to Landor, Hopkins, Belloc, De Quincey, and Jeremy Taylor at their very best! I'm nearly ill with laughter at their opinions. Aching. – But what a state of things! – and the pick of the College unquestionably. Where are we and what am I doing? Who lecturing to? Why do I feel, not salved but exhilarated by the discovery. I feel as though I had just read *Candide* again. Alive to the real world and remarkably hungry.[23]

The Davidson prize essays had re-energised Richards, writes Constable, changing and charging his interest in Cambridge, renewing his sense of purpose: 'Here was something he could actually *do* for his students, here was an explanation of the falsity of the would-be-professionalism of the literary men: the reading public, perhaps many of the men of letters themselves, were barely able to distinguish the worthless from the valuable in their reading.'*

* * * * *

Back in my Magdalene corner room, I open *Practical Criticism* and begin to read it with an eye on utility. Throughout *Climbing Days* Ivor's practicality is noted – be it treating injuries or recognising symptoms of shock, doling out Brand's Essence of Beef or mixing up concoctions of jam and snow to boost Dorothea's blood sugar levels, discovering paths, discerning routes, or planning future sallies when away from the rocks. His expedience exemplified by the four-yard silk scarf he always carries in the mountains 'to meet all emergencies' – such as the disappearance of the seat of one's breeches during a glissading descent.

'Good craftsmanship was at the heart of his delight in mountaineering, particularly in the Alps where so many different skills combine,' wrote Katharine Chorley in Ivor's Alpine Journal obituary. 'A well-made snowstep

---

* Richards, *Selected Works, Volume 4. Practical Criticism (1929)*, ed. Constable, p. ix. John Constable goes on to say that A. C. Benson, writing in his diary, remarked that the result was 'most curious and interesting', and wondered that the candidates showed 'no critical faculty, no taste', and were 'taken in by a shoddy sonnet', adding that 'It shows how little our teaching trains discrimination.' A. C. Benson, 19 November 1923, Magdalene College, Cambridge.

deserved to be respected like a well-made poem.'*

His work was 'directed to action', writes Dr Luckett in *Selected Letters*, whether it was teaching Cambridge undergraduates 'to read in such a way that they did not prefer Woodbine Willy to Hopkins, or Chinese students to speak English in the hope that this might contribute to world peace'.† One of the main reasons he disliked history so much was that there was nothing that could be *done* about it now.

Fundamentally, he was an inventor. Sat in Magdalene, that statement made a sense it hadn't previously. It struck me how inventive he was, and how lucky to have had the support of people like Benson and Forbes. He took quite astonishing risks – controlled, managed risks perhaps – but it was a truly revolutionary act to teach from an egalitarian baseline of a naked text rather than the privileged position of accepted prestige and established authorial credentials within an institution like Cambridge. There's a brilliant insouciance to it all.

Ivor began teaching Practical Criticism in October 1925. The lectures lasted eight weeks. He opened the series with these words to his audience:

> This course is an experiment. I'm going to spend most of this hour explaining what it is the experiment might do and

---

* Katharine Chorley, 'Ivor Armstrong Richards, CH (1893–1979)', *Alpine Journal*, 1980 (see Appendix I, p. 339). 'His talent for planning expeditions was of a high order and he and Dorothea made a remarkable team, picking up peak after peak, often traverses, as the seasons went by, mostly alone but sometimes with friends.' In the same piece Dorothea is quoted – 'He had great pleasure in telling his second (me) how to do an awkward move as though he were analysing a mathematical problem.'

† Dr Richard Luckett's introduction to *Selected Letters of I. A. Richards*. In Rye, Dr Luckett had stressed this point: Ivor was an *immensely* practical person, to the extent that he'd even stepped into the breach to sort out John Pilley's divorce – at the behest of Dorothea, he suspects.

what the conditions are, and in imploring you to follow the conditions. [It is an] attempt to do something which so far as I know has not been tried before. That being so it's very likely to go wrong. Both you and I shall try to do [something] new.[24]

'He rushes forward, as if some gap had opened on the future', wrote Frank Kermode of Ivor. 'We shall never, I think, have a true sense of the man unless we understand this gay calculated audacity.'*

A perfect description of climbing; gay calculated audacity

---

* In a wonderfully illuminating article ('Educating the Planet', *LRB*, vol. 2, no. 5, 20 March 1980), it is notable that Kermode also invokes the poem 'Hope' as a bridge of accord between worlds: '[W]e shall never, I think, have a true sense of the man unless we understand this gay calculated audacity. He rushes forward, as if some gap had opened on the future. He wrote *Interpretation in Teaching*, a difficult book of over four hundred pages, in six weeks, and in the leisure time of those same six weeks turned out the none too simple *Philosophy of Rhetoric*. To bring that off you cannot afford to make a cautious survey of the path before you dash down it. All you can hope for is that you are well enough programmed, or "taped", as he used to say – that you have adequate "feed-forward". And you must be very inventive. From *The Meaning of Meaning* on, Richards prodigally invented new terms; some, like the "Canon of Actuality" and the "Utraquist error" of *Meaning*, died young; others, like the "stock response" of *Practical Criticism* and the Tenor-Vehicle distinction of *The Philosophy of Rhetoric*, have stuck. All were expendable; what mattered was the forward movement. One thinks of the lines, addressed to Mrs Richards, which recall the descent of a glacier, the scrambling across innumerable half-hidden crevasses before being overtaken by darkness on the abrupt edge:

> At the stiff-frozen dawn
> When time had ceased to flow,
> – The glacier our unmade bed –
> I hear you through your yawn:
> 'Leaping crevasses in the dark,
> That's how to live!' you said.
> No room in that to hedge;
> A razor's edge of a remark.

– a cord between his writing and climbing, a link too to Dorothea, whose inclination was similarly adventurous. When Ivor travelled to China between the wars to teach, perfect and promote Basic English, an 850-word version of English developed in Cambridge with the linguist C. K. Ogden, Dorothea went with him – indeed, she was there when she started to write *Climbing Days*, as she notes in her preface – 'I began this book in China, being homesick for European hills.'*

* A note on Basic English – I'm afraid there isn't very much about it in this book, although it was undoubtedly one of the main reasons for Dorothy and Ivor's many visits to China, America and beyond. At the start of this project I had intended to travel to China to research the pair's working and climbing lives there but the cost, together with the realisation that China, Basic English and much else of great biographical interest fell outside the scope of this book, precluded such a move.

Dr Luckett described Basic English in my interview with him in Rye in 2013: 'The essence of the invention was really the idea of a simplified English; [C. K.] Ogden dealt with the vocabulary, Richards did the grammar. It's interesting, Ivor always said that he could have been a mathematician.'

By the time of the publication of *Basic English* in 1935, Ivor had become 'absolutely, totally involved with China' as Dr Luckett put it, but the couple first visited China in 1929, after the period related in *Climbing Days*, which closes in 'The Great Year' of 1928. Ivor had an extraordinarily free hand at Magdalene, Dr Luckett told me, so much so that he was able to spend long periods in China and America and simply substitute his teaching: 'As I say, there was always this distinction between the English Ivor and the American Ivor; and America was vital to him because of his concern for China – which was, I think, more a concern *for China* than it was a concern for Basic English, although I don't think one could ever prove that . . . but he never showed much interest in Basic English in India, Basic English in South America or whatever; it was *Basic English in China*. Now, Ivor's theory was that that was the biggest single ethnic population in the world and that they had proven gifts, extraordinary gifts, of comprehension, so if it were possible to teach Basic to China you'd be off on a world movement. Of course it never happened like that, and I say "of course" but the disappointment caused to Ivor by Churchill's taking up Basic and then dropping it, being voted out of office, that disappointment was enormous and that emerges in the correspondence at Magdalene.' ▷

* * * * *

Next morning I walked around the college perimeter to look at Wentworth House, the house where the pair lived for so many years. Viewed across Chesterton Road, a late eighteenth-century detached Georgian house the colour of condensed milk, it looked the sort of place where comfort is sought in gothic novels, pitched up by the Cam. Slightly lopsided, but difficult to explain exactly how – the jaunty wooden cornice is only the start. It looks like a great many attempts have been made to spruce and fix up the property which have actually only exacerbated its naturally mouldering manner. There's something in its face that's . . . sardonic.

Behind it, willows parade down to the river along which, to the right, stands Magdalene College and the Pepys Library, where Dr Luckett used to live. I imagine him lying awake each morning wondering what Dorothean set piece might befall him that day.

In 1974, when Ivor was eighty-one and Dorothea eighty, they decided to move back from Harvard – Cambridge,

---

The genus, nature and impact of Basic English – both globally and to the person of I.A.R. – is expressed and explained with great clarity by John Paul Russo in *I. A. Richards: His Life and Work*. Rodney Koeneke's *Empires of the Mind: I. A. Richards and Basic English in China, 1929–1979* (Stanford University Press, 2003) provides a hugely readable, inspiring account of Basic English and Ivor's time in China: 'Koeneke considers Richards's project in the light of current theories about imperialism: Did Basic English anticipate today's multicultural aspirations for global exchange? Or did it advance new "empires of the mind" whose spoils are language and information? Ultimately, the history of Richards's time in China offers a crucial window onto the postcolonial complexities of our own.' – sup.org (reprinted by permission of Stanford University Press). I also recommend Frank Kermode's *London Review of Books* essay 'Educating the Planet' (vol. 2, no. 5, 20 March 1980) as a brilliant, funny and lucid appraisal, and John Haffenden's 2005 work, *William Empson: Vol. I: Among the Mandarins* (Oxford University Press, 2005).

Massachusetts to Cambridge, England – and endow a fellow-ship at Magdalene, 'a very expensive thing to do', in return for which they got the lifelong leasehold of Wentworth House. This is where they lived, their last four and a bit years together, Dorothea living alone there after Ivor died until 1986, still ferociously independent and determined to do what she wanted. It looks a big house for a lady on her own but then I remember she had lodgers upstairs – I pondered what Dorothea would be like as a landlady and I'm afraid, in that moment, the image of Maggie Smith as Miss Shepherd in *The Lady in the Van* clanked through my mind.

Standing in front of the house I thought of Richard beside his harpsichord in Rye – in 1974 he would have been a few years older than I am now, unmarried, living alone in Magdalene, beset by a furiously dissident octogenarian whilst all the while trying to study for a music history PhD.

'I mean, one could only admire her spirit,' he'd told me, 'but it meant that she would try and do the most *tremendously impractical* things. I would see her daily, try to make practical arrangements. I was not quite sure what I was doing.'

He related how, when Ivor died, a makeshift committee of Ladies' Alpine Club members was assembled. 'They got together and took it upon themselves to look after Dorothea and then they found that they really couldn't manage, chiefly because they were in London and Dorothea was in Cambridge "being Dorothea". So I had a letter from Janet [Adam Smith] that said, "Okay. Right, well, sorry; over to you!"'

I'd asked him if Dorothea had always been financially independent as well as so personally . . . mercurial and he had said, yes, that had always been so.

'And that's important, I think, in accounting for the rela-tionship which you're discovering and describing. Once you've grasped that there was complete financial independence it makes a lot more sense. Ivor was a university teaching professor at Harvard with a good income, a good pension when he finally decided to retire, but Dorothea's money, the inherited money, that was her money . . . and that was what she left to Magdalene. I was their executor and I remember – I don't know whether any of this came down to you – packing up pathetic little things, you know, objects, penknives and so on, so that people in the Richards family could have something.

But the entire . . . it was about £1.8 million went to Magdalene, and it could have been far more had Ivor retained his copyrights; but he didn't, he gave them to Harvard.'

This was quite a lot of new information to me. I think I must have stared at Richard rather, made a funny face at least, or turned the colour of Wentworth House, because at that point on the tape he asks if I'm alright and offers me a fresh cup of tea.

* * * * *

I didn't climb any belfries whilst at Magdalene, tempted as I was. My room had a window onto the roof and one night I walked around the college environs noting possible routes up to beckoning cornices, drainpipes and porches . . . but no, I didn't chance my arm. My feet remained down on the ground.

A couple of weeks after my trip to Cambridge, sat eating rhubarb crumble in a Norfolk bouldering centre cafe, I ponder the gymnastics and elegance of climbing at close quarters. I watch the stringy student types with bungee muscles hidden under army surplus jumpers; the hulk-armed, pecs-and-singlet pull-up merchants who hardly use their feet; the girl who spends an hour trying to crack one route, those who flash up a route first time, them that buzz from pitch to pitch apparently at random. The groups, the laughing beginners, the lone wolves who take it all a bit seriously – no matter who does it, when a problem is tackled well, the universe aligns for a moment, something clicks and the climber often seems to glide up with a mesmerising grace.

Climbing in a bouldering centre is different from climbing outdoors. It's usually warm and dry, there's always something soft to land on and there's often music playing. When you're tired you can go to the cafe and eat rhubarb crumble; few of these things occur naturally in Portland or the gritstone of the Peak District. No, bouldering is more like vertical gymnastic chess. At its purest, trad climbing is a balance of strength and pathfinding trial-and-error against unmoved, indifferent elements. But the walls inside this industrial-estate hangar possess a subtly different cruelty because everybody knows that someone, some unseen dap-shoed Übermensch, has set and climbed each and every route here – some iron-fingered monster has mastered it – and the trouble is they're possibly here in the room, unassuming, smiling, helping the novices, making suggestions. An awful thought.

At times it felt like I was climbing in a fishbowl, deficiencies laid bare, but luckily it seems that everyone feels this at some level because at one point, unexpectedly, the music stopped and almost every climber froze then looked around, spell broken, zone dispersed. Several dismounted, puzzled. 'What's going on?' one asked. Music was a safety net. Without it the exposure became unbearable.

W. R. Neate, in his book *Mountaineering and Its Literature*, places such things under the heading 'Simulation' and explains how the great demand for outdoor pursuits after 1945 led to the development of artificial climbing walls. 'The first in Britain was constructed with concrete flanges and ledges' and the best example of this type is at Liverpool University, he tells us. But another form is the sport of wall or roof climbing. This is 'stegophily', more commonly known as 'buildering' – although I can't imagine I.A.R or D.E.P. ever calling it that.[25]

Geoffrey Winthrop Young – who we'll meet more fully in the next chapter – published *The Roof-climbers' Guide to Trinity* in 1899, a book which details his adventures on the cupolas, gambrels and gables of Cambridge colleges in the years before Ivor took up the challenge. A humorous history, Young's *Roof-climbers' Guide* is none the less very practical, with hand-drawn maps and diagrams, and still in print; hopefully because it's still used as a manual and inspiration. Such roof climbing as he describes, Young writes, stems 'of enormous antiquity, possessing extensive history and a literature that includes the greatest verse and prose writers of all ages'.

More recently the urban explorer Katherine Rundell, writing in the *London Review of Books*, described how she fell in love with night climbing, a love which began when she was an undergrad at Oxford, 'crawling out of windows and up drainpipes' with a few friends –

> Oxford can be an uneasy place for teenagers not reared on self-belief and champagne, and it was emboldening to walk it from above; the closest you could get to conquering the city. But it was more than that; I have always loved to be up high, and I have always loved the electricity it puts in the blood . . .
>
> Night climbing, when it goes well, works on the joy of quick and necessary decisions, on improvising in the two

seconds in which your stomach and brain are in conflict. It is unmooring your sense of fear and self-preservation from your sense of hope and danger and adventure. There are moments that can't be replicated anywhere else; nowhere at ground level offers the same pleasures as sitting with your back against chimney pots, or walking the apex of a rooftop, or looking down on the Tetris pattern of masters' gardens and college quads.[26]

I'm sure such feelings were the reason Ivor buildered rather than bouldered; the fact it dealt in the realm of the real and set a figure within landscape *to some purpose – archi*-tonic rather than *tec-* – a necessarily secret urbex pursuit,* testing himself in the dark. Self-contained, thrilling and truly frightening – no simulation there. I can understand that need, that love, that sense of quest – his mortality in his own hands, for once. As with so much of his life and work, he went out seeking fresh perspectives on the supposedly solid and familiar.†

Famous as the first to climb Napes Needle on Great Gable in 1886, Walter Parry Haskett-Smith is often credited

---

* Urban exploration (often shortened as urbex or UE) is the exploration of man-made structures, most usually abandoned buildings, industrial constructions, ruins or hidden components of the man-made environment.
† In her essay 'Fare Forward, Voyagers!' Janet Adam Smith recalls the famously even-tempered Ivor was once visibly angered in the company of fellow climbers 'when the lecturer, describing some difficult climb she had made, showed she knew nothing of of the peaks and valleys round her own particular ascent: to her it was nothing but a physical achievement . . . for the Richardses the mountains were never a battleground or a stage; they are simply the place where they are completely at home.' Janet Adam Smith, 'Fare Forward, Voyagers!', *I. A. Richards, Essays In His Honour*, ed. Ruben Brower, Helen Vendler and John Hollander, Oxford University Press, New York, 1973.

as being the 'Father of Rock Climbing' – one of the first to advocate and pursue climbing 'as a sport in its own right, as opposed to a necessary evil undergone by mountaineers en route to a summit'. However, Haskett-Smith thought that climbing ought to be to some purpose, a journey or route to an end, and he poked fun at the emergence and enthusiasm for bouldering in his 1894 book *Climbing in the British Isles*, describing Bear Rock on Great Gable as 'a queerly-shaped rock on Great Napes, which in the middle of March, 1889 was gravely attacked by a large party comprising some five or six of the strongest climbers in England. It is a little difficult to find, especially in seasons when the grass is at all long.' Alan Hankinson, *The First Tigers*, J. M. Dent and Sons Ltd, 1972. For more on buildering and the Napes Needle see the 'Lake District' chapter of this book.

Dorothy's introduction to such climbing, or 'stunts' as she calls them in *Climbing Days*,[27] was more public and occurred on the famous Barn Door at the Wastwater Hotel (now the Wasdale Head Inn) in the Lake District. A classic rite of passage since Victorian times, the aim was to ascend to the first floor of a stable building by means of its rough stone walls.

Harry Griffin detailed the challenge in his book *The Coniston Tigers*: 'Outside the hotel, in the inn-yard, was the *Stable Door* (or *Barn Door*) *Traverse* – quite a gymnastic feat. You had to climb up the slabs on the right hand side of the wall and then make a delicate traverse, on very poor holds, into the open door about ten feet above the ground.'[28] The pictures I've seen of the route being attempted show seconds below in catching positions, a climbing slip cordon.

Dorothy's success on the route is recalled with particular joy in *Climbing Days* since it coincided with another moment of her ascension:

Easter Club meets at Wasdale . . . how I remember the moment when burly, indomitable Philip S. Minor, then President of the Fell and Rock,* told me at Burnthwaite that I might become a Member. We were all doing traverses of the *Barn Door* and I had just fallen off! Enheartened by this news I tried again and succeeded with flying colours.[29]

* * * * *

As I was leaving Dr Luckett's house, he shook me by the hand. 'I think you're in for a great adventure,' he told me. 'The essence of Ivor and Dorothea's relationship was climbing. Dorothea was always at pains to say that they *did not* come up two sides of Tryfan, encounter each other at the top and immediately fall in love.'

En route home from Rye I'd pictured Dorothea mischievously stirring that myth, fiercely denying it all the while, and now I'd found Ivor climbing on Magdalene's roofs and belfry turret before setting his mind to a comparably anarchic revolution within its walls.

In light of these trips I wanted to put those images together and explore somewhere the pair were more completely at home; somewhere they were on an equal footing; somewhere more intrinsically Dorothean; somewhere she was principally the climber 'Pilley' rather than the academic's wife, Mrs I. A. Richards; because, for all the work Ivor did in Cambridge, it seemed to me that both he and Dorothea spent a lot of a time there trying to break out.

---

* The Fell & Rock Climbing Club of the English Lake District, to give it its full title.

The Pinnacle Club

October 2013

It was dark when I arrived in London. I'd travelled up from
Bath with my purple Haston sack, coil of red rope, antique
nuts and slings, emerging laden from the underground to
meet my friend, Emily Benton. Emily is a brilliant climber,
the type who sweeps up sheer walls with seeming ease, arms
like lariats, lithe and sparky: just the partner to properly
show me up in front of the Pinnacle Club ladies.

We'd missed the 7:10. No matter, we caught the next
train north, walking out into the gloom of Euston's concrete
hangar where our red-and-yellow Pendolino waited. We
settled ourselves as the train heaved out. It was raining. As
our speed increased the rain assailed the windows like iron
filings drawn toward our solenoid streak.

Maps unfolded on the table, fingers hovering over mountains, lakes and contoured undulations, we were already
lost in Snowdonia as, outside, London's geography slid by,
hidden – but for floodlit sites like Wembley which flared as
we sped past, beyond the capital's fuzz-orange environs.

When we arrived at Llandudno Junction, well after midnight, it was deserted; starless and bible-black. As the train
left the station it drew all the warmth and life of the night
away also. We stood on the empty platform, watching its
tail lights fade, sensing silence settle thicker in its wake.

Dorothy Pilley. *c*.1932 (I. A. Richards/RCM)

The station's taxi office had a large Welsh dragon on the window but no taxis. We asked how long a cab would be. No one was sure, so we jigged up and down beneath the wrought-iron awnings to keep warm.

Eventually a taxi arrived and the man ahead of us in the queue – the only other customer – offered us a lift. Once in Conwy, the driver became inexplicably lost so we drove around the empty town a while in fraught silence. 'Conwy isn't actually this big,' explained the front-seat passenger during the second circuit.

We reached the hostel shortly after. They'd waited up for us and after signing our names in the book we floated up to bed in green-covered bunks, asleep before our heads hit the pillow.

* * * * *

Next morning we ambled down to the harbour, washed in Vango-yellow sun. Cupping paper coffees we sat on hefty bollards. The estuary waters slipped past the quay and the tethered boats out in the wash which tugged at their ropes as if anxious to get gone. To our left the river passed beneath the castle's three bridge spans, set side by side – new road arch, old road suspension, railway tubular.

Emily quizzed some children about their bacon-baited string; how were the Conwy crabs this morning? Before we left we posed for photographs in front of a massive red-and-white-striped CONWY buoy whilst, above and behind, the castle loomed, curtain walls topped with ramparts: a man-made mountain stepped wall on wall. The fact of it was terrible: a beast so solid as to seem of a piece with the monolithic world about it.

The tinpot local train to Blaenau Ffestiniog chugged out of Llandudno Junction about an hour later, veering off the main line in a hail of clickety clack. The rails sang out our tempo as the train ran up the river's rim, skirting the reeds and silver rills meandering out the banks to join the main flow low in the thick brown mud. The tide was out and the riverbed dashed with the mad massed tracks of bird feet. Ahead rose wooded mounting steeps in hazy fern and peacock hues, some with their head in the clouds, others peering down, over the lower hills. Sheep stood in the fields of the opposite shore and watched us pass. Ahead clouds streamed off Snowdonia like smoke. The day seemed set for sun showers.

Emily knelt up on her seat to see the changing landscape pass, as the wheels' beat slowed and we came to rest at the first of several country stations. Small groups stepped on and off at each, the doors rattle-banged, a whistle, then on, trundling beneath sheer forests, along turf embankments, our flickering shadows ghosting over canoes on the clear waters below. A Blyton journey – Dorothy's world between the wars, a time when railway companies published plush booklets proclaiming Snowdon and the Welsh Highlands 'synonymous with scenery of ravishing beauty. Ancient story, sweet murmurs of mountain streams and soul-stirring music of peasant people add to the delights of this romantic region as a holiday ground.'[1]

Peasant people, dear oh dear. In climbing terms, that was me, of course: rude and unsophisticated – all lineage and no competence. Emily would be alright by the Pinnacle Club, I was sure of that, but me . . . well, that remained to be seen.

* * * * *

Margaret Clennett picked us up from Betws-y-Coed station. She was compact, early fifties perhaps, with bobbed, no-nonsense hair. Her movements had a supple poise which spoke of years on rock and, as she welcomed us and helped load bags into her car, I noted knotty arms beneath her pale pink fleece.

As archivist, Margaret was one of my first points of contact with the Pinnacle Club – the first climbing club founded by women for women alone, which Dorothy helped establish in 1921 – having written them a speculative email earlier in the year, introducing myself and asking if the club might have an archive of records and documents from the 1920s on. Hazel Jones, the PC's Honorary Secretary, responded the same day, expressing delight to hear about the project, introducing Margaret and confirming they had handbooks and journals from the club's very beginnings in its hut. There might even still be members who had personal memories of Dorothy at PC meetings and dinners, suggested Hazel, ending her email: 'I don't know if you're aware but the Pinnacle Club held its 90th birthday in 2011 and to celebrate a mass ascent of Lockwood's Chimney was organised, in 1920s climbing gear. Personally my own costume was greatly inspired by the images I found of Dorothy Pilley.' This felt like an excellent start.

Lockwood's Chimney was one of Dorothy's earliest climbs and appears very early in *Climbing Days*. One can hear the jubilation in her voice as she tells of the exploit – which also serves to sketch the garb she wore for those first jaunts in the Welsh hills:

> Greatly venturing, I went up 'Lockwood's Chimney', a dark chasm under Pen y Gwryd, alone. With what wild glory in my heart did I wriggle out of the hole and find myself in the sunlight on the giddy upper wall . . . By this time I had become the proud possessor of an Alpine rope (from Beale's, with a red strand through it!). How I had studied all the particulars about its strength in George Abraham's *The Complete Mountaineer*. How ashamed I was of its brilliant newness; it had to be muddied at all costs. A first pair of climbing boots shine like twin stars in memory, too. They were large, much too heavy and too high in the leg, but the whole village used to come to see them. I still did not dare go about Beddgelert without a skirt, and was rather balloony in a thick, full pair of tweed knickerbockers under a billowy tweed skirt which I put in the sack at the foot of a climb . . .[2]

Somewhere between climbing and caving, closer in fact to a wet spelunk, Lockwood's Chimney, as Hazel would later explain, is traditionally tackled by large parties walking home from the pub. The route carries strong historic associations for the Pinnacle Club since it was the classic scramble's founder, Mr Arthur Lockwood, who, as well as running the Pen y Gwryd Hotel where the inchoate PC first convened, had previously managed the power station at Cwm Dyli whose adjacent outhouse came to be the club's permanent home and base. The *Pinnacle Club Journal* for 1932–4 begins with an account of 'The Opening of The Emily Kelly Hut, 5th November, 1932':

> [A]t the Easter Meet, in 1932, the cottage of Cwm Dyli was noticed by a party returning from Lockwood's Chimney. Lowe immediately recognised the possibilities of the little place and, with characteristic promptitude, started negotiations with the owners at once. Seven months later our Hut – as we could at last call it – was ready for its official opening. The sturdy little building had been transformed from a storehouse for all the odds and ends of the North Wales Power Station, to a neat habitation . . .

The Pinnacle Club was established in 1921 by Emily Kelly (or 'Pat' as she was better known to her friends) and Eleanor Winthrop Young ('Len') whilst the group's kernel was formed by Dorothy ('Pilley' long after her marriage to I.A.R.), Lilian Bray ('Bray'), Blanche Eden-Smith ('Gabriel' on account of her being the Hon. Sec. – recording angel), Evelyn Lowe ('Lowe') and E. H. Daniell ('Mrs Daniell' in deference to her seniority in terms of both age and climbing experience – a great supporter of the club though not a committee member). The PC was unique as a female enterprise – a club for women first and foremost rather than a later annex of an already established men's organisation, such as the Ladies' Alpine Club (LAC), which had been founded in 1907, fifty years after the AC.*

The Lake District-based Fell and Rock Climbing Club (Fell & Rock) had been established in 1906 and had the distinction of being mixed-sex from the first but the fact remained that women were generally excluded and discouraged from the pursuit. In 1908, British women did not have the vote and would not get it for another decade. The Equal Franchise Act was another ten years hence. They could not speak in a pulpit or serve on a jury. The two hundred or so female doctors could not treat men. The police, judiciary, government, military: all were uniformly male. 'One had really done something drastic by becoming a climber . . .' Dorothy wrote, years later, in the Fell & Rock's jubilee journal, recalling her journeys alone on the night train from Euston to the Lakes – 'even the dreariness of drizzling and smoky dawn at Carnforth was somehow irradiated by a belief that one could actually already taste the mountain air':

> The loneliness and oddity of those night journeys enhanced
> one's feeling of how strange it was to be a climber – nobody
> else was – except climbers, of course! But then the only
> climbers one knew one had met through climbing – other-
> wise they were mythical people in unadvertised, little-read
> books and as remote as Redskins. When I started, there
> were none in the ordinary walks of life, none in the family

---

* The Ladies' Scottish Climbing Club followed a year later in 1908.

circle yet, none among school friends, none came by the office. One had really done something drastic by becoming a climber. Heaven alone knew how, and climbing wasn't in the least like playing tennis, which everyone more or less did. And it wasn't smiled on either – not with smiles you like to see. In those days, even up in the Lakes, a girl couldn't walk about a village in climbing clothes without hard stares from the women and sniggers from the louts.[3]

Early LAC Vice President Ellen Pigeon recalled how male AC members would often ignore and refuse to speak to LACs. One can easily imagine the old guard, sat in their patriarchal Salic clubs, having manfully ignored the upstart women banging on their Marylebone doors for so long, freezing them out once within.

But the first LACs sound resolute and exceptional. Institutional chauvinism was not going to stop them. In many cases they'd already climbed widely throughout the world – Mrs Aubrey Le Blond, the first LAC President (1907–13) is a supreme example: born in London, the daughter of a third baronet, she grew up in Ireland. When her father died she moved to Switzerland and established herself as a pioneering mountaineer, film-maker, photographer and respected author – making twenty first ascents and writing seven books on climbing.

At the time, Fanny Bullock Workman held the female altitude world record in mountain climbing – the 23,300-foot summit of Pinnacle Peak in the Himalaya. A superb climber and stalwart suffragist, she'd flown a 'Votes for Women' banner atop Karakoram, the picture of the moment much printed in the papers of the time. A tough, polarising figure, Workman seems to have taken great pleasure in defying the climbing patriarchy. She famously found the AC unfriendly, more so than their American equivalents, something later addressed by former AC president Captain J. P. Farrar, in his 1925 obituary of her: 'It is possible that some unconscious feeling, let us say, of the novelty of a woman's intrusion into the domain of exploration so long reserved to man, may in some quarters have existed . . . there tended to arise . . . an atmosphere, shall we say, of aloofness.'[4]

Yet the antagonism can be overstated. Whilst it's true that the mountaineering achievements of women at the time were generally reported in terms of novelty, impropriety or vexatious provocation to the natural order, such lurid tabloid spin was neither new or chronically distressing. A hundred years on, gender bias and sexual stereotypes continue to inform the press – albeit in a less overt or openly hostile fashion. By 1921, women enfranchised by First World War work had a new confidence in their abilities. Some had the vote and there was a definite feeling that social attitudes were shifting, suffrage was working and women's liberation was no longer beyond reach.

Reading early Pinnacle Club correspondence and minutes, it's clear that it was not formed in desperation, retaliation or last resort but rather a start-up rooted in youthful optimism and sincere love of mountaineering. 'It had been a long conspiracy,' writes Dorothy in *Climbing Days*, 'prompted by the feeling we many of us shared that a rock-climbing club for women by women would give us a better chance of climbing independently of men, both as to leadership and general mountaineering.'

Rather than defining themselves in opposition, the impression I got from the PC archive was of enthusiastic rather than downcast women, rallying to begin afresh – not in spite of overbearing, stuffy London clubs but because they simply wished to do as they liked and climb together on their own terms to the best of their abilities – away from all previous clubs, organisations and institutional bodies; away from the old order, both male and female.

Nor would it be correct to suggest that all men were opposed to the PC. Geoffrey Winthrop Young – who we last met espousing stegophily on the roofs around Trinity College, Cambridge – former president of the Climbers' Club, future president of the AC, was an enthusiastic champion from the first, as were members of both the Rucksack and Fell & Rock clubs; and so, it turned out, was the *Manchester Guardian*. In 1920, Emily Kelly wrote a letter to the *Guardian* stating that it was proposed to form a club for women rock climbers, provisionally titled the Women's Rock Climbing Club, and inviting those interested to communicate with the writer. To her delight, the letter was not only published but benevolently approved in a short leader by the editor, C. E. Montague.

From the very beginning the Pinnacle Club was to be a purposeful fresh start, an idealistic youthful venture shorn of convention – rival to the LAC only in terms of alternative; radical by default since it had no precedent. This was no mere feminist gesture, it was a rooted sense that training in the fullest responsibilities of leadership in all aspects is one of the most valuable things that climbing has to offer, and that women could hardly get such training unless they climbed by themselves. A woman's club could make such climbing seem normal, would collect those who shared this aspiration, would help them form real climbing ropes as distinguished from strings of people who happened to be climbing together . . . But from the idea to the reality seemed a long step, and without Pat Kelly's powers of inspiration it might have been indefinitely delayed.[5]

* * * * *

The road out of Betws-y-Coed was lined with alternating cafes and outdoor clothing shops, windows stuffed with Gore-tex trousers, telescopic walking poles and neon ruck-sacks. 'All Day Breakfast' and 'SALE SALE SALE' signs strobed past the car for several minutes as we wound away from the town.

As the train had hugged the Conwy, so the A5 skirted the Llugwy through blue pine forest and meadows, past heavy gorse verges and herringbone walls, the tarmac glistening after recent rain. We were to meet Hazel at a cafe equidistant between Betws-y-Coed and the Cwm Dyli hut, in a village named Capel Curig. I knew only two things about Capel Curig before our visit and they were that it was reputed to be the wettest place in Britain, and that 'Bottleneck at Capel Curig' was a song by the band Half Man Half Biscuit.

Upon arrival I learnt a third: Capel Curig is home to the Pinnacle Stores, Pinnacle Pursuits and Pinnacle Cafe, the three housed in a solid pair of Victorian shops, stood on one side of the triangular road junction which forms the village hub. I'd been surprised when Margaret had said we were meeting Hazel at 'the cafe in Capel Curig' since it seemed to imply there might only be one, when experience told me there were always at least six cafes and outdoor clothing shops in every Snowdonian village, irrespective of size. In light of the Pinnacle Stores, Pinnacle Pursuits and Pinnacle

Cafe, it all made sense. Where else could Pinnacle members converge but at this Pinnacle panacea?

Hazel was waiting outside the stores. She was quite small, steely-eyed and purposeful. Not much for small talk, I was to learn, but welcoming and warm once you got to know her a little. Early on, I decided that it wasn't Hazel who was brusque but I who was verbose, so determined to shut up and listen. After a quick cup of tea in the cafe, we all piled into Margaret's car and set off up towards Ogwen, and the slabs of 'Hope' – the weather was turning, Hazel suggested, but we might get some climbing done before it got too bad.

En route to Ogwen, Hazel asked Emily about her climbing experience and it turned out she had quite a lot of it, all over the world – staggering stuff I'd no idea about: Europe, North and South America, New Zealand; sport, trad, caves, teaching, pioneering new routes. God, it was bloody terrifying, not least because she was clearly playing it down! I shrank down into the back seat and hoped the car might forget I was there. I suddenly foresaw the weekend going very badly wrong; I wasn't a climber, nor a woman, but was in the teeth of a women's climbing club trip arranged for my benefit. This might not end well, I thought.

* * * * *

We arrived at Ogwen car park in light drizzle. It was good to be back but the sky looked foreboding so we hastily unloaded our kit from the boot and regrouped in the shiny new visitor centre.

Left alone in the atrium whilst the others went to the loo, I began to mull the coming hours, automatically picking up

Hazel's rope, which she'd earlier noted was badly wound. Rewinding it about my neck, I drifted off, pondering how the slopes above would be, whether the weather would clear up, how dark the valley would be this time, should I put my over-trousers on?

I came to with a jolt to find Hazel returned and staring at me with a face like thunder. She blinked and, raking me a look somewhere between revulsion and pity, advanced and took her rope from around my shoulders, before rapidly relooping the line with the deft automatic movements of a seasoned pro. In no time at all she'd formed a neat, symmetrical, unkinked spool devoid of twists – the opposite of what I'd done. Her idea of 'badly wound' I now realised would have been a major accomplishment for my ham hands.

The silence that followed was loud.

Emily and Margaret had now returned too – mourners at the wake of my self-respect. Even the day trippers inspecting the scale models and video displays around us seemed to be holding their breath.

Rain spat on the roof.

'Shall we go?' suggested Margaret.

The four of us walked out from the tourist centre into strengthening, blustery rain.

I carried some kit in a nylon bag which got steadily saturated and heavier as we went. Margaret had already raised the question of whether I was going to carry my kit in 'that bag, like that' and I had replied cheerily that 'yes, yes I was'. Now it was becoming clear that I had made a bit of an error but, determined to brazen it out, I strode on, arm aching, implausibly jaunty.

We stepped up our pace along the stone path which follows round the lake. Wind swept past like buses, pushing us off balance. It became obvious to me that, after the rope incident, someone was now going to fall into the lake and die. Probably Margaret. That was all I needed.

First the rope debacle, now a death.

Hazel would never forgive me. It would be written up in the Pinnacle journal and I would not be allowed back to the hut, or Wales, ever again.

I walked on in resigned dudgeon and drizzle.

Earlier on our group had passed a man coming down the path who knew Hazel and Margaret. Wherever were we going? he asked, bemused. 'To climb the slabs!' we'd chorused, brightly . . . over-brightly perhaps. 'It's good practice to carry the kit up and back anyway,' said Hazel with a tight smile.

That's it, I thought to myself as we stumped wretchedly on, that's what they'll write: 'Humouring the idiot who'd already destroyed a perfectly serviceable rope, the put-upon representatives of the Pinnacle Club carried all their kit up to Hope in a monsoon, during which fool's errand Margaret drowned, Emily froze to death from shame and only Hazel's volcanic rage spared her serious injury . . .'

At the slabs the weather was horrendous. The wind was blasting a vuvuzela cacophony. The rain thumped about and water sluiced down the sliding face. The rocks looked slick and soapy. We were not climbing here, that was clear. Yet we still stopped and took in the scene rather than turning on our heels and I was suddenly grateful for everyone's forbearance. Emily took a hopeful stance upon a low flake pitch but the sodden ropes stayed bagged and looped about shoulders. A Promethean Joe Brown might have shinned up the glassy rock in socks without a backwards glance, but he was not around so, stopped, we stood. Too wet to sit down, we huddled to discuss how one might have gone about the slabs on another day – were the day a better day; were the day not bloody awful. Then we turned and started down, back the way we'd come. It was too miserable for the scenic route – a bloody awful day to be out.

Oh! To be sat in a nice warm car! Oh, for a car-park view of the hills with the sky's din checked by a windscreen. Oh, to be elsewhere, beneath a tin roof, snug, knees drawn up near a fire – a day for toast and climbing stories – hot soup, talk and tea.

But here we were. Out here: Hazel in red, Margaret in purple, I in black and green; Emily darting ahead, taking pictures, fair hair streaming from her hood.

On the walk up to the slabs the wind had been at our backs so we were pushed along – because even the elements enjoy a joke. The rain had ricocheted off our legs and packs and hats but we'd felt warm. But on the way back! The deluge soaked my cotton trousers and stuck them, cold and chafing, to my thighs. The feeling of soaking trousers and the miserable slop and friction was uncomfortable, unpleasant and wearing. Sopping, we walked – I hadn't put my waterproof over-trousers on, *obviously*, and I was still carrying my nylon bag, now drenched, holding it by the rumpled neck and tramping on, wordless, past the thrashing waters of Llyn Idwal, back to the car park and a longed-for change of clothes at the site of my rope misdemeanour. I had to smile. The whole episode, the quiet stoicism of all concerned . . .

What would Dorothy have said?

She'd have laughed.

Yes, she'd have laughed because laughter was the only sensible response, faced with such a scene.

I imagined the internal monologues of the other three, then flinched and tried to think of something else. The rain began to ease as we approached the car, by which point I could hear my boots slurping and my head was the only dry part of my body. Doubtless my ears, burning red beneath my Richard Thompson teacosy hat circa 1975, had helped.

Wool! Good old wool.

Wool, regret and paranoia. Never fails.

* * * * *

Driving back to Capel Curig, the day felt bleak indeed. The sky was slate grey, all four of us were sat on plastic bags to keep the seats dry and the windows soon steamed with our body heat. Fine Idwal rain had soused us to the bone so, despite stuffing as many of our saturated layers, coats and kit in the boot as possible, there was little respite from the wet. Conversation was scattershot. I smelt like damp dog and wished I could've wrung myself out like one, but as we neared the Cwm Dyli hut, thoughts of tea and towels revived us, so it hardly seemed to matter that, lull over, the sky reopened as we parked and stair-rod rain began to batter the car anew. We took it in turns to jump out with a bag and pelt up between the trees and through the picket gate which led on to a megalithic tightrope of a bridge, below which thrashed a stream in spate. Scampering over the bridge, we ran on, up the path to the hut's porch, keys in hand, green door opened and in, lights on, door shut, the white noise suddenly less, the downpour left without. Panting, laughing, wet, relieved, we put the kettle on. The

Cwm Dyli Doorway
– Hazel Jones, Dan
Richards, Margaret
Clennett, October
2013 (Emily Benton)

best hut in the world and we were in it. The Emily Kelly
Hut: heart of the Pinnacle's kirk.

The downstairs of the hut is one big room, the kitchen to
the left, a long table with benches in the middle, and a large
fireplace forming the right-hand wall. The *Pinnacle Club
Journal*'s original account of the hut's opening made special
mention of the fireplace and its huge, rough-hewn cross-
beam. Then, as now, in the centre of the beam, hangs a
beautiful oak panel bearing, in carved relief, the inscription:
Emily Kelly Hut, Nov 5th 1932. Above this hangs a long-
handled, shallow-toothed ice axe of the type favoured in the
early twentieth century.

We lit the wood-burner which now sits in the hearth and
hung our wet clothes in the humid drying room – a vast air-
ing cupboard for kit, built as part of a recent extension to the

Pinnacles outside
Cwm Dyli, *c.*1933
(RCM)

cottage, which has grown and evolved much since its thirties inception. The walls are clad with tongue and groove
and built-in storage, bookshelves and boxes. Notice boards
of photographs record the club's endeavours round the
world. Where once the ground floor was divided in two by
a stairway and held only a tiny recessed kitchenette, now the
stairs have been resited to one side of the building and a
well-stocked substantial kitchen occupies one third of the
room. The long airy dormitory which originally formed the
top floor is now filled with solid bunks rather than the inau-
gural green sailcloth hammocks and cots – 'gaily bedded
with scarlet blankets, proudly displayed by those who were
going to sleep in them for the first time that night'.[6] A photograph in the 1933 club journal has a maritime air, the
beams and eaves looming like an inverse keel, the

woollen-hatted ladies kipping meshed like cabin boys.

Now the place is insulated, watertight and warm and hard rains on the hills behind don't spring up through the floor. There are skylights in the roof which flood the once dark loft with light. There are indoor toilets and hot showers where once hot water was boiled up over an open fire. Yet the building, though much had changed, was familiar to me from *Climbing Days* and Dorothy's diaries. For all the cosy mod-cons, the original spirit endures. I thought of how delighted she would have been with it today as our damp boots steamed beside the ticking stove and rain hammered bootless without. Her diary entry of Friday 18 May 1934 seemed particularly close to my own experience:

Up at 10AM. Very fiercest Welsh rain. Thank goodness no one else has arrived. Naked, with only a mackintosh over me, padded out to get water. Stove lighting – breakfast, washing up, cleaning – Funny life.

Soon romantic views of bright gorse bushes + just unfolding bracken get hidden in potato peeling + the stern practicalities.

Soup + off to Llanrwst to order new pair of climbing boots . . . (upon return) Found Gabriel & Lowe – Wilson and Taylor had arrived. Deluge getting wilder. Great supper cooking all the evening. Molly Barnard from Manchester,

Cobham Watson & Fairfield – Later 10:15 Biddy Deed, Harper, Allaun.

Awfully like being back in a school dormitory – there are to be 21 – 15 sleeping in – the rest out.[7]

I picture the Pinnacles assembling – travelling to North Wales by train and motor car, collecting each other like raindrops on a window pane, funnelling down the valleys to converge at the hut in a hail of hugs and climbing sobriquets. I imagine the joy of seeing the cottage lights aglow from the Beddgelert road, the warmth of the long room, its smell of soup and woodsmoke; chill dusk and rain shut out with the solid thump of the door and snap of a latch.

I'll remember my weekend at Cwm Dyli for the fine misting spray which hung in the air and slowly dove inside jackets, down necks, up sleeves, through socks and into boots – insipid implacable Welsh *glaw mân*: drizzle; or *gwlithlaw* – that gently falling fine rain of autumn which my father has always called 'mank'.

* * * * *

Emily – or Benton, as I should probably call her in the context of the hut – had travelled up to Wales very light and only brought the clothes she was wearing, so I lent her a shirt and pair of trousers whilst hers dried in the other room. On Emily, far more slight than I, my cords took on the look of Oxford bags; an unexpected but apt aesthetic. She put me in mind of Diane Keaton in *Annie Hall* as she moved about the hut – mirroring the pictures pinned to the walls of the club's ninetieth-birthday ascent of Lockwood's Chimney, the ladies replete with tweed knickerbockers, breeches and plus fours – having fun despite the dreich and grainy mizzle. Like us, they'd been climbing the weather as much as the rocks of Wales. To paraphrase Dylan Thomas: *my great-great-aunt's ghost is climbing in the rain.*[8]

That evening, I sat at the long table with Margaret and Hazel and began to look through the hut's archive and collected correspondence. There were a lot of letters to and from club members from the Pinnacle's earliest days – 'Our club will of course be democratic and embrace all classes,' wrote Emily Kelly to Pilley (or 'Pitthley' as she often addressed her in letters), 'the one qualification being that of ability to lead a moderate climb . . . I think there are really very few who have tried – not because they haven't the ability, but simply because they haven't been encouraged. Well, with our Club in view they will have every encouragement to qualify for membership.'[9]

The letter is typewritten but underlined and signed ('Pat') with gusto, the 'coming club of our very own' is underscored for emphasis, and whilst the paper is slightly foxed at the edges it could have been written recently.[10] It still radiated vivid purpose in my hands ninety-three years later: the first proto-PC manifesto, the foundation for the club, the hut and the archive where it's been kept safe ever since, together with the boxes of postcards, photographs, club song lyrics, signed menus, drafts of climbing articles, scrawled notes complaining of sub-par journal submissions, apologies and summations of missed meets in Cumbria. Amidst all of this sits Kelly's single-page fountainhead. I found its survival very touching; all the more so for the fact that she died so young and didn't live to see her club flourish and succeed.

The correspondence written in the aftermath of her sudden death in 1922 – tripping on rocks not far from the Cwm Dyli hut – is full of raw shock and condolence. The question repeated over and over is how someone so alive, so skilled, could suddenly be gone; the waste of it. Dorothy writes in *Climbing Days* that 'It is an ironic commentary on human care and skill that, as so often in the mountains, one of the most prudent and expert of climbers should lose her life while the irresponsible and reckless constantly escape. The accident on

Tryfan (April 17, 1922) was one of the most startling and cruel calamities which are the more dreadful because unprovoked.'

More dreadful perhaps because death and injury in the mountains can be so banal. To walk and climb in such a dramatic place as Snowdonia, the high Pyrenees or Pennine Alps, one might think that accidents would be similarly sensational, the rescues action packed and death-defying in the truest sense, that a sense of Boy's Own valour would attend. It is not so. People trip over and bang their heads, they get lost and disappear, they ski into crevasses, walk off cliffs, they get cold and fall asleep.

Emily recalls walking along a dry riverbed in New Zealand on a clear warm day, en route to a climb which had been years in the planning. She stumbled on a rock like any other rock and broke her wrist. That was it.

A friend of my father's slid off a mountain in the Carnedds. Nobody saw him go. The back-marker of a school party walking the Snowdon Horseshoe – he was there, then he wasn't.

Chance plays a huge part and, for all the best practice in the world, accidents still happen. Take rock fall: if you get hit by couple of pounds of rock travelling at 50 mph you won't know much about it, even with a helmet; and you can't make contingency plans for that, beyond a certain point. One can climb early in the day when the rock is still iced and avoid gullies and couloirs after morning, attempt to stay on buttresses and ridgelines, and avoid climbing below other parties, but that can be fairly limiting if one has a particular goal or route in mind, so people do their homework and take their chances and ride their luck.

But there does seem a real injustice to Emily Kelly's death because it was so blunt and prosaic – unworthy of her extraordinarily vibrant life, achievements and contribution to the climbing craft. Walking down alone from a solo climb on Tryfan, she stumbled, possibly as a result of the new nails in her boot soles, and hit her head. When found, she was rushed to hospital in Llandudno but died from her injuries nine days later, on 26 April.

I found a heartbreaking letter from her husband, Harry, which for all its restraint revealed a shattered man at a bewildered loss:

Bramhall, Cheshire
May 2, 1922

Dear Pilley,

I should like to thank you for your letter of April 30th and what you say therein about Pat.

She was my wife but I think I am dispassionate enough in my judgements to be able to say without any bias that she was the finest woman I have ever met. We lived together almost the whole of the 24 hours of each day. She was always fresh & new. Courage, large-heartedness and love she had in plenty. I suppose I am only now realising what a part she played in my life. To her more than anyone else do I owe a sympathetic understanding of woman's position in life.

. . . Because of her all-embracing character and pure spirit, I am beginning to think that the mts. had a right in claiming her. All that one objects to now is the time – but this comes to us all – when we know not.

Believe me,
Yours Sincerely,
H. M. Kelly

I am returning the letter you so kindly sent & hope the journal will fructify. She had her heart set on it. May the P.C. prosper.

She was the means of its birth & she called it more than once, her child.

I should like to hear from you at one time or other
H.M.K.

* * * * *

There's a famous photograph of Pat Kelly, taken at Castle Naze in the Peak District, balanced on a gritstone pitch known as the Scoop. She is poised on a sloping swoosh of rock. Alert, crouched as if for a starter's pistol. Dapped feet set, body tensed, the fingers of both hands sunk in thin cracks, her face is turned up towards her goal – the climb running left to right. Even in the early 1920s the Scoop appears shiny; silvered by the soles of innumerable feet. Looking at the picture, Margaret noted that many of the routes from that time are now so polished that they often present an impasse for modern climbers far harder than their original ratings – 'better tackled in tights than boots'.

'Milestone Buttress is now a severe climb,' said Hazel, having cross-checked it with a modern guide to the region. 'When the first Pinnacles did them, they'd have had grassy ledges and all sorts . . . they did use to garden routes but they wouldn't have had much traffic, so from one season to the next all the grass would have grown back.'*

I thought about the rocks I'd seen elsewhere, flecked grey

---

* 'Gardening' in terms of climbing means cleaning a potential route of vegetation, pulling out ferns, grass, moss and other slippery 'green stuff' to reveal the rock beneath.

by crampons and nails, roughed and pitted, ghosted white with powdered chalk, stubbed in matt by boot toes and rubber points, or just plain buffed by the passage of a thousand hands and feet so the routes shine and draw the eye stuttering up a face at intervals like a dot-to-dot.

I thought back to Ivor's notes and illustrations, posted to Dorothy whilst both were away from Wales but still dreaming and plotting new paths up its crags – distracted pencil lines radiating out from dismal Magdalene invigilations; Cambridge memories of calloused trial and error – sketchy experiments now recognised as standard climbs, cased as stairs. A route like Holly Tree Wall, which the pair put up with C. F. Holland in 1920, laid a foundation for generations of later climbers to explore and extrapolate, so that the rocks above Hope would now look a tangled web were each palimpsest variation marked. As such, Dorothy and Ivor's early endeavours are still discernible on the rocks hereabouts – the red strand through the rope. And whilst, today, such routes are destinations, classics to be polished off, that was not the case back when the Pinnacle Club first assembled in their newly renovated hut.

Then it was a lightship in an unknown sea.

* * * * *

The next morning, the skylight was a glaring square. I blinked, remembered where I was, and saw the hill behind rearing, seemingly set to tear down and break over the hut. I had no idea what time it was but there was a steaming mug of tea at my elbow. The others were awake.

We'd turned in late, the night before, having pored over the archives downstairs and seen slideshows of the club's recent adventures in Morocco and traversing *via ferrata* in Italy – which translates as 'iron road'* – a cross between climbing and hiking where the participants clip themselves to fixed steel cables along engineered routes which often snake for miles along, up, down and through precipitous alpine regions. It looked brilliant fun, the cable providing a secure vantage to wallow in the vertigo and drama of a sheer ravine or massive stapled 'stemple' ladder climb. Developed by the Italian army as First World War supply routes, the *via ferrata* were appropriated by climbers in the years that followed. Looking at the sandy, bleached images on Hazel's computer, I was struck by the fact that these trails could be tackled safely solo, following the hawser course with just a carabinered lanyard and harness, ranging alone for hours in the Dolomite sun like a high-wire rigger or an acrobat. How Dorothy would have loved that freedom. Perhaps she did? I made a mental note to check her diaries for edgeways Italian zip lines.

Outside, it was raining. The only things bleached here were my retinas, so I slid down onto the cold wood floor and dressed in the quiet of the dormitory, recalling how, last night, Benton had hung jauntily from the fingerboard affixed to one of the beams, pulling herself up – one, two, three, four – languidly, easy as you like. Now, chilly, bleary, half-naked, I hooked my own fingers into the wooden slots and raised myself off the floor: Once. Tw-ice. Thr–ee . . . I'm not sure if the sound of my fall carried downstairs. If it did, the others were good enough to ignore it.

I finished dressing and drank my tea.

Day Three had begun.

---

* *Klettersteig*, in German – 'climbing path'.

* * * * *

Without wishing to bang on about it, the weather really wasn't very good. Several months later, working to write up this chapter, I discovered a Welsh phrase for such sodden days, *Mae hi'n bwrw hen wragedd a ffyn* – 'It's raining old women and sticks.'[11]

All the old women fell out the sky that day. They fell in waves and strafed the hut, tapped on the windows with their sticks and rattled in the chimney whilst the four of us ate breakfast. The one benefit of the inundation seemed to be that it was not freezing cold. Too warm for frost or snow, the autumn world outside was chock-full of brick-brown ferns and Bovril bracken, flocked and trooping up the slopes around us, mixing with the greens of the moss and the grass and the duller, hard blue of the knotted rowan and haw-thorn trees steel-rooted in the hill.

We decided to venture out under the loaded clouds and scramble up behind the hut. It wasn't a day for rock climbing and we didn't want to go too far from the snug of the bunkhouse, but neither did we want to just sit and listen to the rain. So, dressed in our warm-dried outer clothes, we began to tromp up to the horizon, all boot-slapping fronds and damp smoky smells. Heads down, picking our path beside the stream as it dove and swept down its jet rock flume. We clambered over drystone walls, lichen-furred and greasy. Listening to the waters rush, we became aware that the rain had stopped and the wind had apparently blown itself out. The constant pitter-patter had been replaced with our hard breathing and the low hum of a car on the Beddgelert road and, below it all, the soft sound of the percolating mountain – an underfoot hubbub of oozing hiccups, coughs and ticks.

We stood, apparently alone, the only people in Nant Gwynant, drinking in the panorama. 'To write about Wales is to describe a series of particular climbs, of plans, explorations, disappointments, renunciations, renewed hopes, changes of "form" and weather, and sometimes eventual triumph,' wrote Dorothy in *Climbing Days*, ' but actually, when one is there, the dramatic fabric of those scenes is overlaid by the massed impression.'

This was how it was with us then. Would the other three have set about something vertiginous had I not been there? Possibly, but I'd like to think that we were all content to spend the morning scrambling and rambling, apparently aimless.

Without a mission we drifted up to look into Snowdonia as civilians rather than climbers, still soppy from the warmth of the hut, and stood on the threshold of a wild place, gazing into the teeth of the Carnedds.

Now high on the hill, we turned to look back over the dwindled cottage to the glossy power station beyond. It was easy to picture the nascent Pinnacles standing hereabouts when they first spied the ruin that would become their hut. There it was, sat next to the electricity plant which, I now saw, had an Arts and Crafts air – more chapel than industrial plant. Not all is as it was in the thirties, however, for, whilst the waters of the stream still disappear under the complex and doubtless spun some turbines in the past, a large pipeline now zigzags away and disappears over the ridgeline, which, when reached, reveals a plateau beyond – boggy, pocked with boulders and all the time the ashen pipe eels on, horizon on horizon.

Something about its presence rendered the scape around it bleaker. It ran like a Vorticist strike across the marshes, between the corrugated crags, streaking towards unseen Llyn Llydaw and behind that, looming Snowdon, cowled as if it too had taken umbrage with the weather and decided to have a steam inhalation.

* * * * *

Emily slept on the fast train south. I read, curled up in canine comfort under low light whilst the world flashed past outside and the day spooled out behind us, happy to be carried off and arc like a thrown thing towards London. Strange as it might sound – not having actually climbed anything during our time there – Wales had rather knackered us. I felt as if I had not slept for a week. In fact, I could barely credit that we'd only been there a few days. It felt like a month, so completely had it enveloped us. There had been an uncanny magic about it – a sense that it truly was a world apart – so now, swaying gently at 100 mph, I vaguely imagined our speed as a necessary escape velocity to break from Snowdonia's sphere.

I felt closer to Dorothy having visited the Pinnacles and a great sense of pride at how the club had grown and thrived in the hundred or so years since its formation.

Margaret had kindly given me an original copy of the club's first journal, which contained an account by Lilian Bray of one of their first *en cordée feminine* expeditions, titled 'Three Pinnaclers in the Alps'. 'In 1921, guideless mountaineering for women, *sans hommes*, had hardly started,' wrote Dorothy of the same venture. 'Lilian Bray,

Annie Wells and I discussed a programme of guideless climbing to open the 1921 season.' The group took great pains 'to incur no legitimate criticism', knowing that a rope of women would arouse unprecedented scrutiny and they had not only to achieve their stated objectives but do so flawlessly in order to prove their point and be deemed a success in the eyes of their male peers and the public at large. 'We felt ourselves to be pioneers. The doctrine that women could and should take full responsibility for climbs within their powers was to be tested.'[12] Indeed, this was to prove a watershed as the Pinnacle Club blazed *cordées feminines* trails throughout the Alps during the 1930s whilst the Ladies' Alpine Club stuck firmly to guided expeditions.[13]

Now, as the train sped on and our distance from the hut increased, I recalled scenes from the visit like a slideshow: the discovery that Dorothy was a paper and stationery hoarder, like me, and in old age would amend old PC headed notepaper so it read, 'The Pinnacle Club, *Once* Editor :: Mrs I. A. Richards' – the *Once* added in spidery pencil.

The smell of steaming boots on a stovetop.

The pale curtain which we watched inexorably pushing its way up the valley towards us – an imminent wall of old women with sticks. I tried to picture Dorothy waiting for us in Ogwen car park as we arrived as drowned and thwarted rats. Was she old or was she young? Was she stooped with sticks and that battered black hat or was she the youthful woman in the PC journal, dressed in a smock and beret, plus fours and roll-top boots, feisty and glamorous? How had I envisioned her to be, walking down?

Smiling. That was it. She was there and she was smiling and the thought of that, the thought that she'd have been

pleased to meet me there, in her domain, that was important.[*] If I was on her track and she was on my side, all would
be well, for the more I learnt about her life, the more I liked
her. I determined to send the current Pinnacle cohort a
hamper by way of thanks, as Dorothy so often did – a gift
from us both to the club she loved, still so vital and strong
and unique.[†] And I smiled to think of Hazel's incandes-
cence and Margaret's devotion to the archives and the hut,
and I remembered the sound of the wind lashing the valley
around us the previous night as I lay awake in my bunk and
the feeling of being safe aboard ship in a storm.

Dorothy and Emily Kelly and all the founders would
surely be so proud to see it now and amazed by the scope of
the Pinnacle's activities in mountains all over the world.

It remains perhaps Dorothy's greatest achievement – a
tangible, living legacy in a landscape she adored.

* * * * *

[*] Originally I'd imagined Dorothy laughing and said as much in a postcard
to Anthony Pilley, who responded a couple of weeks later with a letter –
'You picture her as laughing. For the book it probably doesn't matter, yet
perhaps for *you* it does as I sense you have a genuine wish to know her. If
I consciously think about it, (which I have to), I can't remember Dorothy
ever laughing openly with abandon – in a relaxed and solid way she was
quite considered and restrained. What I remember is her bright, enthusiastic
inquisitiveness and her wry knowing glances when she would purse her lips.
Also, a very very warm and welcoming smile. She would have wanted to
hear your impressions and maybe her words would be accompanied by a
firm chuckle. And she would have been doubly excited for you as a young
family member. But she never treated anyone as special, nor what anyone
was doing as special. If a Martian came down the hillside, she would be most
likely to suggest they try using different boots. But who knows? Children
and young adults laugh more than old people and perhaps if I had known
Dorothy at 22 she would have been roaring continually.'
[†] The current Pinnacle Club membership is 156 – November 2014.

The cliffs, the oblique rain across the slopes of the Carnedds, the purple chaos of rocks heaped out into a gusty Ogwen, the spongy masses of sphagnum in the swamps, the clean sheep-bitten turf, the drier shelves above, the endless crying of the streams and the dark gulf at evening of the lower valley. Mornings when Y Garn and Foel-goch soar up out of the shrouds of lifting cloud and the Lake glitters through the curtain of the rowans with their dark coral berries. The stringiness of the bilberry clumps as you lie in the sunshine on the Heather Terrace, the squeak of the lambs as you wind down between the long-snouted rocks. Out of all these is composed a bodily feeling, nameless and definite and irreplaceable, like a scent or a taste or an ache. When one is away, some accident – a sheep's baa, a lichen patch on a stone wall – will awaken it; but it is none of these things. It is the reverberation of one's life among them, known completely only to those who have lived the same life among the mountains . . . Such evocations as I can attempt are at best a hieroglyph to be read in other terms as you please. But in each case the sense of an uncapturable significance will arise, and its secret – for the mountaineer as for any pilgrim passion – is almost an open one. Therein, reflected, is the experience of being ardently alive.[14]

The Cairngorms

As my train edged out of Waverley – below the serrate spire of Scott's Monument, castle bristling on its granite plug above – I recalled how I'd seen Radiohead years before at the Edinburgh Corn Exchange: travelling up from university in flat Norfolk, staying in a hostel high on Cockburn Street, in a room atop a helter-skelter staircase. I slept in a bunk bed next to a window which I climbed through next morning, out onto a slate roof overlooking the sleeping city. Perched near the parapet, my back to a chimney stack, breath steaming, six storeys up from the cobblestones, I sat with gooseflesh arms, watching the dawn begin to gather purple beyond the floodlit castle and the sky clear blue.

A small spot of buildering.

My first Scottish ascent.

Now I'd returned to climb higher, further north in the Cairngorm mountains and take part in a Conville winter mountaineering course to better equip myself for the challenges ahead. If I was going to follow in Dorothea's steps, I would need some instruction and guidance.

The Conville courses were established by Jonathan Conville's family in the wake of his death on the north face of the Matterhorn in 1979. He was twenty-seven. A trust was set up to provide training and subsidy to enable young mountaineers to enjoy the mountains in greater safety; 'to encourage and assist young people to train for and pursue their love of the outdoors in the spirit of adventure, which Jonathan embraced during his life.' Programmes run in both Scotland and France aim to provide the uninitiated with the essential skills required to travel safely in high mountains, with the specific, heuristic advantage that Conville course instruction usually happens 'in the field', be that the slopes of Aberdeenshire or the Chamonix Valley – what better classroom than the mountains themselves?

I've found no record Dorothea ever climbed in the Cairngorms, although her great friend Janet Adam Smith often did and would sometimes break her journey back from London to her family home in Aberdeen to walk into their mass – taking a sleeper train to Aviemore, Kingussie or Blair Atholl before crossing over the mountains to Braemar.¹ The nearest *Climbing Days* gets is the Cuillin of the Inner Hebrides – detailed in her chapter 'The Misty Isle of Skye', where Dorothea writes of traversing the black gabbro stegosaurus of Sgùrr nan Gillean amongst the many climbs and scrambles registered despite 'five weeks of wind and hail, rain, mist and snow'. But she'd definitely recognise the techniques I was shortly to discover and deploy: how to handle an ice axe, belaying and general rope work, avalanche assessment and winter survival skills; she would surely have read about them if not employed them herself, such was her hunger. In the same Skye chapter she sketches this peculiar facet of the mountain passion:

> Dreams of other ranges filled my days. I haunted second-
> hand bookshops for climbing literature . . . I would go far

out of my way to look, for the hundredth time, at a photograph of the Meiji or of Mont Blanc on a poster at Victoria. I showed, in fact, all the symptoms by which this obsession manifests itself. So, when out of these dreams the actuality of a visit to Skye began to develop, there was fuel enough ready to be consumed. . . . To the really sublime devotee the fascination of the peaks spreads itself to whatever else can conceive to become in any way ancillary to their attainment. Not only equipment, boots, ropes, lanterns, ice-axes, or maps and literature, but even railway timetables acquired a derivative but desirable lure.[2]

It was true: I'd experienced something of the same mania in the days leading up to this trip. A pile of kit began to accrue in the hall. I'd gone to outdoorsy shops specifically to discuss socks. I found myself packing and repacking my rucksack distractedly, checking the SAIS Snow Report for the northern Cairngorms each night before bed, dreams full of the colour-coded roundels forewarning of avalanche dangers. Reading this back, I see that I'd possibly begun to develop a panicked mountain OCD or 'Cairngorm psychosis' rather than the genteel enthusiasm Dorothea describes above.

At some unseen point in the journey beyond Perth, the train crossed into the Highlands and, to my tired and child-like mind at least, began to gain in height. As time and sleepy stations passed and traveller numbers thinned, it had occurred that I might be surrounded by others on the course. With nothing to see in the mirror-backed windows I dipped into *Mountain Navigation* by Peter Cliff, required reading for the days ahead, a book chock-full of orientation nous whose bright purple cover turned out to be a good Conville emblem because, as soon as it emerged, several previously impassive folk in the seats about me made themselves known.

It turned out there were six of us in the carriage – Ella from Coniston, Sam and Freddie, friends from Yorkshire, Baiba from Cardiff (originally Latvia) and Paddy who'd bussed and trained over from Bratislava (originally from Manchester) – wearing his massif boots the whole way to save space in his bag. Experience among the group ranged from winter alpine treks to summer hikes and indoor bouldering, but all were excited by the prospect of the blue cairns slopes and lofted pristine snows.

By the time we'd introduced ourselves and shaken all the hands, the train was slowing for Aviemore and we alighted into chill night air, each hefting a rucksack, tin mugs and other such gear clipped and clinking, orbiting satellite-like. I was glad to see that I'd brought neither too much nor too little in the way of kit. Over chips whilst waiting for the day's last lift, I scanned the bags propped up in the cafe. Suddenly the thing was real. Earlier, changing trains, I'd clocked a few odd looks which I'd put down to the Chouinard Zero ice axe strapped to the back of my sack – unusual and unwieldy luggage in Birmingham – but here, now, it made sense; the axe was in its element even if I was not. As the minibus stopped in the station car park and we loaded in, I felt an excited camaraderie which went some way to quell my nerves. We were definitely at the start of an adventure.

As we drove north-east toward Grantown-on-Spey and the Ardenbeg bunkhouse where we were to stay, I could vaguely make out a black heft to my right, lit by the starlight of the cloudless night. There it was, imminent now, the Cairngorm range as weighed by Nan Shepherd in her poem 'Summit of Corrie Etchachan':

> No vision of the blue world, far, unattainable,
> But this grey plateau, rock-strewn, vast, silent,
> The dark loch, the toiling crags, the snow;
> A mountain shut within itself, yet a world,
> Immensity.[3]

I was introduced to Nan Shepherd by Robert Macfarlane, who presented me with a copy of *The Living Mountain* the morning we drove down to the Dorset holloway.[4] Recently republished with an introduction by Robert – researched and written in the National Library of Scotland – the book seemed to augur well for my current situation, both as object, bridge and reference, since Shepherd was a tousled contemporary of Pilley, her mountain writing similarly rooted in the territorial imperatives of that scape. Meandering and sensual, Shepherd's Cairngorm record mirrors the intense narrative and energy within *Climbing Days* but with the emphasis firmly on the tension between elemental geology and individual ambition, concerned with mankind's place in the broader scheme and the traces left behind but not bound by such matters. Where Dorothea climbs and arrows, Shepherd explores and ambles; where the former seeks specific heights, the latter joys in 'essential nature', revelling in the wilderness – those innumerable mysterious aspects of a wild totality. Shepherd rarely talks of venturing *up* but writes of walking *into* the mountain. The Cairngorms were one entity to her, a living thing. The mountains, a multiverse of innumerable dimensions and sensorial possibilities, but principally just *to be there*, within their scope was all. *Being there.*

To my mind, the two complement each other wonderfully well: Dorothea's mountaineering, itinerant and questing, and Shepherd's mountain literature, intent and provincial. Both voices beckoned me to rove and write of my roving.

* * * * *

The next morning we woke before dawn. Fortunately I'd dreamt all the worst-case scenarios overnight so felt slightly more prepared for disaster. Spurred by a strong cup of sweet tea, I blearily dressed in the thermal base layers I'd laid out the night before – long johns, wool top, first pair of thick socks, salopettes (mountaineering dungarees) – with all the braces, zips and fastenings that involved. A merino mid-layer top, a second pair of socks, fleece top and two-part plastic boots – lacing the boxing boot-like inner, then pushing that into the rigid plastic outer before lacing that too. This was made more cumbersome by the fact I'd begun to resemble the Michelin Man as the clothing mounted. Next I put on gaiters with their elastic straps, velcro and snap fasteners, enclosing the shins to sit over the boot laces and tongue, the strap passing under the sole and fixing the other side. A fiddle. But eventually I was dressed and, feeling toasty, clomped to the kitchen for breakfast and a briefing on the day ahead.

There were nine of us in all, the six from the train together with Louie from Bedford, who'd arrived early the previous day, James from Preston and Sam from Sussex, who'd travelled up sideways overnight on the

Euston sleeper.* All of them seemed unbelievably cheery considering it was still dark outside – relaxed and raring to go – whereas I was getting the yips as to how I'd fare taking bearings or tying bowlines, or whether I'd skewer myself with an axe.

Sat round the large wood table, we introduced ourselves to instructors Jonathan Preston and Mark 'Sammy' Samuels – nice, fiendishly knowledgeable chaps, as it turned out. Jonathan was very businesslike, composed and trenchant, whereas Sammy seemed to crackle with an enthusiastic energy just south of manic. I was placed in Jonathan's team. Together we looked over the printouts of the day's weather

* Norman MacCaig, 'Sleeping Compartment', *The Poems of Norman MacCaig*, Polygon, 2009; *Train Songs*, Faber, 2013.

> I don't like this, being carried sideways
> through the night. I feel wrong and helpless – like
> a timber broadside in a fast stream.
>
> Such a way of moving may suit
> that odd snake the sidewinder
> in Arizona: but not me in Perthshire.
>
> I feel at right angles to everything,
> a crossgrain in existence. – It scrapes
> the top of my head and my footsoles.
>
> To forget outside is no help either –
> then I become a blockage
> in the long gut of the train.
>
> I try to think I'm an Alice in Wonderland
> mountaineer bivouacked
> on a ledge five feet high.
>
> It's no good. I go sidelong.
> I rock sideways – I draw in my feet
> To let Aviemore pass.

forecast and then collected the rest of our kit – packing spare warm mitts, goggles, helmet, thermos, laminated Cairngorms Map 1:50,000 OS Sheet 36, compass and head torch in my rucksack. Pulling on my wool hat, waterproof jacket and gloves, and carrying my crampons and ice axe, I made my way out to the stiff dawn and the bus.

Then, driving into the hills below smattered mackerel cirrocumulus, air warming, light welling – the sun rose as a saturated Polaroid developing before us; the day scrubbed clean, Brautigan blue: 'the blue of human eyes, waiting for something to happen'.[5]

* * * * *

The twin lochans in the bowl of Coire an t-Sneachda were invisible, buried. Our cohort stood with backs pressed behind a large boulder, which provided some shelter from the wind that thwacked and swirled about us. The wind had been spoiling for a fight since we'd set out from the Coire na Ciste ski centre an hour or so before – constantly hassling, outright opposed to our progress, bowling gusts in twos and threes with just enough interval to recover balance before the last knocked you over again.

Although not snowing, the wind whipped and strafed us with powder from the slopes. Dashed and peppered, I zipped my collar over my mouth and pulled my goggles tighter and began to develop an eye for the rolling waves of snow ahead which showed the gusts to come, bracing before they hit.

In the lulls I heard our boots on the snow, in step, crisp as Visa cards swiping frost off a dozen windscreens. We were a crunching peloton, trooping over sastrugi and the teardrop drumlins formed behind rocks – frozen velo-drome helmet lumps, shaped by the squalls which luffed my hood, rasped my ears and ripped the hat off Jonathan's head, sending it racing away behind us. As one the group turned and watched it go, streaking down the valley like a frighted hare and out of sight, never to be seen again.

Now, behind the boulder, I pushed up my goggles. Their sepia tint, which had given the cirque and rock field a Martian aspect, instantly turned to dazzling neon blue, as if a flare had gone off. It took a good minute for my vision to recover. I spent that minute rather blindly fiddling with loose gaiters and creeping salopettes, a dance I'd repeat at intervals throughout the day to come.

Around us rose the cliffs of Coire an t-Sneachda – 'Corrie of the snow' – whose colosseum tiers shot sheer into the low cloud, their snow flanks steepening until they dovetailed into bare granite outcrops, fissured and quartzy, mean. Their darkness was such that it burnt through the white around them, their severity hypnotic.

Jonathan pointed out climbs above – Jacob's Ladder, Aladdin's Mirror and Crotched Gully – deserted today, unfancied in this weather, but many climbers have come unstuck in this place . . . and I've written 'come unstuck' there, but as I look at it now all the Wodehousian chutzpah drains away and it stands mealy-mouthed and hollow – for to come unstuck in this charged white hanging space is often to die. This place will eat you.

In early 2007 alone, five climbers died here in four acci-dents, either caught out by the conditions or falling from the routes overhead. 'Young people have always been driven to go out and have adventures, and that's a good thing,' said

Roger Wild of the Mountaineering Council of Scotland in a *Guardian* article about that winter's spate of fatalities.

> But mountains aren't a commodity you can put in a super-market trolley . . . There's nothing wrong necessarily going climbing in the face of a bad forecast. You would perhaps set out earlier, or climb something easier. But you can't point at these lads and say they did something wrong. You can say they were a bit off the mark in one or two areas. But we should be proud of them, going out and having an adventure.[6]

Later in the same piece, John Allen, a Cairngorm Mountain Rescue Team Leader, spelt out the dangers of seeking instant gratification without thorough grounding in the Cairngorms' nature – 'A lot of younger climbers have not got that long apprenticeship in winter climbing . . . They may have a good knowledge of rock climbing or climbing on indoor walls and be technically proficient, but they're not necessarily prepared for what the weather in winter can do.'

So back in the wind we practised step cutting and walking zigzag paths up snow slopes – ice axe always in the hand nearest the bank and so ready for an arrest should one slip. En route back down and round the corrie's floor we passed debris from a recent mini-avalanche and again our eyes swept up and over the cliffs and their freight of ice and snow.

The wind had dropped and a steady dust of flakes began when we took off our bags and set to digging a snow hole, kneeling down to tunnel with the adze end of our axes. As luck would have it, someone hit upon a previously excavated cave so all six of us were inside drinking thermos coffee in relative comfort within a few minutes. I can thoroughly recommend this hermit crab approach as a time-saving device since the next day I dug a hole in a hard-packed drift and was hacking away prostrate, knackered out, legs waggling, for half an hour before anything approaching a burrow was made; but that cramped cocoon could have been life-saving in a blizzard or if injured and awaiting help. That was the crux of the Conville course: the idea that whilst risk can never be eliminated in the mountains, it can be managed; that you 'need enough in your locker' – to quote Sammy – to survive and return to safety if things get out of hand.

'Risk was the salt,' wrote Dorothea of her Skye climbing, 'but he or she would be a stupid cook who thought the more there is of it the better!'

And so, mindful to avoid being stupid cooks, we set about learning our place within the Cairngorm's wild sphere so that to walk into it and witness its stark beauty was not to jeopardise the eggshell flesh beneath our high-tech layers.

'The Mountain Rescue service does its magnificent work, injured are plucked from ledges by helicopter, the located, the exhausted carried to safety,' wrote Nan Shepherd in *The Living Mountain*'s foreword. 'And some are not rescued. A man and a girl are found, months too late, far out of their path, the girl on abraded hands and knees as she clawed her way through a drift. I see her living face still (she was one of my students), a sane, eager, happy face. She should have lived to be old.'

If this sounds morbid or hectoring – Robert Macfarlane diagnosed a 'macabre fascination' in his introduction to the 2011 reprint – then it might be qualified by the fact Shepherd considered the Cairngorm landscape kindred and intrinsic, so it's perhaps unsurprising that her writing sometimes mirrors the cold dispassion of the mountains – a savage, oppositional territory – oscillating like the range itself between extremities. 'All these are matters that involve man,' she wrote. 'But behind them is the mountain itself, its substance, its strength, its structure, its weathers. It is fundamental to all that man does to it or on it . . . to know it in itself is still basic to his craft.'

Here, small events snowball and gather momentum: the weather turns, someone has no over-trousers, the bearing's off so the wrong path is taken, it gets dark early, you run out of water; little mistakes born of inexperience or carelessness accrue and catch you out later on . . . none of this happens on a climbing wall, those perpendicular ring-road gyms. Mountains are uncivilised.

'They sort people out,' my father told me, having read a draft of this book. 'They're not joking. They sort whole teams of people out . . .' He described walking on snow slopes in sunshine and, within a few minutes, being completely swallowed up in whiteout, besieged; stripped of all normality. 'It's like having your head in a white bucket. No landmarks. Suddenly you're completely isolated, you lose the horizon, it's loud, it's freezing, the ability to judge time fails you, your ability to judge distance goes; you forget where you were, you doubt how many are in the group, you flail, you grope about. Exhausting. Total disorientation . . . struggling not to panic. Imagine hours of that. It's like nothing else.'

He stopped. 'All the kit in the world,' he said slowly, 'all the kit in the world will not get you out of that. It's like nothing else. That's the issue with people walking onto mountains who've only ever been on walls; it's often not the falling off that hurts you, not often. People worry about falling off; they worry and they plan and buy all the kit and they forget about the journey to the face or the summit they

Ella Sadler-Andrews, the Cairngorms, 2014 (David Cooke)

want to tackle: the walk there and back. They think the kit will save them and go out unprepared for the sudden changes of weather, light and temperature.'

There had been snow blowing hard about us on that first journey up to Coire an t-Sneachda but it was akin to hard rain and we'd been able to see where we were going: the people in front and behind, the onrushing gusts, the sky, the ground. Whiteout blizzards aren't like that. Only when I encountered one firsthand, later in my travels, did I fully appreciate their extreme, overwhelming uncanniness. When it struck, I felt as if I'd been pushed into a massive tumble drier full of snow. The peripheral world closed down to become a granular stereogram. The light flattened out, a dimension short, and as the powder ambit drifted I felt myself begin to spin head over heels, yet I was still stood frozen, wasn't I? I stamped my feet and they struck unseen snow but all was fuzzy and obscured, as if by swirling ash. All but blind in the teeming storm, I squinted in hope of seeing through the pall but the pall was all there was.

'Ladies and gentlemen, we are floating in murk.'

It was indeed like nothing else; at once hugely frightening yet beautiful – more so once out of it and back in the known world with renewed dominion over my eyes and legs, able to think back and conjure the eerie unseen scene at one remove.

Even digging that snow hole, earlier in the day, my mind had begun to play tricks. Buried, the light seemed to be seeping through from all directions. Nose to the snow, I had no horizon and soon began to doubt my senses, up from down. I knew my legs were outside but which way were they pointed? Suddenly claustrophobic, I squirmed out backwards several times to check myself. Outside in the light it was ridiculous: I'd been totally lost and baffled inside a sleeping bag-sized hole! But I'd felt a rising panic and I had not liked it. 'Were I really buried in an avalanche or snow cave, I'd struggle to dig myself out,' I thought with sudden clarity; and the thought scared me.

* * * * *

We worked with maps and compass all that afternoon, calculating bearings, estimating journey times, allowing for contours – chivvied on by Jonathan to improve our accuracy, conferring and amending our position on the slope, focused on the paper landscape, zoning in to such a degree that we might have seen ourselves below as microbe mountaineers.

I was fairly rubbish at orienting myself to begin with, 180 degrees out at one point, but quickly got the measure of it. Embarrassment spurred my improvement. It definitely helped that the course was always moving toward a practical end and there was a fair bit of jeopardy on the day – to the extent that without a decent compass bearing we'd have struggled to find the burn which flowed down to the goat track which led back to the bus. It was dusk, and both burn and goat track were hidden by snow, so our heading had to be accurate or someone would inevitably fall through the floor into icy water. It was notable that Jonathan hung back at this point and our group walked out with all the trepidation of Indiana Jones crossing the cobbles of Iehova. Fortunately, when the stream emerged it was well to our right and the journey down picked up speed – but the same skills could have got us to a hut if benighted or kept us clear of crevasses in the Alps.

That night, after supper at the bunkhouse, Sammy gave us a talk and slide show about his climbing life. He took us onto the verglas of Ben Nevis's long, exposed Tower Ridge, sea climbing in Wales with his future wife, ski touring and ice climbing in Norway – fresh out of Trondheim Airport. He spoke about tackling warm cliffs in Spain and Greece, eulogising all the while about Dachstein's heavy-duty wool mitts. He waxed lyrical about a man named Toolbox, and the Swiss Jura, and closed with his ascent of Annapurna IV as part of the British Joint Services Expedition in 1993. The main thing we took away from the evening was an image of Sammy at the summit in a rather plush aubergine Berghaus onesie and the fact that part of the deal with the climb was that he had his blood taken by the team's doctor at thousand-metre intervals because the expedition's remit included the testing of new blood-thinning altitude agents for a pharmaceutical company – as if climbing the thing wasn't hard enough! Sapping, in all senses.

'Don't set your heights low, set them high and then work to make it happen,' closed Sammy, switching on the lights; 'Any questions?'

We asked questions, mainly about the purple onesie, then left for the pub feeling inspired to get out into the world.

* * * * *

The group had a relative lie-in on Day Two and only awoke at half past seven.

Again, I geared up with treacly tea. Day One had gone well but for loose gaiters – whose velcro straps stayed stubbornly undone once ripped off, the fastenings snowed up – and the irksome salopettes, whose braces, zips and fastenings baulked at being braced, zipped or fastened. So on Day Two I deployed gaffer tape and safety pins to fix that . . . and changed my crampons because they'd kept falling off too. Other than that, I was King of Kit!

The group's experiments with crampons had been fun. There's something about having massive spiky feet. Emboldened, we'd begun rollicking up hills and yomping about, impervious to ice . . . and a couple of people managed to rip holes in their trousers and gaiters inside ten minutes. After that we'd simmered down, chastened.

That second morning the bus parked at an abandoned chair lift below Coire na Ciste. The place had a post-apocalyptic, Cold War feeling – slightly threatening, gloomy, rusting, falling apart – a perfect setting for a remake of John Carpenter's film *The Thing*.

We walked in single file up a gravel path beside the defunct wheelhouse, getting used to the pull of our sacks and weight of our boots – slowly ascending beneath the moribund pylons, sloshing in the melt streams, frozen chairs creaking overhead.

Here, beneath the thaw line, the path was soft mud and shingle but it began to harden up as we ascended and the temperature dropped. Inside a disused generator shed we practised figure-eights and half-hitch knots as a sleety rain spat and the wind banged doors nearby. The sun had gone when we emerged, replaced by squall – soon to pass, but the weather was restless all day.

At the next big wheel-set, we took to a wooden walkway which led down into a high-sided gully. Here we learnt about snow belays.

Belaying is a technique where one climber anchors another with a rope against a fall whilst ascending a snow slope or climbing a rock face. This is what Ivor was doing on the roof of Magdalene for his flailing friend below – a 'body belay' where friction between the belayer's body and the rope is used to arrest a tumble. It's not ideal and can result in injury to the human anchor or both climbers falling, so, out of shot, Ivor probably tied off around something solid, like the belfry tower, to provide a bit of extra protection.* But here on the gully slopes there were no handy spires to fix our ropes about so we had to improvise and anchor in the snow with the kit we had to hand.

We paired off into belayers and climbers – I was to belay

---

* One of the benefits of a body belay is that it requires no hardware to execute – a similar technique to classical abseiling, i.e. without a harness, using rope alone.

James using a technique known as boot-axe.* Following Jonathan's lead, I trampled a level doormat-sized platform in the snow for my feet then rammed my axe shaft-first into the ground† at the back of the flattened area before planting the side of my uphill boot firmly against it for support. I then knelt sideways to the slope front, leg braced. Meanwhile James, stood on the bank below, had tied on. His rope ran up to me and I looped it over my back foot, below the T of the axe head and back to form a bight over my boot laces. Something about this stance and the coils at my side brought to mind a cartoon detonator box, as I crouched, top hand bracing the axe-head plunger tight behind my boot, the other gripping the rope. Low to the ground like this I was able to reel James in as he ascended, all the time poised to lock off by my ankle and secure the line should he slip.

Next we tried a 'stomper', which involved standing on the head of a similarly driven axe but with the rope passing through a carabiner strung around its neck. In this upright position the rope passed over my shoulder, round my back, down to the carabiner and on to James. It was certainly easier on the knees.

After that we deployed the 'buried axe' method, where the axe anchor lies laterally in a thin slit sliced a foot deep into the snow, with a strop secured halfway down its handle running out onto the slope at right angles so as to form a T. Joined to the main rope by means of a carabiner, the stropped

---

* Aka the New Zealand foot break.

† I want to say 'to the hilt' but apparently axes don't have hilts; in fact it was the opposite of 'to the hilt' since the head of the axe – the sharp end – protruded from the slope whilst the shaft was buried . . . but still, 'buried to the hilt' seems to carry something of the right emphasis. In short, the spiked end of the handle was stabbed as far as possible into the ground.

axe provides a strong mooring behind the belayer, who sits in a sculpted bucket seat, as if driving – leant slightly back, legs apart, heels dug in. A second axe can also be pushed down vertically in front of the first to bolster further.

And so the day went on, stopping at intervals for thermos coffee and chocolate from our sacks, gloves off, velcro reapplied; checking watches to find hours snuck past – Cairngorm time being woolly.

After anchor drills came snow mechanics, digging pits into the surface to inspect the strata formed by drifted, thawed, refrozen snow and ice and check the avalanche conditions; prodding each layer with our gloved fingers to ascertain its relative density and, from that, the slope's stability. Having zagged up the glaring steeps onto shallower slopes, we'd become aware of a new noise as the snows slabbed beneath us squeaked under our boots – subtly sliding as the different bands broke apart, a dangerous unstable sound.

As we left the area, Jonathan spotted the professional avalanche forecasters of SportScotland Avalanche Information Service (SAIS) arriving on Coire na Ciste to profile the area for their daily forecasts, later to be posted online. They were two red dots receding, lost in the billow, as the wind roused and snowflakes surged about our legs like ardent dogs in need of walking, playful outliers of the pack beneath our feet.

* * * * *

Shortly after this, Jonathan slid down the mountain – echoing the actions of a Pyrenean guide named Salles with whom Dorothea climbed in the early 1920s: 'When he had eaten, Salles picked his giant limbs up and took a sitting

The Cairngorms, January 2014 (Dan Richards)

dive into the valley. Down he swept, with a brave crest of snow-spray shooting out on either side of him, and soon he was a mere black speck winding away and away from us . . .'[7] This is how we travelled too; sliding on our behinds, streaking down the peak at speed – leant back, feet raised – whizzing in the sheen of our leader's wake, rekindling the antic childlike spirit which propels so many up to this white world atop that endless Powell and Pressburger staircase.

The pleasures of a really long, steep, sitting snow glissade have points of advantage over even the best of ski-ing. The ease of the thing, the absence of all call upon one's prowess! Careless of Telemarks, Christianias or even Stemming turns, one floats in cushioned ease! Snow-foam does, it is true, work its way up one's sleeves and down one's neck, but this seems better than the giddy somersaults of the would-be ski-runner . . . And when at last the glorious motion slackens,

there you are down in your valley, your point of departure
hangs behind you almost out of sight in the sky . . .[8]

For all the slog to get oneself fit and up the mountains, to
temper wild urges and risk, there is much fun to be had
sliding down the banisters!

Serious fun, such as the sheer joy of axe arresting: lined
up like Pathé penguins to dive headfirst down the mountain, axes held out to one side, slope rushing. Then pushing
the pick down, steel teeth first rasping then biting, gripping,
the chest-lunge checked – pulling in the sharp adze so its
wrapped blade digs into one's shoulder, pick buried in the
ground – pivoting about that dagger point, body taut. And
stop. Blinking in the silence.

Or the trick of halting the slide unarmed by turning and
arcing onto all fours, raking your toes and fingers so you
pull up in the pose of an angry cat. In every case these exer-
tions induced laughter, a childish delight in temporarily
taming the quicksilver terrain.

To quote Dr Seuss –

> It is fun to have fun
> But you have to know how.[9]

* * * * *

Dorothy ends her Skye chapter by describing the sudden
shifts in weather which illuminate (but more often shroud)
the Scottish peaks; the heavy golden mists and fierce down-
pours which defined the only visit to Scotland recounted in
her book.

She wrote of Tower Ridge on Ben Nevis that:

It gave me views of the greatest cliffs in Britain which made me hunger to return, but they seemed to miss the sheath of ice and snow that at Easter makes them our finest Alpine climbing-ground. As we reached the summit a wintry cloud drew over and a wild hail-storm drove us down. I have rashly promised I.A.R. to go back some Easter and climb from an igloo at the summit . . . And I will go back to Skye too some spring, to redeem those promises that I had watched disappear behind the water veil.[10]

As my last day drew on, the sunlight stalled, walled off by Cairn Gorm's bulk, so that the slopes of Coire na Ciste became a shadowed blue. Ahead of us the glowing flanks of Craiggowrie, Creagan Gorm and Meall a' Bhuachaille stood tawny demerara before our frozen field – sprung toasted coffee beyond the Glen More forest, with only Meall a' Bhuachaille sporting a white snow hat.

At times like this, raising one's head from the tromping cold to see the extrasolar blush of quite another season, coexisting parallel, the landscape felt uncanny, as if we were inhabiting an illusory space suspended just beyond the bounds of the real.

The vague thought of our umbilical minibus – sat waiting to ferry us back into the familiar warm world of Aviemore's gear and chip shops – was broken up by the tremolo whump of an unseen Sea King helicopter. Indeed, the whole walk back to the bus felt a sensual inundation of the landscape and its language – each feature's name an honorific, reaffirming the scape as a magical, musical other: corrie, coire, cwm, cirque – cascading akin to Shepherd's gleeful register – 'birdsfoot trefoil, tormentil, blaeberry, the tiny genista, alpine lady's mantle.'

Down we strode and all at once, it seemed, earthy smells hit us, hoods undone: heady, stoutish, malted smells – baroque after the brusque austerity of the hatched snow slopes. The black grouse who burst up on our approach; the omni-ache of bruised shins born of the shunting bang-bang-bang of stiff boot tongues; the unexpected stillness in the hill's lee and the soft new sounds of our susurrus retreat. The sudden snow line – crystal drifts subsiding all at once when tackled by a picket fence; a white ha-ha beyond which the mountain fell in fern hues through the gloaming.

Walking out of the mountain, the thought occurred that our Conville team had been roaming on the buttress of a far more mighty mass sat unseen behind us – that 'grey plateau, rock-strewn, vast, silent' – and here we were retreating off, relatively worn out after a few days on the outer 'gorms.

I too will come back some spring, I thought, and explore this beautiful, savage new immensity – as Dorothea later returned to Skye and Ben Nevis – but before that I was set for Spain and a meeting with Anthony Pilley, Dorothea's nephew.

Barcelona and Catalonia

June 2014

As we descend over the Pyrenees, the mountains trail off into sandy hills, sides banded tight as contours so, from the cramped view afforded by the cabin window, it feels again as if I am descending into a colossal map.

A minute later we bank around so the blue Mediterranean fills the frame and begin our approach to Barcelona Airport, over the flat-roofed apartments of Castelldefels. In the peach distance dock cranes monster like a herd of AT-AT walkers.

Swooping over power lines and landing-light stands, skimming the perimeter fence and long grass outfield, a moment of weightless tension, then the wheels hit the runway, stomachs totter and the plane is down.

* * * * *

Anthony Pilley was wearing a green T-shirt when I met him at Barcelona Sants station. The green T-shirt was key – 'I'll be wearing a green T-shirt,' he'd told me on the phone before I'd left Bath. 'I'll be wearing a green T-shirt and looking like an exasperated Pablo Picasso' might also have been helpful because, at the moment of our meeting, he looked so exactly like Picasso that I double-took and almost checked his hands to see if they were made of baguette.

I was late reaching Barcelona Sants since I'd passed through the station and out the other side on the train from the airport before realising my mistake and returning. This was partly because I don't speak Spanish and was a bit confused by the pocket map I had of the city, and partly because the platforms at Barcelona Sants are underground and it was difficult to see it as the city's main railway station. Whereas Barcelona's Estació de França is a beautifully light vaulted space, Sants Estació is a cellar and the sense of arrival accordingly dimmed.

This can't be it, I thought, so stayed put and waited for something aesthetic to happen. Perhaps foreign visitors baulk at London Euston's similarly tomblike murk. I don't know, but by the time I'd backtracked, I was an hour late and ran around the station concourse like a headless chicken asking random men in green if they were Anthony Pilley.

I found my man by a bank of pay phones. 'Are you Anthony Pilley?' I asked, panting. 'Yes. Why? Who are you?' he shot back curtly in English. A Scottish accent, bright blue eyes. An open face, lined with time but youthful for all that. Mussed straw-blond hair. Mad eyebrows. Smaller than I'd expected but definitely him – a grumpy Scots Picasso. Super.

We shook hands. He *had* begun to get a bit worried, he admitted. I explained that I'd become confused in the Sants gloom. 'Yeah, it's a hole,' he said. 'You want a coffee?'

* * * * *

Anthony lives in Sants-Montjuïc, not far from the station – a district in the south-west of Barcelona. After coffee, we walked to his flat through a grid of roads. The heat had hit me like a wall as soon as we'd passed through the station's automatic doors. The car park asphalt, pooled around its Rubik's Cube bulk, was baking. We crossed bus lanes and disappeared into the safe maze of Santa Maria de Sants – a formerly independent industrial town long since absorbed by Barcelona as it spread south. Here, the air was cool, the neighbourhood quiet. The roads, like the stone and brick-built apartments walling them, narrow and shadowed – streets like deep drained stone canals. Some of the ground floors were shuttered. Closed shops? I wasn't sure. Modern metal rollers jostled with criss-crossing grilles and louvres. Thin concertinaed slats like old lift doors, collapsable gates, scaffolding, garages, graffitied breeze-blocks, blacked-out windows backed with dusty sun-bleached boxes and news-papers, old signs, peeling murals, crumbled brickwork, the chatter and clink of a hidden bar. It was as if we'd suddenly slipped back a century. These seemed the Catalan equiva-lent of British terrace houses, but how many were parti-tioned flats or still whole houses I couldn't tell. We passed below blinds, canopies and awnings; metallic, rusted, oxi-dised, overpainted. To look at the shutters was to hear the clatter of them tumbling at siesta and the end of the work-ing day, unrolling, honeycomb link on link.

There was a lot going on architecturally above the first floors, I saw, craning my head to see. Elegant flourishes which hinted at the expansive Modernisme and Catalan art nouveau for which Barcelona is so revered. Wrought-iron balconies, beautiful and organic, wooden shuttered win-dows set in baroque facades, Moroccan mosaics and geo-metric grates juxtaposed with industrial extractor-fan hoods and wire mesh and everywhere the red-and-yellow Estelada flag – draped from balustrades and hung from windows, flag of Catalan independence. 'This is not straightforward Spain,' the flags said. 'This is somewhere else.'

Cars parked on the tiled pavements leant into the street to form small chicanes. Nobody seemed to mind. Everyone just wound round them as the pastel mopeds slalomed. The grid of roads made new vanishing points at every turn. The sky was a narrowing pale blue line, opening out at crossroads and open sandy parks. The traffic sounded soft and sleepy.

Although surrounded by the city's buzz, this quarter felt latent and laid-back, waiting for the night. Everyone was dozing or at work, I thought, but no, if one looked and listened there were people everywhere – talking to each other across the street, above our heads; leaning out of open windows, standing on leafy verandas. Here was warm modular living, a loved and careworn ward of people piled on top of each other, spilling out into the sultry afternoon. People stood talking in the middle of the road, among skips and rubbish drums piled with unusual trash – old chairs, floorboards, mannequins, broken record players. Occasionally a modern block would rear over the old town's three-floor tenements but the more we walked, the more I thought how the quarter was a miraculous survivor.

Anthony's flat was the last of four single-storey buildings set at right angles to the road – stable-like quarters behind a metal gate, down a rough stone drive with studios and workshops at the end. Former police lodgings, Anthony explained, as he nodded to his neighbours – sat out on bleachers under beer-branded parasols – and unlocked his front door. The room was large and high-ceilinged. An orange-striped bed framed by an anglepoise lamp lay in the far left corner, beneath a tall window now washed blue in the sun's low glow. The walls were white with a band of cable conduit acting as a utilitarian picture rail. Paintings were hung at intervals – Anthony's own and gifts from artist friends, I learnt.

A low flat-top dresser ran beside the bed, on top of which were books. The floor was a mixture of chessboard tile and concrete. Broad black lines told of internal walls having been removed at some point to allow an open plan. A table with pens and a cutting board and various papers and folders occupied the centre of the room. Behind it, through double French doors, I could see a courtyard with a high wall and, beyond that, the framed fronds of a palm.* A kitchenette took up the corner opposite the bed. A tall fridge; pans hung from hooks on the wall above the sink, below which were cupboards. Anthony had built a stage from salvaged wood above the kitchen area on which were piled old crates and suitcases. Other than this, a few shelves and steam-bent birch stools, a couple of fans and a couple of lamps, there was very little in the room. He lived light.

My bed was a fold-out sofa. The bathroom was out back in a small extension.

Anthony put the kettle on and I sat down on the edge of my bed and began to unpack. My first thought was that I hoped we'd get on because, were we to have an argument, the lack of privacy might make the weekend untenable. The second thought was that it was a remarkable space, timeless and slightly Trappist, and that I was very lucky to

---

* 'I don't know if you remember the large Chinese rug in the flat,' Anthony wrote to me, having read an early description of his home. 'Blue and ivory. It was from the drawing room in Minto Street, Edinburgh. I loved it as a child; it was one of Dorothy and Ivor's bits brought back from China.'

Anthony (centre) and the Fantoms, 1964 (Anthony Pilley)

have been invited to stay. The room shored up the picture of Anthony I'd developed since meeting him an hour before. The ascetic aesthetic put me in mind of another Scotsman I'd met, the artist Bill Drummond, whom I'd spoken with several times for a previous book. He lived somewhere similarly spartan in Stoke Newington. Yes, I thought, they'd probably get on.

For the next few hours we talked and we talked mainly of Anthony's life in Spain, and memories of Dorothy's visits to Scotland in her later years, and as we talked we migrated round the flat – from the main room, out to the courtyard, then stood with more tea in the tiled kitchenette – circling with the conversation; getting the measure of each other as much as anything else. And as we talked and settled into talking he relaxed and his brusqueness melted away.

It turned out that he and Chris received the same cap gun, leather cartridge belt and Davy Crockett hat from Ivor and Dorothea as my father and his brothers. 'As a teenager I used to wear that belt on stage with my band, the Fantoms,' he told me with a grin.

* * * * *

Before going climbing in the Cairngorms, I'd met up with Anthony's brother, Chris, in central Edinburgh. Whereas Anthony moved to Spain in his early thirties, Chris still lives in the city where he grew up and has recently started sorting through the family archive of correspondence between his father, John Pilley, Dorothy and Ivor, as well as digitising the recordings and films in the collection. Over lunch, Chris told me a great deal about the Pilley family's life. In common with my father's recall, his memories of Dorothy and Ivor are coloured by childhood – framed at a child's height, intensely felt observations over dinner tables and in gardens, communal moments of pause when everyone in a household interacts: entrances and exits, stations and airports:*

'I think we were all in awe of Dorothy, partly because my father was a bit in awe of his big sister . . . they used to fly in at Prestwick at some ungodly hour. I remember we got up at

---

* 'I don't have many memories of Ivor except as an occasional visitor with Dorothy to our house, but one moment stands out, and I felt it then even at that young age. I remember watching him as he was quickly looking up some reference in a book. I noticed the way he handled the book and his level of concentration with it. This object, the book, seemed to have a quasi-religious symbolism for him. I saw a man holding a thing he loved, as if it were a coded capsule of information from some other planet. And it's not as if anything had really happened, but the memory has stuck with me for all these years.' Author interview with Anthony Pilley, Barcelona, 2014.

T. Burns, Marjorie Pilley, Dorothy Pilley, John Pilley, Anthony Pilley, I. A.
Richards. Scotland, *c.*1965 (Christopher Pilley/RCM)

five! Admittedly it was June and so light and quite nice, no
traffic around, but I remember my father – I used to go with
him – and we used to sit around and use the photo booths.
We took some nice photos together . . . but it was quite a business getting up at the crack of dawn; anyway, that's the best
example of exactly what your father was talking about. They
would usually be the last to get off the plane. There was a
viewing platform and you could see the people getting off the
plane, come down the steps and walk to the terminal building, and they would be the last. First to come out would be
Ivor, carrying masses and masses of bags and, behind him,
Dorothy, carrying probably nothing . . .' He laughs.*

---

* It's interesting that both Chris and Anthony knew Dorothea as Dorothy
– perhaps as the result of their father having grown up calling her so. My
father, Tim Richards, had an 'Aunt Dorothea' who everybody called 'Aunt
Dorothea' and who was only spasmodically called, properly, '*Great*-aunt

This was in the early sixties, recalls Chris, and it mirrors very much my father's recollection of them from that time. How does he remember them *being* together? How were they as a couple? I ask, and he pauses, rifling his memories; trying to find the right words. 'They weren't, in any sense, enmeshed as a couple,' he says slowly, 'although they were clearly very fond of each other.'

He remembers that Dorothy had a very special way of saying 'Ifor' and explains that, whilst there is something in the family known as *the Pilley lisp*, her voice was interesting because she was quite difficult to place – 'there was a very slight hint of Cockney, a slight transatlantic drawl but mostly it's just *Aunt Dorothy* . . . but how were they together? That's a very interesting question. He doted on her, I think that's true.'

Unlike my father, Chris has memories of Dorothy and Ivor discussing mountaineering although, by the time he was conscious of it, Dorothy had been in the car accident of 1957 which so damaged her right hip as to effectively end her climbing life. They still went to the Alps, he remembers, but more to go up téléphériques and tramp in the foothills below their halcyon peaks.

Perhaps they spoke about climbing whilst staying in Edinburgh because John Pilley had accompanied them on climbs in his youth, I suggest.

'Oh, they all climbed! Yes,' agrees Chris, lighting up rather. 'My father's in *Climbing Days*, hidden away. He's in one of the photographs and he's mentioned a couple of times and so is Will, Dorothy's other brother. All four, I think, are

Dorothea', and the Pilley boys had an 'Aunt Dorothy' – Dorothy Pilley, the name she published under. In this chapter, with a few exceptions, Dorothea will be Dorothy.

mentioned: Dorothy, Vi, my father John, and Will.' As he speaks he taps the table to emphasise each of the four so their names become a familial mantra. 'Dorothy was born 1894, Violet, *Vi*, was born in 1895 or 6 – although she died in the thirties . . . John in 1899, and Will in 1900.'* Closely packed.

I ask about Vi but her death is something of a mystery, he says. She possibly died in a sanatorium after a period of mental illness. But like so much of Dorothy's story outside the tramlines of *Climbing Days*, the picture is granular. So I add Violet Pilley to my list of people to pursue in the Magdalene archives when next I visit Cambridge. Another puzzle to solve.[†]

---

* Several of Dorothy's diary entries of 1915 refer to occasions when either John or Will accompanied her on early mountaineering trips. Karen Stockham notes that the accepted etiquette of the time 'continued the Victorian tradition of expecting unmarried women not to consort with a man to whom they were un-related without being chaperoned either by their brothers or father'. (Stockham, *Women's Mountaineering Life-Writing*, p. 123.) In this context, the sudden interest taken by John and Will in the mountains of North Wales seems likely to have stemmed more from the family's need to keep an eye on Dorothy than simply join in with her mountaineering. Note also Dorothy's remembrance of John's grumpy description of climbing as 'a mug's game' in the Lake District chapter of *Climbing Days*.

† A note on Violet Pilley: Anthony later wrote to me to say that he clearly remembers Dorothy, when questioned, talking about Vi becoming 'totally obsessed with some man; camping out on the lawn of his house and all that'. She became unbalanced, he said, and may have have been certified. 'Dorothy told me that Vi had certainly visited Carl Jung. Dorothy was not a great believer in shrinks, however, as she didn't feel it had really helped those friends who had tried it. Anyway, I'm pretty sure a sanatorium was involved.' He half remembers, aged fourteen or sixteen, finding 'a black-and-white studio photograph of a beautiful young woman from a bygone age'. He's sure that's how he got the story about his aunt. In any case, he grew up knowing she had committed suicide.

When I do find a death certificate it states that Violet died on 3 August 1936, at Horton Hospital, Epsom: 'Evelyn Violet Pilley. Female 41 years – Tetany and a tumour of the left suprarenal gland are listed under cause of death but neither is normally fatal. There was a post-mortem. Her death was

Four Pilley
children *c.*1910
(Pilley family
archive)

'We had a family album from my father's side,' Chris
remembers at one point, 'and Dorothy went through it and
wrote captions – where the pictures were taken and who

---

registered on the 11th. It's all signed off.

The only picture I had of Vi at the time of this discovery was a photograph
of all four Pilley siblings as children, arms round each other, laughing and
indomitable with Dorothy front and centre but Vi too, looking happy,
athletic and well. I couldn't square the image with the story Anthony had
told me. I could believe that she'd grown up to be beautiful because all four
Pilley children have been remembered to me as striking, handsome adults,
but something of the joy and togetherness of that picture had a haunting
aspect in light of what was to come.

The truth, when I sat down to seek it in the Magdalene archives, seems
to have been slightly more complex but no less sad. Dorothy was in China
with Ivor when her father wrote on 12 June – a letter reproduced in her
diary of the time – to say that 'V. continues to suffer loss of weight – In one
month decreased from 9.5 to 8.3 & the Doctors can give no explanation.' She
has been moved to a ward on the ground floor where her bed is on an open
veranda and is in the care of 'a lady Dr. to whom she is less hostile'. But she
continues to decline and Dorothy writes to her brother Will on 15 July: 'I
was v. shocked and disturbed to get your letter about V.'s decline. One always
remembers her as she was as a girl & not in her present sad state.' ▷

they were of – holidays on the Isle of Wight when she was a child . . . but she's getting up to things, even in those photographs, you can tell . . .' and he laughs but then he catches himself in the moment of thinking of Dorothy as a child. 'But, of course, they always seemed awfully old to me.'

He stops.

They were Edwardians, I suggest.

'Absolutely. They both had a great presence in their different ways. I remember Dorothy used to smoke cigarettes . . .'

Did she?

'Camels.'*

Right.

'Yes, it seems a bit surprising. I wonder if I could find a photograph of her smoking a cigarette . . .'

On 30 July, she writes to her father: 'From many points of view, one couldn't help thinking that Vi's life as it has been for the last few years was much worse than no life at all + that a relief would be merciful. But it must be too awful to see + and sad beyond means to cope with. I wish I was there to help with this tragedy.' Her diary of 5 August records: 'I.A.R. received a 7AM cable "Violet passed away last night." He broke it gently when I went to wake him at 8.30. Though expected & a merciful release it comes as a benumbing shock.'

Violet features several times in *Climbing Days*, climbing with Dorothy in Wales and the Italian Alps. Page 300 contains the intriguing fragment: 'The summer of 1927 was to bring the Himalayas. My doctor sister Vi, then a radiologist in Delhi, I.A.R. and I, with a few porters, had a wander vacation among them.'

Her death, disturbed and emaciated in Horton Hospital less than ten years later, is hard to understand and painful to relive in the letters and telegrams of her brothers, sister and father as Dorothy recorded them in her diary. I'm particularly struck that, like Dorothy, she too escaped the confines of her Victorian home and expectations to become 'a radiologist in Delhi'. What an amazing achievement and story in its own right! How sad, having broken out, to end up in an institution in Surrey, with Dorothy thousands of miles away in China.

* 'Yes, Camel Plain,' remembers Anthony. 'And she used to tap them on top of the packet, just like in the movies. She certainly wasn't a heavy smoker but she did use to punctuate her days with them and I can't remember her ever giving up.'

Did she smoke all her life?

'I don't know. I can only comment on what I saw. Everybody smoked.'

Did Ivor?

'I'm not aware of that. I just remember the packet in the house because they were so alien. You didn't see them over here. Camels. That's American, isn't it?'

And so the picture alters and I see Dorothy smoking. It shouldn't really matter but it does, it changes things a little. Apparently incidental details are often the ones which resonate most with me on this quest for her. Now I see her talking through a cloud of smoke, using the cigarette to gesture, arm crooked, thin plume rising past her Queen Fria buns. The Dorothy of my imagination will now, forever, be on the point of lighting up – in defiance, in triumph, distant and ruminating, or simply because she fancied a fag. Having been done, it cannot be undone. Waiting outside the Pinnacle Hut for others to arrive, writing in her diary . . . I see her leaning over the page, pen in her right hand, cigarette in her left. I make a mental note to see if the diaries in Magdalene smell of smoke.

Why is it so resonant? It struck me as soon as Chris told me, perhaps because it was a facet that was habitual and universal and furnished her character that little bit more; to smoke is to rebel just a little.

> I am with the roots
> of flowers
> entwined, entombed
> sending up my passionate blossoms
> as a flight of rockets
> and argument

wrote Charles Bukowski of smoking,[1] and doesn't that sound just like Dorothy?

These days, with the knowledge it'll do you in, it's more than ever a youngster's game and you're meant to see the error of your ways. Then, less was known about the dangers to health but, still, to carry on into one's sixties and seventies is a bit bloody-minded. To smoke around Ivor, a TB survivor, hilariously so – although he's sometimes to be found with a pipe in posed pictures. Was she smoking in her eighties? Was she stopping for a smoke halfway up Alps at her peak, during *Climbing Days*? The thought made me smile. Such moments expand my image of Dorothy. Small asides of memory and spots of information join together to form a pointillist picture of a human being. The incidentals which go to make a life; the humanity of the apparently mundane.

* * * * *

Anthony's stories and remembrance are full of emotion and vivid scenes. There is a tension when he discusses his father, an undercurrent of anger and sadness. He tells me that he never knew him well.

'We had very different interests when I was growing up and Dad tended to focus all his attentions on my elder brother, Chris, which was not healthy for him, nor for any of us! Dad died unexpectedly just after I'd arrived in America to spend summer with a family in Berkeley, California, and I was not told about Dad's death until after the funeral had taken place. That was a difficult end to a pretty non-communicative relationship. It was 1969 and I was nineteen. Ten years later, after Ivor had died, Dorothy began to spend Christmas and New Year with Chris's family in Edinburgh. Chris and Odile were very busy with two young children and I began organising trips with Dorothy because she loved adventures and it seemed a very good way to link with my past and a father I had hardly known. Soon I found out that we got on rather well.'

So, in his twenties, scratching a living as a musician and artist in Edinburgh, Anthony decided to encourage and embrace his aunt and a great friendship developed. He would travel down to visit her in Cambridge and the pair drove off into the Scottish Highlands several times, most memorably to Skye at Hogmanay for Dorothy's last New Year.

'I was running an eight-track recording studio in a turret called Barclay Towers in a tenement in the Bruntsfield area of Edinburgh. This would be in the late seventies, early eighties.' He thinks the early demos he recorded with Aztec Camera were the most exciting session from those years. 'They never quite captured the same simplicity and emotional intensity again.*

'The logo of Barclay Towers was a lightning bolt hitting the tower of a mountain-top castle because, some years before I installed the studio, a bolt had smacked a hole in the

---

* 'An unknown Glasgow trio with a great name came into my attic studio and recorded four or five songs. The singer and composer was seventeen and the magic of those few songs made an impression on me like no other recording I had made. "How can he have written this!?" I asked myself. I don't feel they ever matched the stripped-down intensity of those demos when they were recorded commercially. He was an artist who quickly got into arrangements and production, but those songs were so strong that simplicity was the best approach. Someday the Aztec Camera demos ought to be released. I've just never had the time to make it happen.' Author interview with Anthony Pilley, 2014.

domed roof of the turret. For that reason a Frankenstein-like energy pervaded all the recordings.'*

It's easy to imagine Dorothy and Anthony hitting it off and her affinity with the bohemian atmosphere of the crow's-nest tower – an echo of her desire to be off with the raggle-taggle gypsies. Anthony mentions waking up to discover Nick Cave asleep on the kitchen floor, and working knelt in the circular control room with recording equipment arranged on the floor (he always used to work kneeling, he says, and now it's playing havoc with his knees, decades later) surrounded by his collected reel-to-reel players and analogue kit. As we sat talking in Barcelona I began to think that Anthony might be the closest thing to Dorothy left in the world and once that thought was in my mind, the symmetry began to stack. They were both non-conformists with a strong stubborn streak; both enthusiasts for the impulsive and unorthodox side of life.

As their friendship kindled, he told me, differences of age ceased to be important. 'I identified with her. She may have been daunting and demanding on many occasions, but I remember her as twinkling and playful. Physically, yes, of

---

* Ron Butlin, Scottish poet, novelist and fellow resident, described it thus: 'Barclay Towers was a split-level flat, five storeys up from the main street. Five wearying flights of hard stone steps. The tenement was well over a hundred years old and, when northerly gales swept down from the Arctic, its floors shook, its largest windowpanes billowed in and out like sails, and our top-floor flat swayed in the wind like a bird's nest in the topmost branches of a century-old tree. Running straight ahead from the front door was a corridor – on the right, an internal staircase which led up to the Electric Boy's recording studio, Hume's cupboard came next [Hume was another tenant, who famously lived under the stairs] and finally the communal kitchen; on the left were bedrooms one, two and three. The corridor ended at a frosted glass door – a small bathroom. All the rooms could be slept in; if the sleeper was well padded and under five foot four, the bath was reckoned to be very comfortable.' From *A Seat at the Rich Man's Table*, Ron Butlin, 2015.

course she was slow. I have a vivid memory of how she would move around, rather crablike, pivoting herself on that walking stick and swinging the other hip around her. She must have had little mobility on one side, due to the Stateside car accident. And, yes, it was hard to imagine the extraordinary agility she must have once had.* Luckily, due to my intellectual ignorance of her mountaineering career, I got to know Dorothy in her eighties without the baggage of her achievements.'

He wanted to know the person, not the persona. Perhaps that was a real advantage for both of them, he muses, breaking off. And I could see his point, for what do I have of Dorothy but her book and her memory, passed on by the people who knew her? Our common ground is an interest in landscape and a wish to know more about Dorothy, a generation on from Anthony – now perched on the end of his bed, riffling the page corners of *Climbing Days* with his thumb. He began reading the book in preparation for my visit, he tells me, but the more he reads the more he wonders if it isn't actually the first time.

Anthony remembers that his aunt had a similar aesthetic wonder at the natural world to his own, a kindred artistic sensibility which he contrasts with his father's default prosy and reluctance to discuss *feelings* – something his aunt could doubtless empathise with: 'When I was about six I remember the family were out late in the country in my dad's big old American car, which we often used to camp in. The stars came out and I found myself lying in the grass under a dome

---

* The mention of Dorothy's gait reveals another parallel between aunt and nephew since Anthony limps very slightly as the result of a motorcycle accident several years ago which damaged his left knee – as well as general wear and tear and turret twinges.

of twinkling lights. I was overwhelmed by a sense of wonder. I asked Dad why it was that the stars should have such an effect on me, so much more so than dots of toothpaste flicked onto black paper. His answer didn't really satisfy me. I begged my mum to let us camp out the night so I might continue my vigil, but no, Dad had said we had to get back . . .'

Dorothy had an obsession with beauty and the reasons one feels beauty as one does, he remembers. He remembers stopping the car every so often on the trip to Skye so that she could write in her diary. 'It was as if experiences weren't quite fixed or real until they had been written down.'

The idea of capturing moments in time had preoccupied Dorothy since adolescence. 'It isn't merely that memory fails one in the stating of outstanding facts,' she wrote in her 1919 diary. 'No – it is rather that small details escape one, slow changes in scene, subtle ones in people; unless written at once these are clouded by every subsequent change in oneself and one's point of view.' She *aches* to be able to express the beauty of *nature magnificent* 'and to do it, to the sounds of the rushing water' and to this end resolves to 'scrawl any old idea that comes in my head as the days go by' in order to hone the sort of vivid automatic authenticity she craved.[2] Anthony felt a similar need to document his time with Dorothy, aware that she wasn't immortal and anxious to record her memories before she was gone.

'I suppose Anthony and I were a bit unusual in that not only did we have rather elderly parents, but no extended family,' Chris had told me in Edinburgh. 'Dorothy and Ivor were the only family we had, beyond our parents, and they had no children of their own. My father spoke little about his family, beyond his own father, and, after my father died – and particularly after my own children were born in the late seventies – Dorothy became an important link to the family's past.'

On a visit to Cambridge in early May 1985, Anthony made a tape recording of Dorothy in which he gently quizzed her about her life, her climbing, his father, and all the things he didn't know. In so doing, he made the only record I have of her voice.

* * * * *

Listening to the tape now, digitised but redolent of magnetic crackle and crunching – the sound of the recorder and microphone inside Anthony's horsehair artist's bag – I hear Dorothy. What do I hear? An elderly lady recalling the past. Her past. Lamenting the vagaries of glaucoma surgery. More than that. The voice has the wavering pitch of an antique record player, a faintly underwater tone, but through that comes the mix of dialect accents Chris sketched in Edinburgh. She sounds upper class, a little Jean Muir-ish at times, but occasionally a little Cockney *th*-fronting crops up and, more often still, a charming quirk which I now discover is called Yod-coalescence – 'what ju need', 'a month in hospital last jeer' – all slightly Dopplered, a euphony akin to the hoot-hoo-ooh of an owl.

'Anthony, tell me first, you must be very tired,' she begins, offering him a drink, then thanking him for the milk he's brought her in, as the tape squalls and cuts about her. These are the first words I've ever heard her say. No, in fact, the *first* words on the tape, bursting from static and silence are, wonderfully, 'Did ju not know that!?'

For some reason she keeps offering Anthony cabbage and he keeps refusing it. This becomes a recurrent riff.

She wheezes and squawks occasionally in place of

interrogatives and this, mixed with the sub-aqua feel, evokes a puffin; perhaps a penguin. Definitely birdlike, wryly amused, blinking, waterproofed in all weathers, perennially hatted. This is how I see her in my mind's eye.

And smoking now, of course, or considering it. Schrödinger's Camel Puffin.

Anthony sounds very young on the tape and posher than I found him in Barcelona, with a noticeably more pawky Scots accent than he speaks with now.

I've spent all day transcribing this recording and all the time I'm listening and transcribing, thinking how sad it is that Dorothy finds herself confused by her failing body in old age, saying things like: 'I've spent three months being brave, you know, and then I was a month in hospital last year . . . but the doctor hasn't an idea what's wrong with me. I don't feel frightfully ill but I've got no energy, I go to sleep at the drop of a handkerchief and I can't see properly.' And I want to give her a hug, which she'd doubtless have flinched at, and say to her 'You're ninety-one!' I want to tell her, 'You're an astonishing, robust, indomitable lady but the reason all of this is happening is that you're ninety-one and your body is worn out . . .'

I find it so sad. I can hear her on the tape, talking about how she must get back to see her friends in America and would so love to see Switzerland again, and I know that she doesn't get to do either of those things. I know how it ends and I can hear in her voice how tired she is.

Speaking about the tape, Anthony notes that Dorothy showed no mental decrepitude or lack of warmth to him on that visit – 'Certainly the same inquisitiveness as ever shows through.'

As I sit in Barcelona, so, in a way, Anthony sat in

Cambridge thirty years before, asking the questions of Dorothy. The tape records that he did a remarkably good job of steering the conversation and several parts are notable since they fill in important biographical details previously unknown to me about her family background, school days and the first time she became aware of the existence of mountains. Memories seem to land in waves, oscillating back and forth between Dorothy's past and present. As details mount, a map of the moments which most shaped her as a young girl emerges – a constellation of memory: the acute aversion to dogma and disciplined routines she judged unjust; the start of a lifelong friendship with the writer Bryher; the wide-eyed childlike inquiry and photographic recall of scenes once seen, so redolent of her published writing – now brought back to light and life like stills from a long-lost film.

Firstly, she tells of how her mother was brought up as one of the Plymouth Brethren and how she remembers her confiding how awful she found it, explaining that 'they were sort of puritans' and took part in public confessions against each other. 'A husband would give away his wife and vice versa . . . pretending to be so righteous and pure . . .'

Then there are her two aunts. She wasn't terribly fond of Aunt Ellen, she says, but Aunt Liz was an angel: 'They took us to church. Mother and Father didn't, but the aunts always took us to church on Sunday morning . . .'

'Was your mother not religious at all?' asks Anthony.

'No,' says Dorothy.

'She didn't believe?'

'No. By that time she regarded all these Plymouth Brethren as fearful hypocrites. Whereas both Aunt Ellen and Aunt Lizzie used to take Sunday Schools; used to collect little things to give for sale to the vicarage, and a very nice vicar –

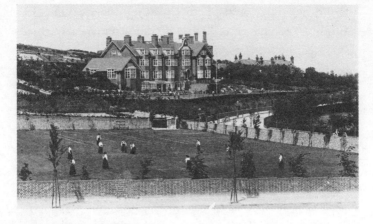

Queenwood *c*.1911 (RCM)

fancy, I was about five when I knew him and I can remember when you ask me now: Dawkes. Mr Dawkes. Of course I thought he was perfect. But then Queenwood,* where I went to school, was frightful. Miss Chudleigh, the headmistress, oh, the amount of religion we had to go through. Every morning we had the collect and all that†; and on Sunday we had to learn the collect by heart and recite it to the headmistress afterwards and then go to church, and then, as we got older, bible class with the headmistress where we had to be able to recite the collect and listen to another sermon . . . And the evening, often going to church in the evening, but that's where I first got to see pictures of the Swiss mountains and sunsets, from the vicar, he must have shown them to us.'

She hesitates.

'And that inspired you?' Anthony prompts, seeking more.

---

* Queenwood was a girl's boarding school on the Darley Road, Eastbourne (1906–40).

† collect¹ (kol′ekt). *n*. a brief comprehensive form of prayer, adapted for a particular day or occasion (Cassell Concise English Dictionary).

'I must have been about fourteen, and then I was at school with the Ellerman girl. She was a millionairess, you see, and we were great friends. She took me on the Marquess of Anglesey's yacht, all round Europe. I was about eighteen when I did that, a schoolgirl. The year before the First World War. 1913.'

'You were living in London?'

'Yes. They got to know the family and the family used to go there. It's pathetic to see the house now – it's number 1 South Audley Street – about six footmen, you know, and a butler, and Father used to love going there to dinner. The dinners were wonderful. Nobody could despise the dinners. But it's now some kind of public office and the windows aren't cleaned and the lights have a dim little electric light and next door they've put a great block of flats, just where it starts on Audley Street, just by the Women's University Club. Of course, Winifred died two years ago, three years ago.'

'And you remained friendly with her all that time?'

'Nearly to the last . . . She had a very faithful Italian maid who could only cook lamb chops, but she could cook lamb chops nicely. She'd been with her about twenty years, looked after her and was really a dear. Faithful to the end. She inherited something, quite an amount, I believe.'

The way she coupled the two episodes together caught my ear: the first mountains and the 'Ellerman girl' – I found that oddly pleasing.

Beyond I.A.R., very few people in Dorothy's life ever compared to the enduring love and influence the mountains held, but Winifred Ellerman was one such person, a soulmate for over seventy years.

* * * * *

Winifred Ellerman arrived at Queenwood School in May 1910, a few months before Dorothy. Both graduated in 1912 and they remained close friends for the rest of their lives.

Daughter of shipping magnate Sir John Ellerman, a several-times billionaire in today's money, Annie Winifred Ellerman would later find fame as a Modernist writer under the nom de plume Bryher. 'School for me was a violation of the spirit,' she writes in her 1963 memoir *The Heart to Artemis*, and then goes on to detail her misery at length:

> I had lived most of my life outside England and I had never had friends my own age. Now I was flung into a crowded boarding school to sink or swim. I kicked and spluttered in an agony of bewilderment and very nearly sank. Nobody gave me any explanations; it was a perfect preparation for Freud. The experience could have driven me to insanity or suicide and it was as crippling as a paralytic stroke. I did not recover from it until after a long psychoanalysis and I survived only because I was tough.[3]

Dorothy arrives a few pages later, in a paragraph describing the achievements of fellow Queenwood alumnae:

> We forget that in 1910 the battle for equal education of men and women was far from being won. Many parents objected to intensive training of the mind and if we spoke wistfully about jobs we were sharply reproved and told that we must not take bread out of a poor girl's mouth. Yet one of the babies of the school, Martita Hunt, became famous as an actress on both sides of the Atlantic, the writers included Sylva Norman and Nellie Kirkham, there was Doris Banfield who created a number of new daffodils, Dorothy Pilley whose name is well

known in mountaineering circles for her climbing books and
her ascents in the Far East and the Alps . . .[4]

Now, none of this is *meant* to be amusing, I know, but
large parts of it are. Yes, the parts which deal with the girls'
playing purposefully bad hockey, or scheming to avoid
enforced rambles over the Downs, or seeking to learn
Sanskrit instead of Latin are amusing vignettes but much of
Bryher's writing is unintentionally humorous, partly
because of the way she takes such a Freudian view of her ills
– both in terms of cause and cure. This somewhat undercuts
the undoubted misery of life in such a controlled and
controlling society. In fact she trumpets psychoanalysis so
often as a panacea to the buttoned-up patriarchal stasis of
Edwardian England that it becomes a sort of subliminal
punctuation.* But the humour, conscious or not, does not
diminish the central point of her record, if anything it
accentuates the bleakness, and whilst both Bryher and Pilley
run the risk of being pitied as poor little rich girls, their
claustrophobic ivory towers were not unique situations:
'The modern world does not understand how narrow
existence was for the Edwardian woman,' Bryher writes.

It was not a question of class, or even money, this should be
emphasised, but of public opinion. From slum to palace almost
everything outside the home was forbidden ground. It was
only after years of analysis, many years after, that I realised how
much of this was due to sexual taboos that were all the harsher
for never being explained or mentioned in conversation . . .[5]

* I know, Freud would have had a field day with *trumpet psychoanalysis* and
subliminal punctuation.

Or, perhaps, *understood* by anybody in unwitting thrall to heteronormative patterns of sexist subjugation, or 'common-sense decency' as much of society would probably have called it. It was 1913 but this was not Vienna, and the figureheads and deliverance of Modernism were far, far away. Pablo Picasso, Arthur Schnitzler and Marcel Duchamp, Virginia Woolf and Rainer Maria Rilke were foreign names in almost every sense.

To read Dorothy's diaries alongside *The Heart to Artemis*, the cultural and sensory suffocation seems to have been almost total. The image of a generation of infantilised middle-class young Englishwomen suffering a kind of dehumanising house arrest is potent – stabled more like horses than people, in dim drawing rooms; breeding machines, destined to be wives and mothers; well-schooled but never, it was to be hoped, to have to utilise that knowledge beyond dutiful rules of engagement and correct deportment. The unlicensed thoughts and actions of independent female minds were to be snuffed out at source – such rebellion was obviously the start of something ill-conceived and wicked and a short step away from setting fire to the king's dockyards. 'Father will not hear of my going over to Kensington alone in spite of my pointing out that I shall have to get used to looking after myself sometime,' writes Dorothy in a diary of autumn 1913, shortly after her nineteenth birthday. 'Evening or train I can understand but not by bus or tram amidst a good many people in broad daylight?'[6]

'I was not allowed to go to public lectures or to accept invitations to lunch in restaurants,' writes Bryher.

I was reproved, aged twenty, for writing a business letter to a publisher to inquire about the fate of a manuscript. 'What do they expect us to do?' I used to ask Dorothy Pilley, the freest amongst us, when yet another harmless pleasure was put out of bounds. Her only answer was to shrug her shoulders . . . We were much too frightened of our parents to worry in the modern fashion about how they might behave. Our rebellions took place in our thoughts, it was only after 1920 that they passed into deeds.[7]

This atmosphere of terminal boredom plays a central role in Virginia Woolf's first novel, *The Voyage Out*, published in 1915. Reviewing the book in the *Manchester Guardian*, Allan Monkhouse noted a 'sense of redundancy' and diagnosed a 'certain insolence of withdrawal from a world condemned as ponderous or meaningless'.[8]

Boredom wasn't an internal problem but an outer containing cage. Boredom was no mere aspect of the world, stagnation was the order of the day, and it's tempting to picture Dorothy and Winifred living Gashlycrumb lives in a stygian Edward Gorey universe – dying of ennui, or wasting away on a chaise longue, or self-immolating by way of light relief.

'I had supposed that I had only to leave school to be happy again but I sweated out the next seven years in complete frustration,' writes Bryher. 'The war was responsible in part; until it ended the pressure to conform increased . . .' The opening paragraph of Chapter 11 in *The Heart to Artemis* – the ominously titled '1914. Life Swept On towards War' – ends with an acerbic flourish.

Was it the golden summer that some say? It was hard to understand the people who spoke of it later as a time of unparalleled beauty because to me as to so many other girls of my generation it was a moment like any other . . . We helped our mothers in the morning, we went for walks in the afternoon; when possible, whatever wishes flowered in us were destroyed.[9]

For many Edwardian ladies, an enlightened husband must have seemed the best way out of their cosseted status quo but it's clear from reading Dorothy and Winifred's diaries and memoirs that they had no intention of playing that game. They dreamt of breaking out on their own terms – which in Dorothy's case meant fighting against housewifery for a career in either horticulture or journalism. Something she could make her own *and enjoy*. But it would be several years yet before they managed to establish truly independent futures for themselves – Ellermann escaping to France to live in a ménage à trois on the Left Bank, reinvent herself as Bryher and take a leading role in the writing and publication of avant-garde Modernist women's literature; Pilley to begin the writing and wanderlust of travel and mountaineering that would set the pattern for the rest of her life.

In retrospect, given the increased constraints of wartime, it seems amazing the pair were given leave to go to North Wales unsupervised at Easter 1915. Bryher writes that it was there that 'Dorothy found her destiny' and spent the trip in a state of ecstatic happiness. It was actually to prove a landmark event for Dorothy since it marked the beginning of her sovereign 'mountain madness', and there is a sense of joyous portent in the way the chapter ends:

'I was there the day that it all began and have always been grateful; she widened my world.'*

---

* Bryher, *The Heart to Artemis*, p. 172. There is a huge amount of correspondence between Dorothy and Winifred preserved in the Magdalene archive. It's notable that of the several soubriquets Winifred used for Dorothy – which included 'Sir Calidore', famed Knight of Courtesy in the

* * * * *

Back in Barcelona the days began to fall into a rhythm of mornings spent walking and exploring the city alone, and then meeting up with Anthony for lunch in La Rambla, where he has an office, workshop and store.

Barcelona was lively and young, infused with all the warm confidence and knowing impetus of the foreign exchange students I'd been so fascinated with as a child when they visited my school. The heat was exhausting. Traffic thrummed. Everything baked and a red V of sunburn bloomed at my open shirt neck.

In the end I kept away from the main drags and discovered hidden worlds in back alleys – a man stood in a carpet of corkscrew shavings, working in an upholsterer's stacked with antique chairs in various states of repair; the terrible hypnotic walls of Plaça Sant Felip Neri, lacerated by shrapnel from Civil War bombs and bullets, the stones still bearing witness. A plaque tells of twenty children killed, having sought shelter in the church. The shaded square before it felt subdued, cool but charged, as if still vibrating with the violence of its past.

The Maritime Museum became the centre of my elevenses. I would sit in the shadow of its ribcage tunnel sheds with a coffee, notebook and papers – across from the *Ictineo I*, a replica of the wooden 'fish-boat' submarine built by renaissance man Narcís Monturiol i Estarriol in the late 1850s, dazzling in the hard white sun, parked like a varnished almond up on blocks. Terrapins swam around a fountain to my right as I read through Dorothy's late letters

---

court of the Faerie Queene, as well as the more prosaic 'Do' – after 1915 letters often begin 'Dear Climber'.

to Anthony, posted from Cambridge to Spain in the early 1980s, and diary entries written in the 1910s – the latter photocopied in haste at Magdalene to be read and annotated under palms in the port of Barcelona.

'Aunt Clara would like to take me up to Wales with her. Do not feel very excited as feel sure I will be disappointed as Father will almost certainly say no,' writes Dorothy on 9 September 1914, but the next day she's giddy with the news that he's telephoned 'to say I might go . . . am very glad to be going.'

Together with her aunt Clara and cousin Elsie McNaught, Dorothy took a series of trains to North Wales. 'Wonderful with cold grey sea on one side and mountains on the other,' she writes on the 11th. The cottage they stayed in had 'splendid views of a giant mountain with a torrential stream running down its face, and always, it seems, a glowing welcoming fire.'

On Wednesday 16 September 1914, the day of Dorothy's twentieth birthday, the three undertook a trip to Snowdon. 'Long drive up to Snowden [*sic*] behind weary steed, eat sodden sandwiches seated in puddles with utmost relish! Sea amidst glow of brass and copper and Pen y Pass Hotel.' The image of the horse, hauling city folk to look at the mountains, grounds the story in an austere and slaty past but the diary pages from the jaunt have wry, comic drawings by Elsie McNaught which undercut such readings. Here are the women sheltering from a heavy downpour beneath a hopelessly inadequate London umbrella; there they go, falling backwards off near-vertical cliffs with disappointed expressions on their faces. Monday 21st sees them scattered about the rocky landscape in various uncomfortable poses. 'View of surrounding ranges grand,' writes Dorothy. 'Watch changing colours while Elsie reads selections from *Punch* and de Balzac!

Discover immediately after lunch the wonderful effects produced by looking at scenery in above striking altitude!' The caption reads 'Admiring the views from Craig-y-Llan' whilst the sketches depict the ladies toppled like skittles.

On 19 September, six months before her unchaperoned trip with Winifred Ellerman, Dorothy records the pair's first independent adventure in her diary. Having gone out for 'an amble', they 'get caught in the twilight and have to come down the bare rock in the dark!' 'Best Day we have had,' she writes, triumphantly.

This was a watershed moment. London and its attendant constraints had never been further away but it's notable that when the same episode is related in *Climbing Days*, whilst capturing the girls' bravado, Dorothy tempers the humour and spontaneity of the original diary entry with a cooler, more assured tone: 'What did it matter that we went up Craig-y-Llan in long skirts and in what the boot-sellers regard as feminine walking boots? We found our way down by the mine-shafts in the dark.'[10]

* * * * *

That evening, one hundred years later in the Sants-Montjuïc gloaming, Anthony tells me about some of Dorothy's last adventures – how they'd set off north in his Renault 4 van the year before they went to Skye. Dorothy was staying with Chris for Christmas, as she'd taken to doing after Ivor had died, visiting her grandnephew and niece, doubtless with exciting and slightly hazardous gifts.

One morning in the sleepy no-man's-land between Christmas and New Year, Anthony collected her in his van and the two drove out into a dawn world of snow and carried on for hours without seeing another car. 'We felt like we were the only two people alive in the world,' Anthony recalls, sat in his flat, on his orange bed, surrounded by the letters Dorothy sent him during his first years in the city. He tells me that she supported his choice to move from Scotland and try to make a living from his painting – always encouraging. Then he picks up a letter and gets back on track – back in the Renault 4, 1985 – explaining how, being of a similarly intrepid persuasion, after a while they both began looking for an off-road experience:

'I can picture the track we found now – straight and steep, the white land and the blue sky. A little way in there was a hill. We made a first attempt to get over the crest, then a second, but the wheels spun on the crushed snow and down we slid to the bottom. I could see that Dorothy was getting determined. There would be no turning back. Besides, there was no place to turn. Renault vans can go anywhere! I thought – light and bouncy – the secret lay in the run-up, of course, so, throwing timidity out the window, I backed up quite a long way and charged towards the incline so that the momentum gained on the flat would carry us over. And it worked! All the while Dorothy was cheering us – me and the van. Onwards and upwards. She had absolutely no doubt that we were going to win the day.'

We go through the letters and Anthony finds, in one of the rumpled envelopes, a card he wrote to his aunt but never sent. 'How funny,' he says ruefully. 'Twenty-first of July, 1981. That's when I first came to Spain.'

Dear Aunt Dorothy,

I always think of you whenever I am in the mountains, or perhaps 'I give the mountains your best wishes' would be a better way to put it. I am in mountains on the West of Spain called Sierra Del Montseny. I have hired a moped and am taking little roads and doing some painting. I'll be away for just two weeks.

I think I really need to clear my head, and the mountain roads are good for that.

I hope you will keep in touch with your movements etc – I will telephone you again sometime soon.

Love Anthony x

There's a letter from Christine Chandler, Dorothy's housekeeper at Wentworth House, written after Dorothy's death. She says the college have been through the house and put locks on the sitting-room door so she cannot get in. She's been trying to get the place cleaned up but with all the comings and goings . . . A young man has moved in for four weeks to go through Mr Richards' letters and papers.* She hopes he's well and having nice weather.

It is not too bad in Cambridge, lovely and sunny and warm.
    Christine.

Anthony nods to himself, remembering.

The next letter is dated Sunday 17 November 1985, from Dorothy – suddenly resurrected and unwittingly comical in her various ailments and demands. She's unwell and annoyed by that, feeling 'like a caged bird' in Wentworth House, 'weak and miserable'. Her hernia operation was successful but instead of coming back into fitness she got

---

* John Constable, cataloguing Ivor and Dorothy's letters and belongings, I imagine.

some flu and then, when she'd just got over that, 'was attacked by the blood infections which nearly killed me in 1984'. She was invited down to Salisbury by Kenneth Richards, Ivor's brother, 'but he is 94, deaf, blind' and rather maudlin, 'which is not easy if you feel it yourself'.

At this point she changes tack and pens:

> I really long for a holiday in the sun. Places easy for me, as I know them, are Egypt and the Caribbean [Anthony laughs] but they are such long expensive flights away. I suppose you are planning to come home and have a family Christmas with the children? Would there be a modest bed near the sea in Barcelona where I could sit in the sun and sightsee gently?
>
> I would gladly pay your expenses but I would want a clean single room for myself.

She enquires about how Anthony's painting is going, then finishes up:

> I'll get a note off now to Christopher and tell him my problems. ['Oh I bet he loved that,' laughs Anthony.]
>
> We've had some good Autumn sunshine but icy nights and leaves all fell dramatically and suddenly when freezing winds blew them. No time to turn golden.
>
> Love Dorothea
>
> P.S. – Did I tell you that I.A.R.'s *Meaning of Meaning* has just been reprinted as a paperback with cover painting by Bruegel? £3.95. It makes you wonder how the young can afford a library.

We read more, taking it in turns to narrate the knotty script, often written on recycled Pinnacle Club or university stationery, the handwriting dogged, the words occasionally crowded over to one side or other of the page. One can imagine her sat in her upholstered chair in Cambridge, spotted hands moving over the paper. Is she alone in the house or is Mrs Chandler busy in the kitchen? Over the course of twenty letters, she writes that she's annoyed with her failing eyes; public transport's turned into a bit of a struggle; she's under the weather but determined to recover; she's been down to London for an Alpine Club dinner which was wonderful; the colours outside are changing, the weather's being fickle, she's anxious to see her friends in America.

And than the last letter – 18 August 1986.

Anthony reads it aloud.

Dear Anthony,

Happy to get your letter with the whole summer's activities. I tried to imagine it all. I like having the mountain colour, also the strange menagerie – as involved as Bruegel.

What is next on your program?

Do you stay in Barcelona?

Dr. Irons won't commit himself but says it's reasonable to go to the States. Unhappily I shan't go back to being able to walk six miles alone as I could two years ago. I missed my holiday that year due to my hernia operation . . .

Did I tell you, the young men at Glen Brittle are very enthusiastic and want to republish *Climbing Days*? Small circulation; real climbers. Hogarth Press also want to do it but in paperback – no photographs, they say, prohibitively costly – so I am torn and taking time to decide.*

---

* Hogarth Press republished *Climbing Days* in 1989 and it's this version

Second hand copies now sell for £35!

Of course it would reach a much larger circle of non-climbers . . . let me know about your progress but probably best not to try to catch me before I fly off to the States as I shall have my last mail forwarded.

Anthony stops. 'Where's the envelope?'
Written in biro on the back of the envelope:

Definitely Dr. Irons has given permission, that is to say, he thinks it reasonable for me to fly to the States on Monday 3rd September 1986. Heathrow 10:45am TWA number 753. Boston local time 12:55. My address there to be . . .

That's it.

She must have died that autumn, he says, straightening up as the sounds of the city flow back into the room. 'She didn't go to the States, I know that. And that was only written a few weeks before.'

* * * * *

Dorothy died in Cambridge on 24 September 1986, eight days after her ninety-second birthday.

* * * * *

After Dorothy's death, Anthony wrote an account of their final trip to Skye in a letter to Muriel Files of the

---

which Anthony owns so, as yet, he hasn't seen the original photographs. I wonder whether Dorothy made up her mind before she died or whether Dr Luckett, as executor of the estate, made the decision after her death.

Fell and Rock Climbing Club.

As with the tapes from Wentworth House, the fidelity of the moment is caught – the gap between the instant then and now reduced so much that Dorothy seems more vital and alive in the telling, as if she's only momentarily left the room.

With Anthony's permission, I've transcribed the letter here since I think it stands as a fine chronicle, an honest, affectionate document of their recent time together – as it was for Anthony, as he felt it.

19th Jan '87

Dear Muriel Files,

My brother forwarded your letter to me and I write just having returned from a trip painting in the Pyrenees.

SKYE

We arrived at the coast on New Year's Eve knowing that if we crossed to Skye we would be stranded for several days. Time was limited and neither of us liked making the decision to take the ferry or not, but as always when I was out and about with my aunt, a feeling of adventure took over. We were on the ferry.

Our stay in Skye centred around the climbing hut at Glen Brittle. As you might expect, we took the small road that leads to the most mountainous region and finally to the sea. These were the hills she climbed as a youth and I took great pleasure in her satisfaction at seeing the great snow-covered peaks once again. We took the road back and forth several times over the two days and she would always ask me to stop at vantage points to gaze once more, describing to me in detail the ridges and routes they had taken. In the village at the head of the road she asked in a small shop about the Post Office and associated climbing hut that had once existed at the base of the mountains, – remembering of course the names of the people concerned. Indeed, they knew of the family, but the Post Office had long since disappeared and the new modern climbing hut had been built on the other side of the road. We made our way there and arrived at the hut as dusk was falling, to be greeted with great warmth by a group of four of five young climbers, and also an older climber, a guide who is one of the chief organisers of the club. Through meeting him that night and finding Dorothy Pilley's name on their journal of records of climbs – his group (who publish beautifully presented small circulation climbing books) offered to publish *Climbing Days* again. Indeed, this was one of her final dilemmas, – whether to republish with Hogarth Press (Chatto & Windus) or with them. The large circulation firm would not print the photographs, but would of course reach a larger public, which was generally felt by her friends to be a great advantage.

On New Year's Eve, we sat around the fire in Glen Brittle climbing hut while my aunt recounted climbing stories. Her audience – an unlikely one, since they would have no knowledge of such a distant era – proved enthusiastic. I was delighted, not just by this, but by the easy way my aunt fitted in with their goings on. Dorothea was a perfectionist and was given to strong likes and dislikes, yet she was lulled and attentive, drinking her 'nip' of whiskey and listening to the Scottish guitar melodies that were played as the New Year came round. I inverted several of the kitchen's pots and pans and joined in on percussion. Later on I took her up to her bunk bed and blankets, and she slept tight along-side a wine bottle that I had filled with hot water.

It possibly explains why in Wentworth House she would still use old camping utensils. In the mountains she was reduced to simplicities, a state of mind hard to encounter, but a continual reminder that sophistication is in one sense superfluous. Drawn as she was to paradox, invention and being at the centre of social activity, she would punctuate her intensely felt opinions with a stoical admission that of course *she might be wrong*. This made her fundamentally provocative, but illustrates how someone so difficult could attract the enormously wide range of ages and types of peo-ple who stood the test and became her friend. Her strong sense of irony, tinged as it was on the one hand by a strict moral code, and on the other by a sense of risk and adven-ture could always make me laugh.

On New Year's Day I cooked her a sizable breakfast of bacon and toast and we said goodbye to the hut. Most of the climbers had taken to the hills by midday. Over the same meal the following day while we waited for the first ferry off the island, she explained to me what I think was almost an obsession with her since childhood – and that is why beauty had the feeling it had.

Why, for instance, she said, should the crystallised snow on a winter tree fill one with a sense of magnificence. She regarded this as a great mystery. I think that whenever she was talking about the mountains, or the view of the garden in Wentworth House, it was this that she was still chasing. For my aunt, all states of mind existed; the dark side and the light, the mean and the generous – but for her they existed in such profusion that she took it upon herself (at, I believe, a very young age) to always leave the last word with the light,

Anthony Pilley,
Barcelona, 2015
(Anthony Pilley)

and to back fellowship rather than the individual, and it is possibly this that gave her eyes such a twinkle in old age.

One other thing she said which struck me was her horror of being influenced in groups, and that she would feel vulnerable in her younger days at being swamped by the ideas of others. An unlikely position for someone of such strong character! The fact is that the opinions of others mattered a great deal to her, although she fiercely guarded her independence at the same time.

Well I hope this may be of some use and that the obituary goes well. I would love to see a copy when it is published.[11]

Best Wishes,

Anthony Pilley

* * * * *

The next morning we woke and dressed before dawn. Anthony took his sticks. The city was hushed and chilly. The metro was not yet running and the streets were being swept as we walked down to Plaça d'Espanya. It turned out we had to wait a little while for the first train of the day so we drank some too-hot coffee in a bright all-night cafe –

feeling filmy, thinking that we could have stayed in bed – whilst, opposite, two Venetian towers framed the National Palace halfway up Montjuïc, the whole scene silhouetted by the three-bar fire of dawn.

We'd explored Montjuïc on the second day of my visit, taking a bus up the hill to see the Fundació Joan Miró – which Anthony and I snuck into via the gift shop without paying, *because he lives here and I'm a guest. You never had to pay to visit things when he first arrived in this bloody city. We're not tourists!* So that's fine – where I saw the artist's fauvist mountain paintings with their lilac peaks beyond corrugated yellow fields and thought of the Pyrenees and stood transfixed watching the cycling silver beads of *Mercury Fountain, 1937* gel, simmer, pull apart and fall for a long time. We walked around the primary-coloured sculptures on the glaring roof terraces – Duchamp-like assemblages of found domestic objects – and mused on Miró's recurrent ladder forms and bulbous raucous chickens. One of my favourite things in the museum was a photograph by Joaquim Gomis – *Objectes al taller de Joan Miró, 1961.*

A monochrome snap of a boggle-eyed rough ceramic sphere balanced on top of a triangular crate-like ladder. The protuberant noggin appeared surprised but content atop its plinth, leant back against Miró's studio wall with an air of relief and contentment, as if having just climbed there with great effort.

'That's probably how I look, up mountains,' I suggested to Anthony.

'No,' he said, quite seriously, 'The ladder is a body and the head is a head. So if it's like you at all, that's how you are all the time.'

In retrospect, sitting at my desk with a postcard of that

photograph pinned to a noticeboard beside my head, the image of my baffled ceramic boggle-face improbably rolling uphill is an entirely apt analogy for the writing of this book.

I was to recognise Miró's tumid forms again when we first clapped eyes on Montserrat, rising in shudders, a distant crazed relative of the Malvern Hills – not quite as serrated as the name suggested, more undulating and corpulent. Jan Morris described it as a 'pile of queerly serrated jags, bumps, and crevices which was hacked into shape by the golden axes of angels'.[12] Green belts of vegetation banded the mountain as it soared, stratum stretch marks, as if Montserrat had mushroomed only that morning as a pink conglomerate soufflé, spilling up into the sky like a mass of worm-cast gyres, recalling the concrete coil sculptures of Anish Kapoor.

At Monistrol de Montserrat station we disembarked for the rack railway which was to zigzag us up the seemingly sheer steeps to Montserrat station. Miró once stated that he had 'managed to escape into the absolute nature', and his landscapes now had 'nothing in common any more with out-side reality'.[13] I had never seen a rock form like this before and the supernatural character of Montserrat only deepened the higher we clacked up it – the train ascending with apparent 'look Mum, no hands' nonchalance although a subtle vibration like a puissant flywheel beneath our feet hinted at unseen moil and grind. The disparity of this below-deck melee and serene snap-happy tourists sat above called to mind a swan pedalo. Pitched at forty-five degrees. In Moominland.

Shooting abruptly from a plain, an inselberg-like island in the air, Montserrat was an otherworldly land apart with an aesthetic and internal logic all its own. Here, Miró's forms made a sense they had not on Montjuïc. Here they were at home and I began to see the powerful influence this fantastic noduled crown exerted on the artist. Apt then that this was Anthony's choice of mountain to climb with me – a peak of surreality revered by Catalonians and artists across the world. 'Montserrat is the Catalan Uluru,' explained Anthony at one point. 'It's sacred like that. They feel it represents their character, their deep-rooted difference.'

The train passed into a tunnel and rolled back out into the sun below Santa Maria de Montserrat Abbey, behind which loomed a wall of friable loessic Hattifattener forms.

Seen in the instant before we dipped into the Montserrat station shed, the massive monastery facade seemed to taper to a point. The sun-bleached mystery and melancholy of Giorgio de Chirico flashed to mind. Once out of the station, I saw the coral blocks of the basilica, vertical walls bolting up to dark windows – surreal pink-faced relation of Conwy's brute grey castle – supremely solid but emphatically dwarfed by the swollen mountain above. A high square tower to the left, risen like a craning snail's head above all else, seemed to be gazing over our heads towards Barcelona, serenely unconcerned by the protuberant chaos of cliffs at its back.

* * * * *

From the station, Anthony and I began our trek to Montserrat's Sant Jeroni summit. The funicular higher to San Juan was not yet running, so we took a winding path out and around the mountain's southern side into a blasted sphinx-form arena. The route had begun as a cobbled way but soon became concrete. Catalonia, I'd noted since arriving, was a huge proponent of concrete. In the past week I'd seen any number of large-scale railway excavations, road- and bridgeworks, polished tunnel mouths and chapped embankments – mammoth constructions of reinforced concrete – walls and grey monoliths baked by the Barça sun. That morning, on the plain out beyond the city's environs, our train had passed a sprawling cement factory, crouched dusty in a mazy mass of ginger ducting – talc powder spider in the centre of the earthwork web.

Yet the sheer amount of concrete up this mountain gave one pause for thought. There must have been hundreds of thousands of tonnes in the roadways and tracks underfoot. Had they driven it all up from the valleys below? Had they helicoptered it up? Surely not, but there it was, set solid underfoot in ten-metre sections. We followed the undulating ashen slabway, rising, meandering, snaking until we reached the San Juan funicular station, at which point, about an hour into the walk, we sat down to eat our elevenses of sauerkraut and pastrami sandwiches.

Directly across the valley from us, shrouded in smoky low cloud, massed a mean domed rank of rock. It was as if a gigantic set of Lewis Chessmen had decided to form a rugby team and we were now faced with their front row – a conglomerate set of ruddy prop forwards, crouched to make a mountain scrum.

All over Montserrat the landscape reared as gömböc domes and pillars; milled pyramids, but always rounded, always sensual – somatic edifices, moulded by the island weather here, high in the air – bodily not just in the recognition of human forms in the terrain but the uncanny sense that the terrain itself was populated, perhaps even created, by enormous otherworldly creatures – kindred of the *espanta bruixes* perched atop Gaudí's Casa Milà, or Miró's boggle-eyed Martian men.

The track we took next wound round a series of pebble-dash cones – the path a shelf cut into their sides. The sun was now high and the day very dry, and our feet beat up talcy clouds as we walked.

Joggers passed us, tight in Lycra, running back the way we'd come. Clearly they'd been up and were on their way down, clutching ergonomic water bottles, focused behind sunglasses, all neons and black. We could hear their rhythmic thump ahead and learnt to flatten ourselves to one side to let them jog on.

In the valley we saw climbers ascending a termite-mound phallus more than a hundred metres tall. Above our heads the tinkle of belt gear told of others, scaling unseen. The place was clearly a Mecca for grit scrambles and climbs of all levels. During the day I watched parties of kids being schooled in rope skills on bombproof routes as well as older contingents – ripped threesomes scaling apparently feature-less plates – moving sinuously between mere finger-crimps in the warm rock.

At one point we passed a family of Americans sat beside the path, taking it in turns to read aloud from the Bible in clothes which made no concession to the heat. In fact they looked like they'd stepped out of a golf catalogue. Round the next corner we overtook a fellow singing 'Goodbye Yellow Brick Road' in a thick Spanish accent. He seemed very happy with his lot.

'*Bon dia*,' we smiled.

'I'd really struggle to be friends with an Elton John fan,' Anthony confided after a minute or so had elapsed and the singer had faded from view and hearing. '*Really* struggle . . .' he repeated to himself, a serious frown on his face.

Under the Pic du Midi d'Ossau, 1924 (From *Climbing Days*. Photo: I. A. Richards/RCM)

We were now quite high up Montserrat. The concrete underfoot had ceded to rock and earth. The middle of the mountain was lush and wooded and we walked in parched runnels overhung with trees in landscape reminiscent of Dorset's hol-loways, albeit overlooked by multistorey figures – la Prenyada (the Pregnant Woman), la Mòmia (the Mummy), and l'Elefant – which really does look like a monstrous oolite elephant.

Gorse flowered yellow. Lime trees, oaks, white pines and maple grew with yew, olive, hazelnut, holly and box. The smells were rich, thick, sweet and sappy as we passed beneath their canopy, very grateful for the shade they gave. In the quiet the clicking of Anthony's hiking sticks became hypnotic, a metronome to birdsong and the distant tolling of the monastery bells. We didn't speak much but there was camaraderie in our synchronised step and the mirrored way we'd both sit down for a drink without needing to discuss it.

Since crashing his motorbike and smashing his left knee, long walks had been a struggle, Anthony explained – not ascending, as a rule, but rather descending – something to do with the way the cartilage flexed or, more accurately, failed to flex in his right knee. But he was feeling alright at the moment since the trail had been of a relatively consistent grade.

He was dressed again in a bright T-shirt, tangerine this time. Looking at him there, I reflected that it was an ageless attire: T-shirt, light trousers, thickish socks, robust boots. Perhaps he'd been similarly dressed when he moved out here thirty years ago, or even before, working in Barclay Towers – only the face changing over time, affirming itself beneath the same thatch of hair, above an ambit of brilliant T-shirts.

* * * * *

I've heard of routes up mountains described as stairways before but generally the term is used to allude to an obvious path or pitch with a ladder-like set of holds. Montserrat's case is more literal – the Sant Jeroni summit is reached by a long grey flight of concrete steps. There are handrails too, in places. The sense is of an accessibility scheme which has got out of hand. The highest point features an observation platform and a 360-degree map with the bearings and distances to cities and mountains near and far.

Below us, Montserrat dropped sheer for several thousand feet to the vineyards, forests and pastures of the Catalan Central Depression, spreading green towards Andorra and the distant Pyrenees. Somewhere, some two hundred miles to the north-west on the French side of that range, was Gavarnie and the Hôtel des Voyageurs, where I.A.R. and Dorothy first met the 'grand old man' François Bernard Salles, who guided them safely through the events related in the *Climbing Days* chapter 'Into Spain and Back Again (1923)'.* Further west stood Pic du Midi d'Ossau, which the pair returned to climb the following year and in whose shadow Ivor took one of my favourite photographs of Dorothy, 'In the daffodil fields under the Pic du Midi d'Ossau at evening'.

Face in shadow, body half-hidden behind rucksacks, she sits looking back at Ivor. A long-handled axe leans in the foreground. But for that axe it could be a contemporary shot; Dorothy in a headscarf and a thick jacket, fir trees ris-

---

* François Bernard Salles was a legendary Pyrenean guide who had climbed with nineteenth-century explorer and mountaineer Henry Russell amongst many others. 'Salles, a big man with a curling moustache, was famous for the prodigious weight he could carry. And also for his ability to sleep; sometimes he fell asleep like a waxwork in the middle of rolling a cigarette. He was never ambitious and when not hired as a guide he continued his work as a shepherd . . . There is a photo of him only six months before he died at age seventy-nine in 1934, still in Gavarnie guarding his sheep, in clogs and beret, holding his shepherd's crook.' Rosemary Bailey, *The Man Who Married a Mountain*, Bantam Books, 2005.

ing behind her, first tightly packed in swathes, then thin-
ning – lightening band on band until they peter out
completely and the snow-defined ridges and grey twin
prongs of the mountain stand alone in the grainy sky.

The light is crisp but nebulous. Were it not for the caption,
it would be hard to know what time of day the picture was
taken or whether the pair were setting out or returning from
the crescent pinnacles which dominate the scene, but the day
is clearly extremely cold, so cold that a chill stillness seems to
escape the frame and the trees seem to steam in the frozen air.

Sat in the centre Dorothy holds our gaze, Ivor's gaze. She's
twenty-nine, her physical peak, and behind her looms Pic du
Midi d'Ossau, freshly scaled that day – like a horned prize on
the back wall of the scene. But now the night is coming on
and the moon is up and they're en route back to their inn at
dusk, about to plunge into a forest by lantern light, but they
stop, just for a moment, and Ivor takes a photograph.

A frozen snap in time.

* * * * *

Sat on top of Montserrat, Anthony takes a small package
from his bag.

'I was staying in the house the night Dorothy died,' he
tells me. 'She was in Addenbrooke's Hospital. I arrived that
day. I didn't visit her there. When I returned to Spain I took
this away with me. I knew they were leaving everything to
Magdalene. I knew I would never see any of the things surrounding her again . . .'

Inside the package is a fountain pen.

'It's for you,' says Anthony.

Switzerland

September 2014

i. Mountains

The red lights on the side of the Matterhorn blinked on and off for several hours. We watched them, perplexed, from our seat on the side of the Dent Blanche. Every so often, freezing cloud would sweep up the valley and envelop us, obscuring the view, but then it would clear and the moon would emerge and the red lights could be seen again.

Sometimes I would fall asleep but only for a few seconds before starting awake again. Swells of snow occasionally strafed across us. Our jackets were frost-lacquered pearly and the rope was frozen fairly solid. The bivvy bag had ripped at some point in the night so, rather than being sat together in a sturdy sack, we had it wrapped around our legs as an ineffective sheet, as if engaged in the worst picnic in the world.

At one point, shifting position with numb feet, I felt myself knock into one of the helmets next to me on the ledge and heard it slide and fall into deeper darkness – down towards Zermatt some thousand feet below. I didn't bother to turn my head torch on to watch it go, I could hear it ricochet away on the rocks beneath us; tick, tick, clatter; bouncing, clunking, fading . . . I followed it with my ears

The Dent Blanche. (From *Climbing Days*. Photo: E. Gyger)

until it was lost in the low humming whistle of the wind.

I knew my father was awake and also listening next to me. Neither of us spoke. Shivering hard, I hugged myself and drew my knees in to my chest.

Ahead, the lights on the Matterhorn flickered on and off, on and off, on and off.

* * * * *

The Dent Blanche hangs over much of *Climbing Days*, the climax of the book. From Ivor's first trip to the Alps as a boy and Dorothy's first sighting in 1921, the mountain, specifically its unclimbed North Arête, loomed in their imagination – 'lurking behind our plans each season, thwarting or favouring them and shaping our climbing lives'.

The mountain is famed. One of the great summits of the Swiss Pennine Alps.

My father, Tim, climbed its West Ridge with a friend in 1981. His guide book from that day, a small red Alpine Club guide which smells of cupboards, age and ink, describes the Dent Blanche as 'A fairly symmetrical mtn, of bold outline, recognisable from afar. It has four ridges, forming a cross.'

Of the North-North-West Ridge (Dorothea and Ivor's North Arête), it says:

> Much the shortest but most difficult of the ridges. A famous climb of uneven difficulty. The crux passage is excessive for the ridge as a whole, for this reason it is not climbed very often. A number of attempts were made before it was finally climbed, when it was regarded as 'one of the last great problems'. It therefore has a certain glamour – enhanced in British mountaineering literature by Dorothy Pilley Richards' account in 'Climbing Days'. . . . First ascent by D. Pilley Richards and I. A. Richards with Joseph Georges and A. Georges, 20 July 1928.[1]

It was not climbed again for fifteen years.

Dorothea called it 'the Witch'. The white witch.

The plan and pictures beside the text in Tim's red book show the mountain glowering dark and massive – less white, more metallic. Pictures of mountains in books are often dubious, queer things, their paper portraits stripped of scale and majesty, as bad taxidermy shames a lion through no fault of the beast's, and I knew better than to trust small black-and-white pictures in books, but one thing the picture did convey was a sense of aggressive mass.

Just as the mountain formed the pinnacle of *Climbing Days*

– the most celebrated ascent of Dorothea and Ivor's lives – the definitive climb and mountain in a book of climbs and mountains, so it forms the centre of this book too. It is the place where my family's mountaineering threads converge. As a child I knew the name. Something great had happened there, something which elicited a pride, independent of knowledge of the specific mountain or the act; an achievement large enough to transcend 'climbing' and the regal alien strangeness of 'Dorothea and Ivor' to become a shared point of family honour. 'The Dent Blanche', like an invocation; or sometimes, 'the White Tooth', knowingly, as if it were a secret.

'The Dent Blanche' was the reason Tim began climbing in his youth, another attempt to engage with Ivor and Dorothea, the conversational approach having foundered. His 1981 climb was a pilgrimage of sorts, he admits.

'I went because of them. I wanted to go where they had been. I wanted to talk to them about these things so much but I just couldn't . . . I didn't know how.'

Which is truly sad when you consider that Dorothea was still alive in 1981 but never learnt of Tim's climb.

* * * * *

When we left our house in Bath, Tim and I were carrying a large box between us strung on a four-foot plank. We got some strange looks at the railway station but at the airport we were vindicated when it weighed in at *exactly* twenty kilograms and *exactly* the maximum size of our hold allowance. The box contained ropes, axes, a frame-sack, crampons, gas stove, penknives and such – the sort of things airport security get testy about if they find them in your hand luggage . . .

although, amazingly, they let Tim keep the plank, which got all the way to Arolla, against all odds and common sense.

The precedent for getting maximal bang for one's baggage buck can be found in *Climbing Days* with Dorothea's description of the postal exploits of E. W. Steeple and Guy Barlow and the 'locally notorious parcels' the pair would send up to Glen Brittle on Skye:

> These parcels were nicely calculated not to exceed either in weight or dimension the maximum allowed by the Post Office Regulations and yet not to fall short of it. They were elegantly encased in a distinctive buff-coloured material and soundly stitched. You could recognise them a long way off. In a stream of such parcels their entire luggage, gear and provisionment would arrive, harbingers appearing some considerable time before Steeple and Barlow themselves. The feelings of the postman, confronted daily with the largest and weightiest parcel he had yet seen . . . may be imagined.[2]

The distance to Glen Brittle from the Post Office was nine miles, she adds, mischievously.

Once landed in Geneva and out the other side, we sat down beside the luggage claim conveyors and broke down the cardboard box, repacking all our gear into two large rucksacks which we further rejigged on the train to Brig as it sped away from Geneva, along the lakeside – below the terraced Lavaux vineyards swathed in blue netting, a ha-ha hillside steeped in wine and crossed by roads which strode alongside us on Bauhaus viaducts.

Swiss trains seemed wider than their British counterparts, more palatial, with more space between the seats to stretch out and stow kit. Their overhead racks could accommodate rucksacks bursting with ropes and Vango tents. We settled down on the seats and looked at the other passengers, none of whom were taking the slightest notice of our eccentric haul of spiky kit – the clanking red helmet, the purple Haston sack with the two Chouinard axes and white helmets strapped on the back, the smaller backpack for water and food, and the plank; British trains were pokey in comparison.

This was how I.A.R. and Dorothea travelled to the Alps, of course: train, boat, train with stops along the way. It felt like we'd dropped in for the last leg of a journey in their stead – on their track around the crescent lake from Geneva to Montreux, the same vines still growing, the waters still reflecting the mountains of Savoy and Valais. As we scooted past Chillon Castle, it looked to be wading out, stone trousers rolled; at Lausanne station my window drew up level with *that* iconic Swiss clock, red second hand wheeling to our moment of departure at which point we left on cue. I thought back to Barcelona as we passed through Montreux where Freddie Mercury's statue punches the air.

Then it was up the swoosh of the Rhône valley, cupped by the canton walls of Valais and Vaud. Mountains rising around and in front; green, buff, blue, steely mountains in a subdued, equalising light.

Never having been to the area before, it was easy to envision it as avenued and ordered – each mountain rising as a single entity, graduating straight up and down from Rhône level like an egg-box inner – but no. The mountains I could see were not the mountains we had come for. Those stood higher, proud as knuckles on a hand held flat. The mountains I could see were only fingertips; we still had a long way to go. Mainly up.

We disembarked at Sion. Tim bought provisions in a nearby supermarket and then we boarded the yellow 381 Car Postal bus which drove across the curiously turquoise river and round the first of many hairpin bends which wound up to the mouth of Val d'Hérens – the hanging valley which leads to Les Haudères and Arolla. In this we mirrored Dorothea in almost every way. She writes in *Climbing Days* that her diligence from Sion station to Les Haudères 'turned out to be a little yellow post-chaise' which 'took most of the day to crawl up the long valley, and the too gallant postman-driver, when not trudging beside his horse, beguiled the way with anecdotes and attempts at flirtation'.

Our Car Postal was the great-great-nephew of that post-chaise – livery retained, horsepower increased, so the twenty-three-mile journey took only an hour; which is not to suggest that it was uneventful – at one town our canary bus pulled away with its baggage hold doors still open and bouncing like stubby wings. Alarmed, passengers shouted to alert the driver before he started decapitating passers-by. I tried to shout something helpful too but forgot the French word for 'Stop!' so made an incoherent alarmed noise instead which drew confused and amused glances from the schoolchildren sat around us and was to set the tone for my linguistic interactions during the rest of our stay. 'I'm sure I *used* to know a bit of French, you know,' I'd say sheepishly to Tim at intervals, as we pooled our schoolboy Franglais and tried to make ourselves understood in the mountains and villages around Val d'Hérens.

As the bus drove on, skirting sunny meadows and abrupt sheer drops, we passed through a great many small towns which became more dispersed the further we went; knots of chalets and hay lofts petering out to the odd interjection of a charcoal shed – eventually becoming so diffuse that they looked more grown or thrown than built; barns stood in the middle of fields akin to glacier erratics or the massive boulders which occasionally dislodge and tumble from the cliffs overhead.

All this we saw en route, craning our heads to see the world pass – sawmills, pine forests, rushing water, wireframe mattress nets to catch rockfalls, mighty reinforced tunnels, roads veering off elsewhere; who knew where? Added to this, in the midst of all the excitement, I discovered that the majority of Tim's shopping for the week ahead was prunes and packet risotto.

* * * * *

'The end of the long drive is Les Haudères, a maze of muddy passages between overhanging wooden chalets,' wrote Dorothea.

> The post gallops in in style with a hissing and jangling of bells. The horses are brought up sharp in a space no larger than a room and all the idlers stand round to watch. I collected a much too heavy sack from the boot of the chaise, tucked my ice-axe under my arm and promptly lost myself in the labyrinth of narrow alleys of the village.

Les Haudères sits below Dent de Veisivi, a mountain wedge which splits the valley in two. The main channel of Val d'Hérens forks south east, rising to the Ferpècle glacier whilst, to the south, Val d'Arolla steps up to Mont Collon.

Our bus pulled up in a tarmacked square and we disembarked, thanking the driver and hefting our bags over to a bench beside a small post office. Around us stood all sorts of wooden buildings built in the Swiss tradition; the largest was a half-timbered, shallow-gabled restaurant four floors tall which occupied one side of the square; an older hostel – closed for the season – formed another. Higher up, ancient-looking *stadel* granary-barns crouched on toadstool legs of gneiss. Their woods were deep coffee, their roofs an overlapping armour of broad stone slabs. Between and behind these vernacular structures jostled newer stucco terracotta-topped apartments, recent arrivals in the maze. But the town had a cross-grained larch-wood heart; beautifully crafted and tightly knitted using a technique called *strickbau* – each part slotting and locking together without need of nails; the utility was beautiful to see. Many buildings in the area, built this way, are still working and solid after hundreds of years, their sides weathered dark over time, part of the landscape – there to see Dorothea ascend in the 1920s and still there to greet us in the 2010s.* There they are, saluted in the pages of *Climbing Days* – 'Chalets of La Forclaz on the way to Ferpècle' – three khol cabins framed against the ghosting bulk of the Dent Blanche which looms over all, the silvered shock of faces and ridges below the summit and the pall of undulating snow flowing out of shot, the long 'easy' ridge of the Ordinary (Wandflue) Route. But there's something about the mountain's inexorable size and gravity which suggests it's tolerating the cabins, for now: the cabins, the people who built them, the meadows, everything else.

---

* In his book *Switzerland Builds: Its Native and Modern Architecture* (1950), G. E. Kidder Smith writes about *strickbau* or *Blockhaus* buildings and notes that 'Although even the exterior walls are unpainted and unstained, protection against the weather is achieved by four, five, or six-inch solid wood thickness. The Swiss actually complain that their stern climate deteriorates the wood buildings after four or five hundred years! Paint, they claim, would shorten this life considerably.'(Reprinted by permission of Tatjana Smith.)

I'm reminded of a cartoon by the illustrator Tom Gauld about a conversation between two hills. 'Hey, Frank,' says one to the other, who has a castle on his head. 'What?' replies Frank, the castle now having turned into a town. 'Never mind,' says the first, as we see that the town has fallen down. 'You had something on your head, but it's gone now.'[3]

'In eternity there is no time,' suggested Hermann Hesse, 'only an instant long enough for a joke.'[4]

Unlike Dorothea, we weren't stopping at Les Haudères, and a few minutes later another bus arrived, which we climbed aboard. As the only passengers, we sat at the front with the driver and a widescreen view as he drove. He had driven this road for a long time, he told us, as he traced his familiar line on the road with the assurance of years; cranking the wheel round to swing through the bends, skimming the barriers and jockeying the gearbox to coax his bus on, revving ever higher – each change earning a shudder and a little burst of speed from the quite-large yellow Car Postal-that-could.

The old road used to run along the floor of Val d'Arolla but now it zigzags up the hillside and threads through concrete boxes and tunnels where the roar of the engine swells and echoes under lights. All the time, to our left, pines flickered past and behind them were thin air and far peaks. The canary-coloured bus swayed on and then – there was the Dent Blanche, a stark dorsal fin at the head of Val d'Hérens. There. Stood in plain sight, staring us down. Sudden, vivid, daunting and now disappearing behind the flanks of Dent de Veisivi; the great white sliding from view.

* * * * *

You might have thought I'd know *Climbing Days* inside out, having read it so often and scoured it for details; be able to recite whole passages aloud and have excerpts circling in my mind the whole time, but this is not so.

I've used three copies in the writing of this book. One a British racing green cloth-covered Bell from the 1930s, one a Secker & Warburg (revised second) edition of 1965 with a Dent Blanche dust jacket and new foreword, and one a shonky recent reproduction with an awful pistachio cover ... with a man on it.* I've read and annotated them all. Each is marked and battered in a different way – highly foxed by age, travel and use. But the things that most stand out for me are atmospheres and images rather than set-piece extracts – the timeline sometimes feels uncertain and I think the fact that Dorothea pieced much of the book together from twenty years of diaries in the mid-1930s can be read between the lines; or perhaps that's just my reading, knowing it to be the case.

For me the book exists as a range of encounters, an archipelago of instants, many of them small. I'm drawn to the way Dorothea notes the small stuff – the recounted speech, strange meetings and eccentricities, incidents and accidents humorously retold, the way she often clearly downplays strain and physical danger – and often find these vignettes more affecting than the set-piece triumphs. Amidst all of this, they went up some mountains, big scary mountains: for fun.

I suppose I'm drawn to quirk, the mountaineering equivalent of a dog running onto the pitch, because the whole enterprise is faintly ridiculous; something Dorothea never forgot and cheerfully observed throughout her life.

* I don't have a copy of the Hogarth Press reissue, which, as well as having no photographs, also has a fairly rubbish cover, now I think about it ... with a man's boot on it!

And then there's Ivor, to whom autobiography and nostalgia were anathema; who agreed to a biography in later years unwillingly and on the proviso that it examine his life through the prism of his work. Yet here he is, not only depicted in *Climbing Days* but contributing to and editing the book, uncredited and behind the scenes – as he pitched in with the Pinnacle Club's journals and, to some degree, Dorothea's diaries as well. Ghosting on holiday.

Dorothea's diary of Wednesday 24 June 1934 records a day spent writing and editing together in the Dauphiné Alps of south-east France: 'Rest Day. Slept about 12 hours & felt glorious. Typed all morning & I.A.R. worked on Picion Epicoun section. Usual tourists up for lunch. We had ours outside but blowy & visited by dogs (so) not very satisfactory . . . Went to bed early after arranging the Dent Blanche bit.'[5]

The next day they climb the Roche Blanche (9,341 feet):

Away at 6.15. As we ascend the Tête de la Maye, curious dry whispy clouds formed everywhere. By the summit were enveloped. Found a party unexpectedly camped up there with nothing to look at – we enjoyed a tin of apricots . . . then on along a pleasant plateau & started up our hidden peak. Reached Summit 11:15. Tour de Force with a bottle:

Charles Tairsay
Maximus Rodier } – 30 Sept. 1912

Charles Heuriot – 29 July 1914

Mr. & Mrs Jean Emil
Mr. & Mrs Faure } – 23 July 1926

Paul Durant – 4 Aug. 1931

Added our Chinese card to mystify the future!

Wondered if we should go on towards Tête du Rouget but it looked long & rotten & a storm was coming up rapidly.

Stayed till 12:40 & then hurried down. Ate peaches under a
rock & took photographs on the Maye for 2 hours. Ran down
as the storm broke. I.A.R. caught his nails in a turned down
sock & took a header. Cut his knee & was heroic.[6]

It's easy to imagine such field notes being expanded to form
the body of a chapter, but the question of how the pair came to
write *Climbing Days* in the first place is an intriguing and
crucial question in itself. A trip to Reading University, which
holds the archives of both G. Bell & Sons Ltd. and Secker &
Warburg, revealed a great deal about the book's early life.

The first mention of a book comes in a letter from Mr
Alan Harris, a publishing friend of Dorothy's brother John,
in November 1928. Harris asks if Dorothy might consider
the suggestion of a book 'descriptive of the climbs you have
done in various parts of the Alps and in this country' –
Mountaincraft by Geoffrey Winthrop Young and George
Abraham's *The Complete Mountaineer* are mentioned as
suggestive models. The penultimate paragraph reads,

> We had hoped that the book might be jointly [authored] by
> Mr. Richards and yourself . . . but, from the publishing
> point of view, it is yourself that is important, because there
> is still something striking and original in such a book being
> written by a woman at all, (not that I want to suggest that
> you should in the least exploit that point unpleasantly, but
> there it is) especially by someone as famous among moun-
> taineers as you are.

Harris finishes by hoping that what he has outlined is
not 'hopelessly repugnant' to Dorothy, adding that he's
certain 'a book on the subject by you, well got up and

illustrated, would be a great success'.*

Dorothy responds in a two-page note written on paper headed 'Dawson's Dungeon Ghyll Hotel, Langdale'. She is 'distinctly interested' in his suggestion of her writing a mountain book, yes. There are many types of climbing chat she detests, she tells him, but once back in Cambridge she'll look through her notes and let him know more definitely what she feels she could do, ending 'Perhaps on your side you could give me some idea of the terms your House had in view of making the proposal?' – a pointed, business-savvy coda which perhaps prompted Harris to rethink his previously knowing, slightly patronising tone.[7] Thus, John's climbing sister with the famous husband rapidly assumed the form of a strong independent lady. In fact it is she who shows strongest in the letters, confident and professional, whilst Harris's writing reads like a verbose undergraduate deploying flash words to impress; hence we get 'fructifying', and 'tantallisingly' (*sic*) shoehorned into the fifth letter between the pair, as well as the familiar refrain 'We should awfully like it if your husband could be induced to share the authorship with you; so I hope you will have a good try.' Does this come from him and Bell or has Dorothy encouraged them, I wonder?

After a month's silence, Harris writes again. He hopes Dorothy hasn't forgotten about the climbing book; perhaps

---

* Alan Harris, G. Bell & Sons, draft letter to Mrs I. A. Richards, 11 December 1928, Reading University. Harris is acquainted with John Pilley, he mentions, and his letter begins with the suggestion that news of his approach might have already reached Dorothy that way: 'I understand from John that you might consider the suggestion, but that you have very definite ideas of the sort of book you are *not* prepared to write.' Another interesting nugget – one which will crop up several times – is the mention of Ivor's possible inclusion: 'John seemed to think that Mr. Richards would not have the time or inclination to take an active part in such a book.'

she's working on a chapter plan, he suggests, hopefully. The letter is short and slightly pleading.

Dorothy responds four days later (19 May 1929) with a letter and synopsis – she's had influenza *again*, she explains. Perhaps she could get the finished manuscript to Harris by the autumn of 1930? 'I am actually leaving Cambridge in two weeks time and then (in) London for two weeks, then Switzerland and Russia, and so to China in August . . . I haven't been able to persuade my husband to join me yet but I haven't given up hope! – He will anyway do an introduction.'

So it was Dorothy's idea! The meretricious wheedling I'd detected in Harris's correspondence is not altogether fair – as much a case of Dorothy trying to get elusive old Ivor to commit and reveal himself on paper as the publishers fishing for a name with clout.

The typed synopsis for the projected book is interesting since it bears so little resemblance to *Climbing Days* as published.* The Dent Blanche is not mentioned. Czechoslovakia, India and Japan *are* mentioned but don't feature in the final book at all. China is mentioned only in passing. The Jungfrau ends up with a scant four pages, and Grivola only

---

* The main headings run: 'British Climbing (The novitiate. Rock climbing technique. First ascents in Lakeland and Wales. The Holly Tree Wall. The Devil's Kitchen. Accidents. Ridge Walking in Skye.) / First Alpine Season (Snow and ice technique. The early women mountaineers.) / Guideless Climbing (Difference between it and guided – Women's particular problems.) / The Bouquetins (Two new routes and escape off Glacier at night.) / Mt. Blanc (guideless) / Jungfrau (2nd ascent by W. ridge.) / Grivola (Ice ridge – see article) / The High Patra of Czechoslovakia / Corsica (camping) / Pyrenees (Pic du Midi d'Ossau. 1st Easter ascent. Col de Boucheron – see article.) / Canada (Canadian Alpine Club camps.) / America (1st Ascent of Mt. Baker. 1st Ascent of Mt. Shuksau.) / India (Wanderings in the Himalayas) / Japan (Fuji) / China (Western hills.)'

eight. Canada and America would be bunched together into the impressionistic chapter titled 'Wander Years' whilst the first 'chapter' mentioned, 'British Climbing', would be carved up to form the first five: *Climbing Days*'s opening run. Of course books evolve as they're written into shape (take shape whilst being written, might be closer to the truth) but I was struck and oddly pleased by the divergence between first plan and finished manuscript.

As in the mountains, Dorothy and Ivor divined a route. Their original Bell contract states that 'The authors undertake to write a work dealing with mountaineering.' Early in the writing process – mostly carried out in China, where Ivor was teaching and at work perfecting Basic English in Peking (now Beijing)* – 'the work' is referred to variously in letters back to Bell as 'the mountaineering book' and, notably, 'A Memoir of Two Mountaineers'/'Memoirs of Two Mountaineers'.

On 12 January 1932, back in Cambridge from China, Dorothy writes to her editor at Bell, Mr Bickers:

> I am ashamed not to have written to you sooner to tell you that house moving instead of taking one week takes months seemingly – plumbers, carpenters, paper hanging, not least architects have been devouring all my leisure hours since I last wrote!
>
> The book is about 9/10ths written but is at the moment buried <u>somewhere</u> among our personal belongings – in one or other of several small mountains that stand in the middle of the still uninhabitable house! I have spent (the)

---

* There are clues in *Climbing Days* that the book took a long time to write and was subject to much revision – the original preface, for example, whilst only a page and a half long, is dated both 'Peking, 1929' and 'Cambridge, 1934'.

best part of today looking for it – without success . . .[8]

In early August 1932, Ivor writes to Mr Bickers with a progress report from Austria, together with several 'suggestions':

I am up here in a high Alpine Hut but having serious weather. However, the snow and wind has given leisure, and my wife and I have been hard at work on the book. It is now within a day or two of being ready for typing. My wife hopes to get that done, on our return to England, quickly, by about mid-September.

I wonder, what would you say was the latest date for you to receive the MSS with a hope of getting it out as a Christmas gift book?[*]

. . . As to the signature – we have been collaborating, but I have a strong impression that a climbing book of this type by a woman would be much a novelty to the general public (and) that it would be best if my wife alone signed it in her maiden name (D. E. Pilley) by which she is *very* well-known in the climbing world, and added her married name (Mrs I.A.R.) underneath. Let me know your views about this.[†]

On 31 August, Dorothy writes to thank Mr Bickers for his 'most helpful letter' of reply (since lost):

[*] Here, Mr. Bickers has drawn and underlined a rather large, rather worried question mark in the margin.
[†] I. A. Richards to Mr Bickers, G. Bell & Sons, written in Mayrhofen, Zillertal, Austria, 5 August 1932, Reading University. An example of this collaboration can be seen in the similarity of the beginning of Ivor's 1927 article 'The Lure of High Mountaineering' (see Appendix II, p. 348) with the top of page 77 in Chapter 4 of *Climbing Days*. 'Grand bits of Ruskinian crag work' all round.

After some discussion with my husband, we have come to the conclusion that you are right in preferring January as a publishing date. But I am making all efforts to get the man-uscript completed and revised by the end of this month so that there will be time to get it read by one or two people and alterations and additions made.*

She expresses uncertainty over the inclusion of 'certain American, Canadian and Himalayan sections with the Alpine & other mountain chapters' – which suggests to me that these were not actually fully written – 'I shall very much appreciate your advice on this when you see the M.S.' (A reminder that Bickers hadn't seen *any* of it until this point and they'd been going three years!) 'As to the signature – I have found it almost impossible not to write it in the first person, and though we have pooled our memories and discussed all the incidents and indeed written a good deal of it together – we both think that the book would have a better chance as coming from me.'

She doesn't think male mountaineers would be put off, in fact they might be intrigued, she suggests – echoing Ivor's earlier letter – ending:

The Austrian Alps have been very charming this season and we have got 9 peaks in the last 5 days guideless.

What a game!

Yours Sincerely,

Dorothy Pilley Richards†

---

* *Climbing Days* was not finished and published until 1935.
† One of the great discoveries of my trip to Reading was a reference in a 1965 letter from Dorothea to the editor of the Secker & Warburg republication of *Climbing Days*. Paragraph 3 begins: 'When the book was first being discussed,

* * * * *

Reading Dorothea's letters and diaries, mountains are always framed as free egalitarian space, territories unencumbered by ho-hum regimen or social baggage.

In the mountains, wherever those mountains were, Ivor and Dorothea were both, first and foremost, mountaineers. They met in the mountains on an equal footing and returned there whenever they could for the rest of their lives. This was perhaps the crux of their marriage for, as Dr Richard Luckett observed, their relationship seemed more akin to devoted companions than married couple; closer to a team – united climbing companions on a rope, their apparently eccentric union founded in the wild landscape of the mountains.

Their match and manner were cause for comment. T. S. Eliot – a friend of the pair, literary confrère of Ivor's and regular guest of the pair at Cambridge[9] – writing to Eleanor Hinkley in 1931, noted:

> I am glad you like Richards . . . I should not have thought of

Mr. Robin Collomb [Dorothea's previous editor at Secker & Warburg] held out high hopes that Penguin would want to follow up? You may remember that some years ago they approached me with a proposal to do it but I wanted a hard-backed republication first.' (Dorothy Pilley Richards, letter to Oliver Stallybrass, Secker & Warburg, 13 December 1965, Reading University). Also in the archive is a letter from Eunice E. Frost at Penguin with a list of missing illustrations. She ends: 'this means that, apart from those mentioned above, we have prints of all the others, which were supplied to us by Bell.' (Eunice E. Frost, Penguin Books Ltd to Mrs Dorothy Richards, 15 August 1949, Reading University.) Penguin had the prints and, presumably, the manuscript but Dorothy wanted a hard-backed republication first . . . which raises one of the great hypothetical questions in the story of the book: had Dorothy not dug her heels in on that, apparently trivial (perhaps slightly snobbish?) point, but instead understood the impact a mass market paperback edition of her book might have, what might have become of *Climbing Days?*

him as effeminate – rather sexless perhaps, just an intellect and a body, but [the] body is a very muscular and intrepid one: at any rate, I, who dislike looking out of a third storey window should not call effeminate such a daring mountain climber as he. Not that Mrs R. is not just as great a climber – I believe quite a celebrity in the Alps – when and if you meet her, inspect the muscular development of her calves – unless she has conceded so far to recent fashions in dress as to make that impossible.[10]

Here, in one short extract of correspondence, there is a real sense of the pair's eccentricity both in terms of relationship and interests. Eliot discussing effeminacy raises odd questions of appraisal – in photographs Eliot always strikes me as timorous and porcelain, a rawboned city bird to Ivor's owl. But sexless, yes, there he hits upon something often remarked upon, their oddly platonic off-kilter otherness in Cambridge twinned with their ardour for the mountains – a wildness veiled from most, effectively disappearing off the map for several months each summer. Whilst their alpine trips engendered wonder, admiration and esteem in many of their contemporaries, as evinced in Eliot's letter, they also distanced the pair further in the collective imagination – the mountains being an abstract scape so large that the sense of 'the mountains', these massive metaphysical landscapes, might seem to merge with 'the sea' as a nebulous gesture towards the epic faraway.

The result of this is that accounts of Dorothea and Ivor's mountaineering are, almost without exception, reported from without – academics sketching Ivor's exploits (with Mrs R.) in passing, as peripheral daredevil addenda to academia in reverential tones of bemused respect. John Constable, writing in his introduction to a recent edition of *Practical Criticism*, exemplifies this game but slightly dislocated approach:

> Before this breakthrough could have any consequences the Richardses went on their annual climbing holiday, during which Dorothy fell in a crevasse, Richards had his hair burnt by lightning, and, on the 20th of July and under the leadership of the great Alpine guide Joseph Georges, they made the first, and by all accounts terrifying, ascent of the North Ridge of the Dent Blanche.[11]

This is not meant to be a criticism of such accounts – my interest and writing is of a rather different sort – but it serves to illustrate the importance of *Climbing Days* as the only long-form account of Dorothea and Ivor's relationship written from within.

'The interaction of Dorothea and Ivor was to become very familiar and yet to remain mysterious,' Dr Luckett wrote in his introduction to the *Selected Letters*. 'The harmony of their social presence belied differences of temperament so great as to seem implausible.'[12]

I doubt either would have cared very much what others thought. Over and again the memories of those who met them tell of two people deeply connected and affectionate. But the fact they found a symmetry and balance in the privacy of the mountains that many other couples might have kindled in more prosaic situations is striking. They seem to have made perfect sense together in the mountains – a sense which very few people witnessed and might well have countered and debunked their eccentric public image 'back home', a sense entwined with place and deeds beyond the ken of most of those in

England, extrasolar from the London/Oxbridge circle.

In light of this, any glib description of *Climbing Days* as 'Dorothy Pilley's climbing memoir' feels inadequate but, of course, that is exactly how she described it herself. Ivor may be in it but it's Dorothy's name on the cover and it seems highly likely it could only have been so – it's very telling that there is no mention of Ivor, I.A.R. or any such soubriquet in the book's index. He is the ahistorical/abiographical man who wasn't there.

Whatever else it is, however much more I can tease out with the aid of retrospect, further reading and archival research, *Climbing Days* is an excellent, generous climbing biography first and foremost, crafted and kindred of the mountains and the landscape it describes – sure and independent of its feet and voice, co-climbed and written as I know it to be.

The images the book inspired in me – reading at home in Bath or at Magdalene College, Cambridge – were visions of distant lands and peaks. The photographs reproduced in its pages helped steady those imaginings, but this is a book which tallies with real-world topography as a symbiotic companion piece. It is no coincidence that the Bell first editions featured hand-drawn maps as endpapers* – an invitation to transcend the book's form. Now, for the first time, I was travelling on those papers, moving into Dorothea's memoir of scape; down from the top of the mottled first page, approaching the black circle marked Arolla.

---

* Another of Ivor's contributions – Dorothy Richards, Diary, 19 November 1934, RCM: 'Very misty and cold. Re-arranging index all day with Ivor but not yet completed. Ivor also did a sketch map of different districts of the alps with the main chains marked so as to make it intelligible – rather tangled affair. Felt better.'

* * * * *

We were dropped off on the road below the village, opposite the Hôtel Aiguille de la Za and a sign for a campsite which pointed down a gravel track through coniferous woods. We followed, unsure what we'd find. The light was dusky in the trees but then the track opened out and passed over a wooden bridge to a terraced area with a few tents and a shower block.

Mme Laurence, the lady who ran the campsite, made us feel tremendously welcome. She had very fine features, like an aristocratic egret. Patient eyes below silver birch hair. Yes, we could stay, she said, we were lucky, this was her last day open for the season. This was indeed a huge piece of luck, we agreed, whilst pitching our Vango in the twilight and cooking up a supper of risotto and prunes.

As dusk became night the world grew very quiet, as if the whole valley was listening. I lay awake keen-eared but Tim's soft breathing and the occasional ripple of wind across tent and trees were all I heard; the silence was deep and I fell quickly in; only to be woken twenty minutes later by the sound of our kit being rifled.

I fumbled for a torch and the zip of the porch to get out and see what was afoot. My thrashing beam caught the tail of a retreating fox, sloping off, dragging our UHT milk.

I stared. It didn't hurry and it didn't look back, nonchalant and calm like a pro, whilst I froze, befuddled, likewise on all fours, hands in cold dew – half in, half out the tent.

'Did you meet our fox?' asked Mme Laurence next morning. 'I forgot to warn you about her. She likes new campers!'*

---

* I later discovered that the Camping Arolla site is famed as being the highest in Europe at 1,950 metres.

As a memento of her visit, the fox had left several bite marks in Tim's leather boots. We had both worn our solid leather boots over – the only footwear we'd brought.

A few days before departure, checking through equipment, Tim's boots had come to light in the cellar grinning, soles peeling back from the uppers. He recalled last wearing them in 1982, the year of my birth, so I went to a taciturn cobbler who, having turned them over in his hands a long time, muttered, 'They're done in, alright. Thursday?' – the way great craftsmen do. New soles and a gallon of dubbin later they were back in the Alps, renewed – in better nick than Tim, one might say! Although that would be terribly unfair.

The fox must have had a taste for the marzipan tang of boot grease and long-life milk, an acquired campsite taste, perhaps.*

---

* Jack Kerouac wrote of comparable dairy-based larceny, but his fox was a bear: 'One morning I found bear stool and signs of where the monster had taken a can of frozen milk and squeezed it in his paws and bit into it with one sharp tooth trying to suck out the paste.' Kerouac stares into the foggy dawn, down the mysterious Ridge of Starvation 'with its fog-lost firs and its hills humping into invisibility', aware that somewhere in the fog stalks the bear. He imagines all the attributes and stories of the bear, its life and times: 'He was Avalokitesvara the Bear, and his sign was the grey wind of autumn.' He waits for the bear's return. It never comes. Jack Kerouac, 'Alone on a Mountaintop', *The Lonesome Traveler*, Andre Deutsch, 1962; Penguin, London, 2000, p. 114.

Letters, *LRB*, vol. 24, no. 10 (23 May 2002): 'In my freshman year at Harvard, I was one of at least two hundred students to take a General Education course in which I. A. Richards was a lecturer (*LRB*, 25 April). He was one of the best I have ever heard. We also shared an interest in mountaineering. He gave a talk on climbing in the Canadian Rockies, the high point of which was an encounter with a bear. It came into a two-storey cabin where Richards was staying and seemed inclined to climb the stairs, up which Richards had retreated. Richards said the way he dealt with the bear was to pee on it from the balcony that overlooked the ground floor. The bear, he said, got the message and promptly left the cabin.' Jeremy Bernstein, New York.

* * * * *

We packed as the sun worked its way up the valley. In shadow the day was hard cold and my hair and skin were taut and prickly. Our plan was to call at Arolla and get our bearings before hiking up to the Bertol hut, then over the glaciers to Cabane Rossier, from where we'd climb the Dent Blanche. Written down like that it sounds simple, of course, like a string of stations to be passed in a train, but we knew it would not be an easy task, particularly since we were neither of us as fit as we'd have liked, nor attuned to the altitude.

Mont Collon looked severe and bulbous in the morning sun, a monster torso with its head lopped off. We walked towards it in the new day's rising heat.

'To the English, Arolla is probably the best known of all the remoter centres of the Alps,' wrote Dorothea. 'Perfectly situated amid pungent scented arolles and at just the right height (6,500 ft.) for general purposes, it offers an extraordinary number of interesting peaks.'[13]

We passed through a number of 'pungent scented arolles' as we made our way up to Arolla – which is to say, having found ourselves on the wrong side of the river and sloshing across, we stumbled through some arollerous thickets of pines and negotiated a couple of electric fences before harrumphing our way up the opposite bank.

Twenty minutes after leaving Camping Arolla, we put down our heavy sacks beside the Hôtel du Mont-Collon – founded in 1862 and managed by the Anzévui family ever since. From 1921 onward, Ivor and Dorothea seem always to have stayed at the Hôtel du Mont-Collon. It appears many times in *Climbing Days* and even, unlike Ivor, has an

entry in the index. M. and Mme Anzévui are described by
Dorothea as a gargantuan host and hostess who 'showed a
remarkable interest in their regular customers [even]
remembering which peaks they went up from year to year'
– and now we'd arrived, slightly foxed relatives. Tim went
inside to investigate and see if the hotel knew where we
could get some cash.

Cash in Switzerland was a bit of an issue. It's a very
expensive country, something shrouded at first by fuzzy
mental currency conversion and the fact one's money disappears in silent increments from cards, but in the mountains
they only take cash and cash machines are few. Now, almost
in the mountains, at the gateway of Arolla, Tim returned
with two pieces of news: the people in the hotel knew of the
Richardses and said that there was a lady living nearby, *an
English lady* named Joan Pralong, who had actually known
them in person and would, they were sure, be happy to talk
to us about that; but this turn of events was rather eclipsed
by the second bulletin, which was that cashback was illegal
here due to money-laundering fears and the nearest bank
was in Evolène, nine miles away. The cash that we had
would have to do.

We walked up to Arolla to see if the Post Office was
open but it wasn't. It looked the sort of place that might
open for an hour every other Tuesday but today was not
that Tuesday so we bought an ice cream and sat down
again. It was now getting on for mid-afternoon, which
seemed incredible since it had been early morning only
minutes ago. Tim bought a cheap pair of sunglasses and
some 'Sherpa Tensing' suncream. Eventually we set off for
Mont Collon along a road which turned first into a long car
park, then a gravel drive and then a ballast track. We

passed below silent chairlift workings and skirted snuffling cows with bells like butane bottles around their gigantic necks whose tonk-tonks could be heard long after the cows themselves had disappeared.

A hydro-power station appeared beside the river, which was now several streams in a wide outflow of sediment from the glacier whose glisky tongue we could now see snaking down to the right of Mont Collon. At this point Tim decided we were carrying too much weight. What we needed, he announced, was to stash our excess somewhere and return for it post-Dent Blanche. So we unpacked and he hid a deal of stuff behind some rocks, then we carried on – across a bridge beyond which the semblance of roadway petered out and we began to twist up a rough path. After an hour of dusty slalom, having gained several hundred feet, we turned east and saw the Bertol hut high on its ridge.

We'd passed a few people coming down our path in lightweight summer clothes – shorts and singlets – most with walking poles, all smiling, jovial and happy. Now, alone, we stopped for a drink. Not long to go, I thought, the hut looked high but close, an hour at most . . .

For the next few hours – as day drained to dusk – we struggled up boulder fields and moraine, suffering what we later deduced to be the effects of altitude sickness. The trek was interminable – we became steadily more tired and bad-tempered. We lost the path. The air became chill. Hour passed hour. We reached an ice field, the exposed crown of Glacier de Bertol, and began to lose further time and energy skidding and sliding backwards down it in the dark. We had no cleats or crampons on. The hard snow was glassy and the falls began to hurt. We'd stopped muttering and swearing, now the only sounds were a gentle breeze and the *thunk* and scrape of a fall. My reserves of enthusiasm were very low, Tim's were gone, and all the while the lights of Bertol, bright above us, seemed to grow no closer. The blinding hot day had given way to freezing night and all I could think of was that we were in a mess, a stupid mess within spitting distance of our goal. The air was so clear that once or twice I was sure I could hear voices from the hut – lit and looming out of reach like a liner passing overhead.

Eventually, past 11 p.m., we reached the foot of one of the cabin's famous fixed ladders. It took all of our resolve to climb the iron rungs without either rushing madly or falling asleep.

The people in the cabin were incredulous that we could get up to such mischief on the easy path up. They thought we must have left Arolla very late indeed. We politely explained, in a mixture of languages, that we were both unacclimatised *and* unfamiliar with the path, whilst rejigging our departure time from Arolla by several hours to cushion our dudgeon; but frankly I was too knackered to care.

The Bertol guardians kindly gave us tea and a strange custard pudding thing left over from their dinner – for which we were later billed.

Once recovered, we prised off our boots and padded downstairs to join tens of others tiered in bunks, crawling over prone bodies in the blanket warmth, seeking empty berths with the aid of a muffled head torch, fully dressed, dog-tired, lights out.

* * * * *

Next morning I woke in the half-light to find the beds about me emptying. As I sat up my body announced it was broken – I felt as if I'd been methodically tenderised with toffee hammers during the night. Everything ached. Sat warily on the edge of the bunk, nursing a Brillo-pad brain, I heard Tim announce to the room at large that he had slept 'really well' and 'actually felt great'. Bully for Tim, I thought to myself – myself, a human bruise. Bully for Tim.

As with the campsite, it turned out we had arrived on the last night that Bertol was manned. The upshot of this was that after a bleary breakfast; after everyone else had dressed, kitted up, shaken hands and descended down the ladders in the sheer dawn to stand on the Mont Miné glacier, which, I now saw, spread crisp like a frozen sea foaming pink at the fringes; after the tick of boots on steel, the cackle of stone-fall, murmur of voices, diminishing chuff of serried feet as the parties trailed off on the glacier's icing; after we'd stood in the sun on the hut's slab walkway and watched them go, striding off in ant lines and followed their courses until they curved out of sight to the south-east towards Tête Blanche or disappeared north over the dark spiny ridges to the finger point of Aiguille de la Za; after they'd all gone, leaving wakes of tread and the glacier was empty and white as the sky was empty and blue, only Tim and I were left with the staff who were packing up the hut in a hurry, making ready for their helicopter home.

The previous night, having taken off my boots, I'd gone outside for a look at this high world – the glacier, the peaks and the sky. I stood on the threshold at 3,311 metres, the front door framing the Dent Blanche in moonlight, cowled magnetic. Walking forward, letting the door swing quietly shut behind me, I leant on the rail. Below, a sheet of ice swept forward and down to the wall of Mont Miné then rose in alternating bands to the knapped silhouette of the Dent Blanche. The sky was clear, the cold air still. In the silence the stars and the moon illuminated a panorama of famed and fearsome mountains: the Dent Blanche, Wandfluehorn, Matterhorn, Dent d'Hérens. I felt as if stood on the prow of a towering icebreaker looking out at a shelf of impossible icebergs – alone on the brink of their domain. Leviathan Alps with a capital A.

Now, from my vantage in the brisk sunlight, as the cabin crew packed up the hut at my back, I pictured a small party scrambling up Mont Miné, 'that graceful little point that divides the Ferpècle glacier' – Ivor, Dorothea, Mrs Daniell and R. B. Henderson in 1921 – gazing up at my position, a century before:

> From its summit we looked across at the smoke from the chimney of the Bertol Hut, hidden on its knob of rock in the midst of the glaciers, and I.A.R. told of how with two equally inexperienced companions he had once waded across to it by night from the Mt. Miné without a lantern. They had come up from Evolène and lingered so long gazing at the Dent Blanche from the slopes below and bathing in a moraine pool, that night caught them before they reached the ridge of the Mt. Miné. So the three of them sat down to let the snows harden! But they soon found it cold and set out without more ado. Their safe arrival towards morning, seeing the route they took, still makes I.A.R. wonder why crevasses are so incredibly kind to the young. Even then the sight of their track in the morning light had made them ready to believe in miracles.[14]

I saw crevasses lurking, ghostly stretch marks in the ice; thin shadow fissures like the marbling of clouds: hidden mantraps, unseen pitfalls, gravitational rendition. 'It will eat you.' I thought back to Tim's Cairngorm caution. Once recalled, it was hard not to think of the landscape in terms of malevolence and hunger.

There are pictures of Dorothea crossing chasms on snow bridges in *Climbing Days* – thin rib gangways, 'curled and knife-like edges' above unknown depths. In a photograph[15] she pads out gingerly, thin thread rope around her knicker-bockered waist, tall axe prodding ahead: a wary stick figure on the rime roof of a fathomless cathedral; a huge glacial maw leering beneath.

Fifty pages later there's a shot of the Cabane de Bertol – the caption reads: 'The Bertol Hut (11,155 ft.) perched like a medieval castle.' It doesn't look anything like a medieval castle; adjoining potting sheds on a silver rock mohawk maybe; 'perched' is right though – a small black building with a pitched roof perched beyond the reach of frozen white horses, on an iron-filing outcrop below a pyramidal nub. T. S. Eliot & Co. would have certainly blanched at the prospect.

Today, by contract, Bertol sleeps eighty on four levels – 'five dormitories of sixteen beds equipped with duvets Nordic' and has 'a panoramic dining room . . .' Things have changed. The sheds are gone, replaced with a multistorey insulated bunk fort. *Now* Bertol looks like a castle, or rather a Maunsell army fort of the type still stalking Red Sands in the Thames Estuary; a martial thought reinforced when a red helicopter approached up the valley and dropped a large net to the Bertol crew.

Tim joined me on the terrace and we watched the staff fill the webbing with luggage and boxes of uneaten provisions – a lot of wine, we noted. A minute later the helicopter returned to collect the filled net on a hook at the end of a cable. One of the guardians – a tall bearded man in his thirties dressed in plaid – manhandled the airdrop hawser in the downdraught, signalling, arm aloft. His hands seemed huge, even in work gloves, and all the time the noise: a thunderous chug – our clothes flayed and saturated in the whipped air. Then gone, away and dwindled in a moment. The staff said farewell and sped off down the ladders to the glacier below. One of the three had a guitar which lent the scene a slightly madcap Beatles air: *HELP!* on a budget – the sort we'd require forty-eight hours later.

* * * * *

When the helicopter returned for a third time it took only a moment to bank around, swing down and hover as the crouched group of three climbed aboard. Then, rising, turning, it flew away towards Arolla – nose down like a thrown paper dart – a flash above the path we'd so laboured up the night before, gone as a streak; judder chop and echoes fading. Tim and I were left alone in sudden silence, quite alone with only the glaciers and peaks for company. The day was blue and already hot. We stared about and grinned, still amazed. Then we made a cup of tea.

Shortly after the tea, having recovered my appetite, I looked through our bags for something to eat and it was then we discovered that Tim had jettisoned most of our food in the kit dump he'd made en route from Arolla. The weight he'd diagnosed as an issue had been the rations. We had packet soup and chocolate to last two days – by which I mean *we had to last two days* on packet soup and chocolate.

Tim and the bircher. Bertol Hut, September 2014 (Dan Richards)

Luckily the hut staff had left us a large container of purple bircher muesli, a mix of porridge oats, berries, honey, milk and apple, so we ate that.

We ate purple bircher for brunch and lunch and supper and breakfast the following day and we carried what remained away with us to eat later elsewhere too, occasionally supplementing it with packet soup and chocolate. Purple bircher saved the day. Although, since my return from Switzerland, I find I'm slightly phobic of it and almost screamed when I recently discovered it in my local supermarket.

* * * * *

Bertol was our staging post and we spent our day there alone but for a few enquiring black choughs and three

Joseph and Dorothy. Bertol Hut, 1928 (Antoine Georges/RCM)

walkers from Arolla who climbed the ladders and paused for a while gazing out at the vista before descending back the way they'd come, like fell runners patting a cairn before dashing off to the next.

Sat out on the concrete sun trap, I read more *Climbing Days*. Bertol was a regular base for Dorothea and Ivor and the book records many visits – trips down to Les Haudères for provisions, passing over meadows shrill with grasshoppers – but it is also central to their story for another reason because it was here that they first met Joseph Georges le Skieur, the Swiss guide who accompanied them on many of their greatest adventures and became a lifelong friend. Dorothea records their meeting in Chapter 7: 'Experiments and Discoveries' – a wonderful description of the encounter, made en route back to Bertol from a climb on the Aiguille de la Za:

> To vary the return and avoid the soft snow we followed the enchanting but long crest of the Douves Blanches, which sends down an easy spur to the North Col de Bertol near the

hut. It was evening as we approached the Col. Two tiny black figures had been standing on the snow shoulder where the track from the Za leads round to the hut. They seemed to be observing us. Presently, to our relief, they vanished; but soon a single figure reappeared and came rushing with remarkable speed towards us . . . We were annoyed. Horrors! An officious rescue party! Such things can be a great nuisance and expense. We were prepared to be haughty; there was no occasion for a search party. It was only just dusk and we had no distance to go. All such feelings, however, were instantly dispelled by the charming smile with which we were met. This Imaginative Unknown produced a bottle of freshly made hot tea – casually, as though such Good Samaritanism were the most usual thing in the world. A slight antagonism often exists between guideless parties and professionals; but this young guide with an upturned nose and bright blue, slightly mocking eyes evidently did not share it. While we drank his tea he explained that he and the guardian of the hut, having nothing to do, had come out to see whether we were coming, that he knew how interminably long the Douves Blanches ridge was and guessed we might be thirsty. This sympathetic intuition we learnt later to be characteristic of him. The meeting was fateful for us, for this was Joseph Georges le Skieur, who was to be our guide and friend thenceforward. By the end of the season we had made two new ascents with him and an association was cemented which has lasted ever since.[16]

It's amazing how prophetic and relevant this passage was to prove for Tim and me.

* * * * *

The next day we set out to walk over to the Dent Blanche hut – Cabane Rossier. We began at dawn, the mountains before us coal-black teeth below pale skies whilst, behind us, above the waxen ice of Mont Collon, the heavens shot back royal blue.

Once down on the plateau of the Mont Miné glacier we found the snows rucked every which way with tracks. It was clear we were the latest in a great many people to pause here and gaze back at Bertol, now looking unexpectedly severe, a sharp-faced box like a lunar lander elevated on a crag.

We roped up – now dressed more fully in alpine kit. I have a photograph of Tim on the hut's veranda: solid boots, red gaiters, woolly trousers, harness with a couple of carabiners, black jacket under which he's got two light jumpers and shirt; topped with shaggy warm hat. He's in the act of swinging his bag onto his back, the same aluminium-framed rucksack he'd climbed with the last time he was here – red crash hat strung on the rear. The sun that cuts across him is hard. Over his shoulder copper peaks snag the first light.

Travelling across the glacier was a new experience. We walked five metres apart, the rope strung between us. The first crevasses we came across were fascinating – fine cracks shooting down who knew how deep, as if the ice had been sliced or slashed. We stepped over these and walked on, seeming to have found our feet at this altitude, the only figures on the snow. We turned south-east, as the parties had the day before, round an outcrop of the Dents de Bertol, onto the glacier's main trunk – losing sight of the Cabane de Bertol behind, acquiring a vast channel sided with jagged peaks and the massive imminence of the Tête Blanche.

We carried on up the middle of the glacier's bulk, the

Tim on the Mont Miné Glacier below Dents de Bertol, September 2014
(Dan Richards)

snow beneath us pitted: sometimes fresh clean, sometimes
mucky, frozen films of crystals which swept up either side,
combed banks mounting into huge meringue quiffs.

We saw broken chasms in the glacier sides, house-high
ruptures appearing as portals into an inscrutable dark
underworld – the ice bursting out in cyan-seamed wounds
weeping lumpen chaff – whilst around and below the chaos
the ordered snows flowed unperturbed, heightening the
havoc with their uniformity.

Approaching the Italian border, yards from the invisible
dotted line, we bore left and began to climb up a long incline,
a contour every twenty steps, winding a route in the shade
of the Tête Blanche, the slope trudgeable but such that one
had to crane to see the sky ahead. Up we went. Up, monoto-
nously up, time passing at a rate it was hard to comprehend,

the sound of boots, a stop to catch our breath, and then up. Pesky snow travelator. It wasn't hard so much as boring! When would it end? The thought occurred that this would be a lot of fun on skis the other way, which only made me more irritable.

Climbing Days has Dorothea, Ivor and Joseph walking this route before sunrise –

> One could see a great deal in shadowy outline without being able to tell in the least how far off it was. Joseph's hat and the tip of the Matterhorn were objects in the same plane floating in and out of a dream. The slope ahead looks a five-minutes affair. Five minutes pass and it is still the same Then you suddenly wake up to find that you have been walking for three-quarters of an hour in a blissful doze and it is still the same![17]

By this point, now off the glacier's highway, we'd unroped and, after a while, began to drift apart: Tim stopping more often, me 'trying to get on with it' as I might have said uncharitably at one point* – battling the interminable powder hill. Then it plateaued, levelling slowly, an expansive view rising as a theatre backdrop. What a fantastic view! Now at a height of around 3,700 metres, 400 metres higher than the Bertol hut, the world opened up to reveal the Matterhorn's dusted gneiss spire and roof, and all around it echelons of other mountains, the Matterhorn holding court. The snowfield in front of me dived down towards the deep green valley of Zermatt. The clouds were below us; most of

---

* A remark for which I later apologised: 'I'm sorry, Tim. I didn't mean it. It's the purple bircher talking.'

Tim climbing on the upper reaches of the Ferpècle Ridge, July 1981 (Pete Healey)

the mountains below us too, oblique sunshine showing off their serrate profiles.

This was a new world, a mythic over-otherworld. Fierce, beautiful, heroic and grand. I, very small, and it, colossal – monstrous big; and I was above it. Not all of it though: to my left in a long swooping sinuous sway was the Plateau d'Hérens – a luxurious, apparently untouched run which sped to the feet of the Dent Blanche. Its long barbed spine was now clearly evident, the ridge we would climb next day.

Where the Matterhorn spears abruptly at the sky like a new sharp keen idea, the Dent Blanche builds slowly like a storm – building up from its valleys and attendant glaciers, up from flanking peaks to dominate its manor, standing higher, more deliberate, solid, cold and imperious. Where the Matterhorn's steeps are bare and dark, the Dent Blanche carries its snow. The former shows itself, the latter hunkers waiting. I didn't really want to think the word 'mean' – all the mountains here were mean, all the mountains here could eat us – but the way that the Dent Blanche held itself gave me pause. This was a serious beast.

* * * * *

A couple of hours later, around one o'clock, we reached Rossier. Our course had taken us beside the Wandflue, where I had seen how the ground fell sheer a thousand metres to the Schönbiel Glacier – *Schönbielgletscher* as it was on our map; as flinty to the ear as the eye.[18] As with Bertol, Cabane Rossier was elevated – this time on a tall podium of loose rock which had to be negotiated whilst tired; almost like they didn't want you to get there at all.

The guardian seemed a bit unhappy from the start and we got off on the wrong foot when we walked into her hut still carrying our kit and were curtly redirected back outside to put it in a storage container on the level below the cabin; back down the icy deathtrap steps. She spoke little English and we spoke bad French but it was clear that, as well as our kit faux pas, she wasn't impressed with our lack of cash – depleted by Bertol, inadequate here. Tim led negotiations and we found we could afford bunks if we shared an evening meal.

This hut was very different to the last, a traditional solid stone chalet like a large cottage with a pitched roof and deeply inset shuttered windows. It stood on a solid stone outwork which gave a view over the amazingly fractured Ferpècle Glacier icefall, back towards Bertol, now hidden behind Mont Miné.

Inside Cabane Rossier, everything was wood. The walls were panelled tongue and groove, the ceiling beamed, the floor boarded, the windows framed: wood. There was a bar, behind which the guardian had a small open kitchen. Stairs ran up to the dormitory. Under the stairs was a boot store. Past the stairs and the bar was a benched area where meals were taken. Everything was sturdy and solid. It was the sort of snug base where I could imagine happily staying for days, drinking coffee and beer, eating hearty comfort food, reading, climbing and marvelling at the views, but I couldn't. We weren't allowed. Bottled water, never mind coffee or another night's board, was beyond our means. Even as I was thinking these warm arcadian thoughts, Tim was outside with a spirit stove cooking cup-a-soups. To celebrate our arrival and supplement the soup, we bought a pot of peppermint tea with the last of our coins, which we drank with milk. The other people in the cabin had a giggle at this, perhaps not realising that, in the circumstances, *free* milk in tea (any tea) was a bonus. The money had gone.

* * * * *

Dorothea relates in *Climbing Days* how, around the Wandflue, Joseph Georges suggested they go up the Dent Blanche by the tougher Ferpècle Ridge, rather than the Ordinary Route – the group having begun their day from Bertol, walking over and past Rossier before setting about the mountain.[19]

Sat warm in Rossier, I open Tim's red Alpine Club Guide Book[20] and find the West (Ferpècle) Ridge – as it's titled there – and read its description, related in the classically clipped shipping forecast format of such manuals, as 'A long straight ridge which in good conditions is entirely rock. It finishes somewhat N of the summit. The rock is fairly good. AD+, pitches of II and IV, not sustained, 850m.'

It notes that, at the time of publication, the ridge had only recently become popular, especially with British climbers, then lists a few people who've died on it.

Tim has circled the title in biro. Next to this is written 'Pete Healey July '81'. That's when they climbed it, Tim leading, the year before my birth, thirty-three years ago now* – sixty years after Dorothea, Ivor and Joseph Georges. Dorothea writes that, once at the top, Joseph 'with the air of a magician producing a rabbit from a top-hat' flourished an enormous tin of pears. 'An amiable trick he has on big expeditions.'[21]

Looked at as a picture in Tim's red book, the Ferpècle Ridge looks severe. Looked at out the window, the Ferpècle Ridge looks murderous. On the page, I trace the route's dashed lines. A climb of four and a half hours, it says.† Descending from the hut to the glacier, a long shallow slope, a cliff to negotiate; then along the top of a black rock spur – still at the base of the mountain, the black gum of the tooth, like a dog's tooth. A dog's mouth. The dashes mount diagonal over snow until they meet a couloir which rises directly west-south-west to the summit:

---

* Tim has long since lost touch with Pete Healey and attempts to trace him through organisations such as Brathay, the Alpine Club and BMC have failed. The only physical evidence he ever existed consists of the note in the red book, two photographs taken on the climb, and a postcard sent back to my mother in Penclawdd from Arolla: '8.7.81 – My dear Annie. Arrived yesterday evening in the dark, the thunder was coming and I put up my tent as the first drops came down. Il tonne. Pete wandered in this morning dazed and very tired. He is sleeping the long trip off – what a ride down here – A sauna from Geneva to Sion. All new things. You would love this place – many small spiders and lots of climbers! Brits! But not many tourists besides. Tomorrow we will go up to one of the huts and maybe do a rock route – we have some lined up – pas difficile. All my love, x Tim. Will write as soon as I can. I am not far away. P.S. Saw the Pralongs and they *were very interested* indeed.'

† Seven hours there and back.

L of this is a broad ledge of scree, leading horizontally L to the W ridge at a point where it steepens noticeably. It is usual to cross the bergschrund near the start of the ledge and from there climb directly up a steep snow slope, then scree and rocks to another ledge line which slants steeply L to the ridge above the first buttress/step at 3700m. (2¼ h.). Climb the crest and with continuous interest and some difficulty (slabs, III),* turning small gendarmes on the L or R. Halfway up reach an obvious ledge which cuts the face to the L. Above is the grand gendarmes. Turn this on the R (III) and regain the ridge by pleasant walls and slabs (III/IV). Continue up the crest, getting easier, to the summit.

How do people write these things? I thought, idly, imagining the Alpine Club in London sending envoys to climb routes, pencils in hand, with instructions to jot concise campaign manuals. Amazing to think Tim had done it, bested it and ticked it off, like Dorothea and Ivor before him. A quite amazing feat. What was the hut like then? I'd asked him. He said he hadn't stayed in the hut – not that he could remember, probably bivouacked somewhere, he wasn't sure; huts being expensive.[22]

The climb accounts for three pages in *Climbing Days*. I reckon a lot of people would hold it as the pinnacle of their climbing lives . . . but I don't know. I was learning that – or, rather, it was becoming clear – I really didn't know very much about this place at all. It was completely alien. I knew it scared me: the extremity and wildness, the hostility of it.

The climber Joe Tasker – who made the first British

---

* Bracketed numerals here refer to grades of difficulty – I being easiest, IV the hardest.

ascent of this mountain's north-north-east face with Dick Renshaw in August 1973 – wrote a book about climbing in the Himalaya named *Savage Arena* – a title both apt and accurate since it not only describes the way the mountains empirically are, but the way they make one feel within them. They dominate everything, looming in the mind, set one on edge, overbear thought. Everything about this place was hard, even the hospitality had a steeliness, as if conditioning you for the peaks with tough love. But perhaps I was just tired and a little paranoid. Perhaps the mountains wouldn't weigh so if I wasn't sitting so inert in their midst. All the same, Rossier put me in mind of a plane where everyone sits preoccupied in their chutes, before going to the door and jumping out. A holding pen for the mountain.

* * * * *

The hut comprised a group of Catalan men and a party of Germans with a guide. Altogether there were eleven of us.

In the evening the guardian gave us two meals despite the fact we'd only money for one, which was kind. During the afternoon I'd observed how her manner was gentle when she thought no one was watching but whenever approached or asked for something or inspecting new arrivals, she projected a tough no-nonsense demeanour, her official face – which then took a while to soften. Even now the food she'd been making all evening with obvious care was set down with a thump on the table. The thump seemed to imply it was, bluntly, fuel but it was actually very tasty – a vegetable soup with croutons, lasagna, and ice cream with pineapple and Swiss finger sponges for pudding. We told her it was lovely and she smiled slightly. I counted that a major victory.

The Catalan men sat on our table for supper. The one who could speak a little English chewed our ears off about the need for an independence referendum 'like Scotland' – as if we were duty bound to help him sort the Spanish out since we, specifically us, had acquiesced to the Scots. It was ironic that the only time at Rossier someone engaged with us in sincere conversation it was to lambast us for personally treating other countries badly.

The three had driven here from Barcelona, they told us. They were friends from childhood and this was their annual holiday together.

I told them that I was a writer and Tim was a sculptor and explained a little about the book, Dorothea and Ivor, and how I'd been to Barcelona recently to visit Anthony. 'Ah,' said the man, 'what Barcelona needs is a referendum . . . like you've given Scotland.'

After supper we went to bed. I attempted to find a plug adapter for my phone charger but failed. Every time we asked questions in our slightly ropey French, the guardian had made a big song and dance of not understanding. This seemed to get more exaggerated as the day went on and her audience increased until, by evening, she was theatrically rolling her eyes and chuckling with other residents whenever we approached. We were left in no doubt that she was humouring us by even *attempting* to understand our meaning and my final effort to talk to her about the charger was batted away with laughter and a 'No.'

We'd behaved badly, turning up without enough cash, seemed to be the gist. We weren't proper paying punters. And no guide either! Bloody foolhardy English . . . not to mention the way we'd personally ruined Scotland.

Before turning in, I went outside to the portaloo perched

at the back of the hut. Communion wafer flakes were falling, pulling down the sky. Visibility was low. Rossier existed as a sullen snow globe, a hostel bar floating in space.

* * * * *

The following day we woke and dressed for the Dent Blanche at 4 a.m. – stirred by the guardian's rounds with her torch. It was time. From the back of the hut we scrambled up an outcrop scratched with the points of many thousand crampons. It was freezing cold and dark but sunrise flared the peaks which rose around us as we reached a steep snow ridge which nagged an uneasy exposure. Above this was a crunching walk onto the col of the Wandfluelucke, ascending round the mountain to more rock, snow-free, loose and friable – large stones held in place with grit, like an abominable Cornish hedge. We climbed roped, slowly working our way higher until we saw a break in the ridge cornice ahead and aimed ourselves towards it. We didn't talk much but we found a rhythm of movement which became more pronounced once back on snow and tackling the ridge itself because we began to belay about our axes. The snow was very deep, in fact snow was all one could see bar a few bare boulders or crags jutting up. You couldn't see where the cornice started, which might have been a problem had not there been the track of boots ahead to follow. The Catalan three were out in the lead, although we could not see them. We had their path to follow though and we did, hour after hour. Occasionally we'd stop and eat a little chocolate, chests and shoulders aching. Axe belays quickly warm you up with the repetitive kneeling, bending and flexing required; pulling in and playing out the rope like mariners, leapfrogging pitches. I would stand ahead, axe down, stabbed in, stance struck, rope around, the tension taken in, then call down for Tim to follow. Up he'd trudge, me reeling his rope, and then on he'd go, climbing ahead in the sapping drifts. Then the process was repeated, innumerable times. And always, five metres to the right, a hundred-metre drop, several hundred metres maybe. It didn't really matter. We kept it five metres to our right.

Up and up. Suddenly it was noon. Then 3 p.m. and we found ourselves panting, high on the mountain cloaked in snow. In truth we were two months late to tackle it in decent condition but we pressed on – belaying pitch after pitch.

The Dent Blanche is a long mountain if you go along its spine, as we did. Every new nib in the journey seemed to beckon as a potential summit but hide a longer, steeper climb beyond. So seductive, such a tease, such a slog.

I didn't really know what to expect; this was not much like the Cairngorms. It was not like anything I'd done before. And it came as a shock when Tim said that he didn't remember it being such a massive undertaking; that he didn't remember it being such hard hard work.

Suddenly time was against us. Now, every pause was a waste, so we stopped less often. The day could not last forever. We fretted that we were going too slowly.

We knew we would still have to get back down once up and we were just talking about how much further it might be when we heard voices ahead and there, on a crest, were the Catalan men returning over a precipitous pitch beneath the steeple of the Grand Gendarme – the icy crux below the summit climb – and making a hash of it.

One was already over, watching the other two. The second man was picking his way back, an axe in each hand, trailing a rope which he dropped halfway across so one end of it fell down the mountain, useless. The last man, the one we'd spoken to the night before, waited his turn, now ropeless, exposed and unprotected if he fell.

Earlier in the day when we'd first seen the party's tracks, Tim had told me they were climbing as individuals, without a rope, each to his own. With no backstop. They'd moved faster and further on the mountain than us because of this but if we'd thought that was due to their confidence and skill – that they were good enough to do without – this scene disabused us of that. They'd clearly no idea how to use a rope. The two on our side of the crux now stood silent, watching their third flail. They offered no help. No words. It was compelling and surreal, but most of all sad – like a rite of passage or a hazing: the others had done it, now it was his turn. So he came, sidestepping iffily, axes chipping, toes kicking little notches for purchase in the couloir wall; fresh air below his boots – the sort of sheer drop pictures seldom convey. Breathing hard he edged and inched, a terminal star-jump.

Turning away, cold from standing, I met the eye of one of the silent two. Had they made it alright to the top? I asked, pointing. He understood. No. They were heading back, it was still a long way. Too far, he said. Too far.

I exchanged a look with Tim. We'd walked into something, a frostiness nothing to do with the weather; and then, behind us, bang on cue, the third Catalonian fell.

Or rather he slid; dropped ten metres until his axes bit into hard snow and he stopped and, stopped, stayed put; nose an inch from the wall.

Tim and I decided the best thing to do was get over and drop him a line. The silent two were doing nothing, even now, and we were keen to keep moving and help so, single axe in my right hand, I began to cross to the man. I dug the axe into the hard snow and stamped my right outstep crampon spikes in, then I stepped on and buried my instep spikes likewise, axe out, hack hack, axe in, repeat. I was higher than the Catalonian and once above him found a good rock bollard to secure a sling. This I did. Then I dropped him a belay. He didn't move. I called out, still watched over by his dour friends. The lowered rope was beside him. It bumped his hat. Nothing.

I balanced above him, shivering now. There was no need for this – we were all getting cold. The day had been overcast throughout and dusk wasn't far away. I shouted, I told him to take the damn rope, and he did – sullenly, slowly. 'Okay, okay,' he said into the snow, as if doing me a massive favour.

'That was all about pride,' said Tim a few minutes later, watching the three walk away. We were sat back at the start of the crux. There was no point in talking about the summit now, it was obviously best to get down. Around us rocks reared out the snow like sandy red finger ends. This was as far as we'd get.

I felt very deflated and Tim seemed similarly glum but we ate some chocolate and our humour returned, concurring that it was better to help and embarrass an ungrateful man than leave him to the mercy of his friends.

Dorothea would have had no truck with them, we agreed, before starting back.

* * * * *

The descent was a release. We'd accepted that we would not reach the mountain top, and that done, we were going

home. I would write 'home for supper' but there would be
no supper and I would say 'home to bed' but that wasn't on
the cards either. Even so, we were making off in haste –
belaying on the soft snow where the ridges were narrow,
but even in retreat everything was still further than one
remembered. The Catalonians were long out of sight.
Occasionally, cloud would roll over us and we'd travel
through mirk until it passed. We were still on the heavy-
going spine when the light, stalling grainy, broke down. We
ghosted to a stop at the cornice break above the crumble
junk flank and turned our head torches on. Under us the
needle marks of crampon nails receded, a slight sharp path
into the rocks. Our beams sought these flecks out as we
descended in the dark. This morning it had been an obstacle
course, a discordant field to overcome, now the night had
made it a maze. The future was rendered illusive and
strangely flat by headlight, sharp shadows shifting and list-
ing with a turn of the head, leaving strident after-glare.
Peppery snow began to fall and again our peripheries
shrank. Depth and distance were hard to gauge and we
soon lost our way. We were tired. We were slow and slowing. It seemed like every running belay we set on a looped
sling caught and had to be dislodged by hand. We were
cold. I'd begun to feel my body as a weight. It was miserable
weather. Time was passing unknown. Sometimes I'd find
myself dreamily detached, listening to the sound of my
strapped axe knocking, of the woozy wind, of the raking of
sleet. I could sense Tim was tired through the rope.
Unbeknownst to me, he was already sure that we wouldn't
get back to the hut that night.

* * * * *

The Matterhorn started blinking red an hour after we'd hunkered down, stopped in the shelter of a small stone ledge which was rather like sitting on the tailgate of a car – our legs dangling slightly, backs to rock. After a short argument as to our plan, I had agreed to stop where we were and bivouac. Tim summed up our position: we were tired and had no kit for a brew. We were low on rations and unsure of our position. The weather wasn't bad but the cloud was low. Our torches were not powerful enough for us to see any real distance. If either of us came a cropper it might be serious and so it was best that we stop and carry on at first light.

My phone was dead. This, we agreed, was bad. Everything else was in our control. We could stop and sit it out and keep ourselves safe but the danger was that those below in the hut would be worried and we had no way of letting them know that we were okay. So, as I sat and tried to make myself comfortable, pulling up my jacket collar and wiggling my cold toes somewhere in my boots, wrapped in the ripped bivvy bag with Tim, it wasn't the possibility of a long drop beneath that worried me so much as the fear of a rescue party.

All night, as the Matterhorn flickered, I listened, desperately hoping not to hear voices or boots or, far worse, a helicopter. All night – and it was *all night* for neither of us slept and we knew that we had to stay awake – as we talked to keep ourselves awake and shivered on that ledge, I thought about mountain rescue, searchlights and worried guardians; and the Catalonians warm in their Rossier bunks. I wondered what they'd said about us at supper and I thought about dawn and I willed it to come.

* * * * *

Funny what you think about stuck on a ledge. My mood oscillated between manic Pollyanna upbeat – alive to the adventure; benighted and bivouacking, just like Dorothea and Ivor often were, 'leaping crevasses in the dark, that's how to live' and all that – and incandescent fury. The Catalonians featured prominently when I had the latter hat on, Boggis, Bunce and Bean; although the disappearance of the red helmet around 3 a.m. provided fresh focus for my rage.

The stars of Zermatt far below; the moon sometimes, rheumy eyes. All the muscles taut in my neck, my throat dry – Sigg bottles having long since frozen solid; no clatter and dink when shaken now, just solid blocks of ice. Rocking back and forth slightly, sometimes shaking hard, alternatively rubbing my legs and arms, crossing and recrossing them, hugging myself, arms held tight to my ribs. I recall the quiet hisses which escaped between clenched teeth, my jaw set, the night dragging endless. 'Your teeth join with all the other unemployed muscles in a counterpoint of chattering,' wrote Dorothy of her night out on the glacier below Epicoun. 'Mercifully a kind of stupor descends to dull the senses.'[23] Memories of nights spent in railway stations having missed the last train home. The dislocated loneliness of knowing everyone you know is asleep, tucked up; thoughts of home. I thought of my mother back in Bath, sleeping, oblivious to our situation – how she'd always wait up for me and my brother if ever we were due home late.

The dream of sleep, the reality of having to remain awake.

All night, we stared across at the Matterhorn, a grandstand view, waiting for day to break. Every so often a brightening seemed imminent but it was only tired eyes playing tricks. When it happened, it was far over to our left behind Zermatt.

The figures of Strahlhorn and Rimpfischhorn growing more pronounced as the sky slowly kindled at their backs.

As soon as there was light enough to see the mountain-side, we made a move. It transpired that the drop beneath us levelled to a wide terrace, beyond which was the plunge to Schönbielgletscher.

We picked up the deep footprints of the track within five minutes – we'd been sat within a hundred metres, obviously so, but the mountain was a different proposition in the day, opened out. Joyous. New. We tromped along the Wandfluelucke, cramped stiff but happy.

I found the red helmet crizzled with frost ten minutes later on the snow. We approached it disbelieving. How had it contrived to skitter ten minutes sidelong in the face of that yawning drop? Who knew. Magic.

Shortly after, we reached the snow slope above the rock buttress which backed Rossier. Now the sun was fully up. We descended cautiously and took our time. There was the hut roof, here was the green portaloo. I had a vague idea that we might get a nap. We'd not slept for almost thirty hours. The first people I saw were the three Catalonians, who told me that the guardian had phoned the police. Did you go to the top? they asked. I said no. They were stumped to learn we'd bivouacked on the mountain and talked it over between themselves, shaking their heads. We were clearly mad. They told me that the guardian had 'suspicions' about us, that they'd all discussed our strange ways over dinner last night – a poor choice of words or translation on their part, perhaps, but in light of what had gone before, and the fact I was so tired that I mostly existed in the third person, I consider it a great achievement not to have brained the man speaking with the crampons I was holding at the time.

There followed an egregious scene. The three having departed, the guardian appeared holding the most passive-aggressive pair of binoculars I'd ever seen in my life. She gave us a prolonged shellacking and we took it. Then, shortly afterwards, having cleared our bunks and apologised to a blank face, we were stumbling down a grim hump of glacier towards the village of Ferpècle, five hours away.[*]

* * * * *

Our route off the glacier and icefields below took us through a range of ruptured landscape: slushy snow which we tobogganed over on our sacks; rivers disappearing through pearlescent tunnels – a reminder that so much around and beneath us was ancient ice, scree and boulders skating on the surface of a frozen sea.

Following a path marked by occasional cols and brightly painted arrows, we made it down to the lower reaches of the Glacier des Manxettes – over milled slabs strewn with malicious grit where we skidded, fell, swore, tottered, skidded, fell, swore – to gain the moraine which forms the higher portion of the Bricolla Alp, moving out of the shadow of the Dent Blanche, below the snow line, into meadowland. The day was now hot and skies again blue after yesterday's overcast chill. Yesterday was still ongoing, of course, we'd bypassed the midfield of today, and were headed – route one, ball over the top – into tomorrow.

---

[*] At least, we'd been told five but Swiss schedules and prophecies had not gone in our favour thus far, so we were minded to multiply every estimate of time or distance by three.

* * * * *

Dorothea's descent of the same path in 1921 was a more upbeat affair:

> We were hoping that Bricolla Alp would be open but it was close-shuttered and empty when we knocked and so was Ferpècle, but we hurried on, rejoicing, through the valley to Haudères. Our ambitions of the morning had been utterly surpassed. Joseph . . . had shown himself all and more than the companion we had hoped for. And he seemed every bit as happy as we were. Already we were spinning dreams of North Arêtes and other oddments in the ecstatic moment of accomplishment that every climber feels after a great mountain.[24]

That North Arête was now at our backs, watching us go, passing down done in. Tim had taken on the appearance of a hollow man escaped from a penal colony and developed a limp to match, whereas I, though similarly knackered, had felt obliged to assume the mantle of 'the enthusiastic one'. We stopped often to drink our now thawed water, the journey measured out in two-hundred-metre intervals.

The thought that I was walking towards a cup of tea sustained me for a good couple of hours. I'd had no tea since leaving Bertol and that had involved foxy UHT milk. 'The perfect cup of tea' and invented limericks about glaciers kept me mumbling and laughing manically along like a man who'd lost his mind.

We found the old Bricolla Alp Hotel similarly shuttered as when Dorothea's party had passed through: a three-storey building with a tall chimney like a tin mine, surrounded by ruined shepherds' huts and pens. Ahead, the valley ran straight to Sion, lush spur ribs interlocking like a zip and, above all, the carry of clouds across the land as bedsheets swing on a washing line. To the left of the Bricolla Alp Hotel the ground fell away to La Borgne de Ferpècle, beyond which the Grande Dent de Veisivi rose vertiginous in baize and fern, cut in diagonal swathes, corrugated outcrops hatched down its flank.

The previously turbulent and shattered landscape was now beginning to compose itself, sprung fervid green – suddenly more grass than rock. There were sheep about, we weren't alone; now passing over wooden footbridges at regular intervals, the path had grown into a dusty trail: a stone wall, a stile, wire fences, a signpost! Outliers of a future involving tea and sleep. Ahead in the valley I could see the chalk line of a road.

* * * * *

Towards late afternoon we were passed by two men, another father-and-son team. They looked very much the *before* picture whereas we were the warning from history. It transpired that the son was a mountain guide and they'd already been up the Dent Blanche that day, leaving the hut before dawn as we had, but making the climb quickly, topping out and returning by early afternoon, so fresh that they'd now overhauled us. Were we alright? asked the guide. He'd heard about our troubles from the Rossier guardian. Would we like a Coca-Cola? This act of kindness seemed biblical at the time.* Having drunk, we stood on the path and explained the situation. He agreed we were right to have bivouacked

* Comparable, I'd say, in almost every way with Coke's appearance in Cormac McCarthy's 2006 novel *The Road*.

as we did, it was always best to be cautious, but was firm about the need for a phone. There was a lot of sage nodding, then we all shook hands, they wished us luck and strode on. What nice chaps, we agreed, refreshed and hobbling tall in their wake towards our Xanadu: Ferpècle.

ii. People

Ferpècle was another dispersed village, spun along the road like meteoric debris. I'd offered to go ahead of Tim to find something to eat before everything closed for the day but it seemed that everything had closed for the season. I pressed on and walked a couple of miles further down the valley, over-shadowed by peaks overlooked the day before, sunk under cloud as canyons beneath a sea – we'd dropped two thousand metres since leaving Rossier, twice the height of Scafell Pike.

Eventually, I thumbed a lift from a local man in a 4x4 who dropped me off a little way along at a place named Seppec, which had a shop, but the shop was shut. At this point, imagining Tim being picked apart by vultures, I started back the way I'd come. His situation was actually much better than I'd supposed for, when I met him coming the other way, he was in the passenger seat of a brightly smiling lady's car. He stuck his head out of the window and waved.

'Hi, Dan!'

'Hello, Tim.'

'This is Rosemary. She was worried about me.'

As well she might, I thought, greeting Rosemary, who had now stopped the car and was beckoning me to get in.

'Rosemary knows somewhere we can stay,' said Tim,

enthusiastically, once I'd climbed in the back.

'Your father looked very tired,' smiled Rosemary as she set off.

'Did he?' I feigned bemusement. 'I imagine he would have been inconsolably tired if he'd had to walk an extra two miles up a road for no reason.'

'Yes, well done about that,' said Tim, seriously. 'I met Rosemary on the road a few minutes after you left to fetch help . . . she's a wonderful lady.'

We drove back through Seppec and on through the recognisably actual village of La Forclaz and on to another named La Sage. Rosemary worked in a gîte guesthouse which was closed, she explained, but she had telephoned the patron, Dominique, and he was going to open it up for us.

Tim had told Rosemary about Dorothea and Ivor, although exactly what he said I never discovered – I didn't ask at the time and he couldn't remember later – but clearly he'd impressed her enough that she pulled out all the stops.

A few minutes after pitching up at Gîte Alpin l'Ecureuil, Dominique arrived with the keys; smiling politely, exchanging glances with Rosemary, solemnly shaking our hands. They made a funny pair – he tall, gaunt, grey, perpetually smoking; she small, round and pink, forever on the phone – we weren't quite sure what was going on but one of the first things that happened, once we'd put our bags down in the restaurant bar which formed the gîte's ground floor, was that Dominique made us a cup of tea.*

We agreed on a price to stay a couple of nights – which seemed very reasonable and, yes, they took cards!

---

* Lipton's tea. Lipton's gets everywhere – I've drunk it in the US, France, Dubai and now Switzerland. I never see it in the UK but the world seems to think of it as English tea . . . what's all that about?

Dominique intimated we could sort all this out later, he wasn't worried. He stood smiling by the kitchen hatch watching us dunk our yellow Lipton's tea bags in focused silence; eccentric Englishmen perhaps but apparently harmless enough. Besides, we were famous, he'd been told; descendants of great mountaineers. Rosemary meanwhile was stood in one corner talking quietly into her mobile – phoning round the Swiss Guides in the area, I was later to learn, to tell them some Richardses had fallen out of the sky. A name which apparently still rang a few bells in Valais.

* * * * *

Leaving Tim talking spasmodic French with Dominique, I carried our bags upstairs. The first floor held a series of dormitory bunk- and bathrooms and smelled softly of cinnamon, pine and larch – relatively low-ceilinged, dark red and soothing. There were antique skis strapped to the walls, long as javelins, framed maps and photographs from Dorothean days.

I sat on the edge of a bunk with my elbows on my knees and felt my torso crunch and creak. Outside the window, balconies ran the building's length, planked verandas with views of the peaks and dusky slopes, the night now welling again. Warmer and more welcome than the last.

Exploring further, at the top of the gîte, I found another twenty beds tucked beneath the beams and A-frame, made up by Rosemary, awaiting the next cohort of walkers and climbers to arrive, as swallows return to a nest year on year. At that moment I wanted to fall forward into them all and sleep twenty consecutive nights.

$\sim$

Returning downstairs, I found Tim had been joined by an expansive man named André 'Dédé' Anzévui – a Swiss Guide summoned up by Rosemary. Wine was out on the table, I saw, as was the charcuterie.

Rising, Dédé shook my hand, gravely. An honour, he said, a great honour.

He was slightly older than Tim perhaps, his skin tanned by the slopes, lined features weathered but supple, a nimble face and a very solid handshake. Spry was the word.

'Dorothea and Ivor were beautiful people, and Joseph Georges . . . perfect!' he told us. Of course, he knew of the 1928 climb up the Dent Blanche, of course he did. Yes, he'd climbed it. He beckoned Dominique to bring us more food, a glass for me, explaining what a pleasure it was to meet us. He himself was an extreme skier, he explained. He'd skied down the northern slopes of the Dent Blanche. Down the very wall our Catalan friend had dangled from the day before – helicopters were the key to this, he told us breezily, nodding to Dominique to refill our wine.*

Did we know André Georges? Joseph's great-nephew? He lived close by, over there (a wave away towards the door); we must meet him. He *was* perfect; a perfect one. He had climbed all over the world. The Best! Dédé looked me keenly in the eye. You must meet him, he repeated. Okay, I said, stunned – this was news. Amazing news. A living link to *Climbing Days* – searching for the right required response, 'I will, yes, thank you!'

---

* By this stage he could have said anything and we would have nodded along, we were absolutely whacked and the wine had us out on our feet. He could have told us that he'd jumped out of a helicopter and skied down the Matterhorn and we would have believed him. Then he did. And we did. So I was right, I reflected later when the memory returned.

You will! He beamed. But first you must sleep – we looked tired, he said. (He said this several times whilst insisting Dominique top up our glasses.) Yes, he spoke in a voice both charming and emphatic, first Tim and I must sleep and then, tomorrow, we would visit him for coffee. Dominique would drive us over to Arolla for nine. He insisted, it would be his pleasure. There, it was decided. Of course, Dominique didn't mind!

We looked at Dominique, who gave a shy smile and a shrug; it was inevitable, said the shrug, and we all knew it. Dédé's enthusiasm was total and we were as twigs borne along in an irresistible torrent.

'Perfect,' beamed Dédé and refilled his own glass. And that was the sixth day done.

I went to sleep mulling the astonishing news of André Georges's existence.

* * * * *

Next morning, as instructed, we drove to Arolla, a journey soundtracked for the most part by Climie Fisher's 'Love Changes (Everything)'. It was a day for power ballads. We had slept and eaten well, and now we were being chauffeured about by the endlessly affable Dominique. 'Everywhere' by Fleetwood Mac followed Climie Fisher. Swiss radio – at least, the Swiss radio played in Dominique's car and gîte – seemed to have decided that music died around 1988 so Roland and Fairlight synths attended the rest of our week. I ate my dinner with Starship and Simple Minds, and breakfast with A-ha. This had the effect of lending the trip a filmic dimension somewhere between *Back to the Future* and *The Living Daylights* – the descent from Rossier reframed as a chase off the mountain under heavy Russian fire whilst riding on a cello.

Dire Straits were fairly ubiquitous on the radio too, which I didn't mind at all since tapes of Dire Straits had been a fixture of car journeys and family holidays from a very early age, so I associate the band with panoramas seen through windscreens. In fact, I was in the womb in Penclawdd in 1982, listening to Dire Straits – probably *Making Movies* – with my mother, Annie, whilst Tim was away in Svalbard on a Brathay expedition, his last big trip after Switzerland in '81.

We met Dédé in Arolla's cafe bar (which was playing Dire Straits.) He looked superbly smart in a buff suit with brown lapels, white shirt, knitted tie and highly polished shoes; the formal dress of the Swiss Guides. Today a new cohort were graduating and he was to attend, representative of a proud tradition. He told us this with gravity but his eyes were shining – this was his life, you sensed, the centre of his being. But whilst his manner was more sober and serious than the night before, his kindness and enthusiasm remained undiminished. He furnished us with coffee and pastries and sourced me a phone charger from one of the patrons, all the while insisting we pay for nothing and apologising for having to dash off to the ceremony and promising to catch up with us again later in the week. Dominique would look after us in the interim, he announced, nodding to him as if passing the mantle of hospitality. All would be well.

Before leaving us, Dédé put in a call to Joan Pralong, the English friend of Dorothea's we'd been told about at Hôtel Mont-Collon. She lived above the Post Office, next door to the cafe. And so, as our new friend Dédé departed, another figure in the story appeared in the form of Joan – she'd been expecting us, she said, having spoken to Dédé the night before and the fabled André Georges as well – and it suddenly dawned on me how close-knit the community round here was. Everyone knew everything and everybody else: our presence had been noted. The cat's-cradle phone lines had been abuzz since Rosemary met Tim on the road the night before.

Sensing all was well and we were alright, Dominique suggested he might go back to La Sage. Thank you, Dominique, we said. You've been so kind, it's marvellous. He smiled his rueful smile, waved an affable hand and left us with Joan, driving off to the sound of Talk Talk.

* * * * *

Joan had a northern accent; she was born and brought up around Durham and her voice still carried the north-east's gentle burr, as she sat talking briskly in her no-nonsense glasses, snug in a puffer gilet. It wasn't a surprise to learn she'd once been a teacher. She could remember having drinks with Dorothy (she knew her as Dorothy) and Ivor ('I.A.') in this cafe, she told us, and she could remember meeting Tim in 1981 because he'd introduced himself as Dorothea's great-nephew and given her a book of photographs. And she remembered how she'd thought it strange at the time that Tim didn't seem to know very much about the pair – at which Tim was suddenly a doubtful young man again because he couldn't recall the meeting at all. 'I just can't remember,' he murmured apologetically. 'All I remember about Arolla . . . I remember being in the sun and eating a yogurt sat against a wall, it must have been just outside here. I can remember bringing the book here but I can't really remember meeting you or handing it over.[25]

'It's funny how the mind changes things. I mean, I did that route on Dent Blanche, the Ferpècle Route, but I can't recall coming down at all. It was far far longer and serious than I remembered it.'

Luckily, Joan had memory enough for us all and, in the course of an hour and several coffees, told us the story of how she came to be here, her recollections of 'I.A. and Dorothy', and the remarkable climbers she'd known – in so doing, opening out the mountain world around Arolla so it reached all the way to Tibet.

* * * * *

The first time Joan saw I.A. and Dorothy, without knowing who they were, was in 1966, she tells us, but they were often here in the early seventies.

'In 1976 they were here in Arolla and I took them out one day, round to the Dixence dam with two young girls from Guernsey; we went through the tunnels and out the far side and we sat around and picnicked. The two girls from Guernsey – one of whom was my cousin's daughter – were still at school at that time, Mandy and Jenny.' The mixture of generations went down very well, she recalls: 'To hear I.A. and Dorothy talking, "Darling, can you remember when . . .", talking about the late twenties or early thirties and there we were, in the mid-seventies, listening in to their conversation. It was fascinating . . . and it would have been then when Ivor and Dorothy, André Georges and his then wife, and my husband and I, we all went for supper at the Hôtel Mont-Collon . . . I can remember that as if it were just yesterday.'

Left: Dorothy and Ivor beside the Dent Blanche cross, Les Haudères, September 1966 (RCM). *Right:* With Swiss Guides at Rossier for the Dent Blanche centenary celebrations, September 1966 (RCM)

Ivor would have been eighty-three and Dorothy eighty-one, I say aloud, thinking about them old – birdlike in hats by a dam.

'Ha! Would she?' Joan asks, delighted. 'For years, Hilary Boardman* and I tried to find out her age but she wasn't saying anything! Sometimes she'd ask people, "Can you go to the bank and get me some money?" so we thought, "Right, passport!" But, no, she would never give me that.' She laughs. 'When she'd go to stay with Hilary, after she'd stayed with me, we'd ask each other, "Any luck?" But no.

---

* Hilary Collins met Peter Boardman in the Cairngorms at a course at Glenmore Lodge, where Boardman was a climbing instructor. They began climbing together worldwide. Hilary left Britain to take up a teaching position in Switzerland and was joined in 1977 by Boardman when he became Director of the International School of Mountaineering in Leysin. They married in 1980.

Hilary and I both tried to get Dorothy to write her memoirs which she strictly refused to do . . . she could be so funny.'

When Dorothy was staying, she'd go out walking during the day, Joan remembers, and once, early on, she'd wanted some cognac to put in her flask of tea. So Joan went across to the small Arolla shop to buy it, and 'I must have thought "poor old lady"; I don't know what I was thinking because I bought the cheapest they had . . . and she knew, of course, knew straight away. Heavens the reaction. "Oh, my dear! Oh! Oh no!"

'The week that she spent here with us here, I think Loughborough University Geography Department were here also and so, on occasions, they were all on the bus together and she had a whale of a time! Talking to the students from Loughborough. And they were fascinated by this old dear with bright eyes, who was walking with a couple of sticks but could tell a good tale.'

Joan herself was never a climber. The only summit she's ever been up was the Pigne d'Arolla back in 1965, shortly after she arrived, she tells us. But in September 1966, there was an event to mark both the centenary of the Dent Blanche's first ascent and a new flag for the guides of Val d'Hérens, so there was a big celebration and people were flown up to Rossier by helicopter. They had a large metal cross commissioned to sit on the summit of the Dent Blanche with a Madonna and all the rest of it, remembers Joan. The presidents of all the local authorities were there, the British vice-consul, who made a speech, the president of the local Guides' Association, who also made a speech. And this all happened to coincide with the summer meet of the British members of the Swiss Alpine Club at the Hôtel Mont-Collon. So Joan, as a resident English person, got roped in to

ask if someone from the AC might like to attend the ceremonies and then when, as luck would have it, Ivor and
Dorothea were found to be staying at the Hôtel Les
Haudères, they too got incorporated as honoured guests. In
fact, reveals Joan, she filmed the events, and could show us
if we'd like to see? So we leave the cafe and walk the few
steps to Joan's house above the Post Office to take a look.

Joan Pralong's house is full of penguins. We drink tea in
penguin mugs overseen by penguin prints on the walls. Joan
has been to Antarctica four times, she explains, to see the
penguins there. 'I've been round Cape Horn three times.
Once it was so rough that we were all sent into our cabins to
wedge ourselves somewhere. Icebreakers are terrible things
to travel in on a stormy sea because they have such shallow
keels, of course. They're flat-bottomed things. We were
heaving forty-seven degrees off the vertical on the one side
to forty-seven degrees on the other; we did that for over a
day. People in Hobart used to say they knew an icebreaker
must be due when they saw the ambulances queueing on
the dockside . . . Yes, we've had some epic times but, luckily,
the last time I sailed past Cape Horn it was nice and flat.'

Joan shows us the penguin board she built for when she
used to give talks. Each type of penguin is silhouetted to
scale. 'They're jolly tall, aren't they?' I say.

'Oh, yes,' she agrees. 'You know, when they stretch up,
they're big folks!'

We set up Joan's projector on the table, reel out the screen
and close the curtains. The motor clatters and a soft light
flickers, then the silent pictures start.

'There they are!' says Tim and we all cheer. There they
are, framed heads and shoulders. Dorothea looks out at us,

a sidelong, enquiring, slightly incredulous look. This camera, the look says; whatever is this camera up to? 'Is it moving?' she mouths before turning to Ivor, who stares at and through the camera for a second, a piercing gaze that pins us before, all steeliness melted, he turns to share a smile with Dorothea – both in shirts and light jackets, saturated and marbled in the Kodachrome blush. It's the first time I've seen them on film – moving, being as they were. In this instance they don't appear affected and when Tim murmurs, 'Yes, that's them,' he means the way they were; quietly amused. A look, a smile, a whispered aside – a tacit world of cognisance, their shared history contained in a glance. The frost in Ivor's stare, the way it evaporates when he meets Dorothea's eye – it's all there in that moment. They must have seemed so distant and aloof when Tim was young but now, knowing what we know, older and at an age to see, they seem so close at hand. He'd only to have asked and they would have welcomed him in, I'm sure. The frost was less than skin deep.

The scene cuts to a glossy helicopter lazily descending towards the camera from a sky of sharp blue mountains cut with snow. It has red and green lights on its belly, flat ski-feet, rotors invisible: a black bumblebee.

'This is the helicopter coming in to pick up the statue and the cross for the top of the Dent Blanche,' Joan says.

Now quite a lot of people clamber into the helicopter – hefting rucksacks, piling in, beaming – as the film briefly blurs and fills with multiple overlaid scenes from the day. 'Yes, I had to turn the film over halfway through so it's got one image on top of another, unfortunately,' apologises Joan, so we watch as the helicopter lands in the midst of a Catholic mass up a mountain. The wind is blowing and snow swirling and the priest's robes flap as he offers up his chalice. There's Cabane Rossier in the background behind the hastily assembled altar topped with axes and aesthetically coiled ropes. There's the new banner of the Guides alongside the national flags of Switzerland and France and a battered Union Jack (*Joan's* Union Jack), all thrashing fiercely in Super 8 slo-mo photobombed by spectral helicopters. It's a rather surreal hallucinogenic scene but what it lacks in narrative sense it compensates for in terms of cold. It looks unequivocally raw.

* * * * *

I later discover that Ivor and Dorothea both wrote accounts of the ceremony in their different ways – Ivor described it in postcards to his family in Bristol, which are doubly interesting because they're fronted with photographs of the pair from the day in and around the Rossier hut. On the first they stand wrapped up and hooded behind the alpine altar, talking with local guides. 'Cordialities in the cold,' writes Ivor to his nephew. 'Note how much warmer the local men look: The Chef des Guides that Dorothy is talking to and the donor of the big iron cross who is smiling in the background. We were *cold*.'[26]

The second card, to George, his brother, shows them eating inside the cabane. Dorothea is wearing fingerless gloves, her hair is bunned and perfect. They're sat on the same wood benches in the same corner where Tim and I had supped forty-eight years later. 'Cosy session most restorative after a long cold spell of standing at ceremonies in a Blizzard,' he begins.

This is the Cabane on the Dent Blanche built in memory of
a man who died from cold about there. The first guardian
was Antoine Georges – our companion on our 1st ascent of
the North Ridge. That is why we found ourselves invited to
be there. You can see that we are being fêted with great fare.
After this, all upstairs the whole company for a snooze
before beginning the descent at 12:00 noon sharp – on foot.
We'd been flown up at dawn.[27]

Dorothea's rather more extensive stream-of-consciousness
account appeared in the Fell and Rock Climbing Club's
journal of 1966, titled 'The Dent Blanche Centenary':

The first days of September 1966 were for me, quite unexpectedly, one of the gayest and most delightful experiences
that ever came to a retired mountaineer. My husband,
I.A.R. and I had gone up the Val d'Hérens to visit the grave
of Joseph Georges, *le Skieur,* at Evolène and to exchange
greetings with the Dent Blanche whose north ridge had
been the scene of his greatest triumph.[*] When a delegation
headed by M. Lucien Gaudin of the *Sociéte des Guides du Val
d'Hérens* called on us, we had heard nothing of what was in
the wind: a celebration through three festive days of the
centenary of the first ascent of the mountain made by
Thomas Stuart Kennedy and William Wigram with Jean-
Baptiste Croz and Johann Kronig on 18th July, 1866. Would
we join them as official guests of the *Sociéte* in the programme to fly up to the Cabane Rossier with the 200 lb.
wrought iron cross they were taking to the summit, feast

* 'Joseph Georges, Dorothy Pilley Richards and I. A. Richards made the
first ascent of the North Ridge of the Dent Blanche on 20th July, 1928.'
(Dorothea's original footnote)

there with the representatives of the A.C., S.A.C., C.S.F.A. and the Guides of the adjoining valleys, be present at the Mass and the Blessing of the Cross and the Guides' Banner, come down on foot for a splendid *raclette* at Les Haudères on the Sunday, attend an open air Mass in the square and listen to the fanfare *'Echo de la Dent Blanche'* played by the local band to be followed by speeches, lunch and a *lotto* (bingo, we would call it) lasting into the night?

In spite of very treacherous weather, this programme was carried out in the highest spirits. Only the simultaneous ascent of the four ridges by four parties who were to meet on the summit for the installation and blessing of the cross had to be abandoned. The flight was horrifically by helicopter, the ceremony took place in a blizzard and the descent was through new snow. But how nice they all were to us, how heart-warming the accord, the Guides' regard for Joseph and his brother Antoine, the enthusiasm and local spontaneity – a glowing memory uniting the past with the present.*

* * * * *

* Dorothy Pilley Richards, 'The Dent Blanche Centenary', *Journal of the Fell and Rock Climbing Club of the English Lake District*, ed. N. J. Soper, no. 59, vol. 20 (III) (1966), p. 297. Dorothy and Ivor also made a BBC Home Service programme titled 'Celebration on the Dent Blanche' which was broadcast at 8.44 p.m. on 9 November 1966. Dorothea wrote an account of the Dent Blanche Centenary for the *Pinnacle Club Journal*, no. 12, 1965–66. And see 'A Cross on the Dent Blanche', J. Byam-Grounds' account on p. 135 of the 1967 *Alpine Journal*, which ends: 'The celebrations culminated in an official luncheon attended by M. d'Allèves, Prefect of Sion, and M. Jean Maistre, President of the Commune, who, in sending a message of good wishes to the Alpine Club, emphasised the close links which had existed for so long between British mountaineers and the people of the valley of Evolène. The cordiality and friendship expressed, and the great affection in which Dr. and Mrs. Richards were so obviously held, made the occasion a particularly memorable one.'

Back in Joan's sitting room, the film cuts to show the splendid raclette at Les Haudères, the open-air Mass in the square and a silent band playing 'Echo de la Dent Blanche'. There are the establishment figures in tweed suits chuckling, here are the sharp-suited guides in dark glasses looking like playboys, every man with a side parting and a Brylcreem contract. Warm gauzy sun, women young and old in traditional dress with embroidered burgundy shawls and apron fronts, with hats like sculpted shellac. White soufflé sleeves, bodices and dark full-length dresses – then 'There they are again!' hoots Tim delightedly. There they are again, sat on folding chairs talking to a small child in a red-and-white headscarf and her mother. Ivor shakes her hand gently, interested, and Dorothea too leans forward to hear what's being said. There are the famous hats, the battered wax bonnet and a careworn grey fedora. Ivor rests on a walking stick, dressed in a navy blue wool suit; Dorothea's suit is faded carmine – they huddle together in talk constantly.

You can hear her voice so clearly, says Tim of the silent screen, and I think back to Anthony's Cambridge tape, the slightly cockneyed transatlantic elegance of it.

'That lady there is Dédé's auntie,' mentions Joan. 'And next to her is Dédé's grandmother . . . and these were different guides. Jean Gaudin, there, he was somebody who pioneered several winter climbs on the Dent Blanche.'* I look at the handsome man in the grey suit, arms folded, face in shadow, the sun at his back. He's listening to a speech, his lips moving ever so slightly as if following the words to a song, then I see that he's whispering to a lady at his side.

---

* Winter climb: north ridge by Pierre Crettaz and Jean Gaudin, 1–2 March 1963.

This is the man, although I don't know it, who, along with Pierre Crettaz, first climbed Dorothea and Ivor's North Ridge in winter, on 1 and 2 March 1963. What a fearsome thing to do.

Did they speak to them, I wonder now. Did he introduce himself?

He looks very solid, tough – rugby player tough. Dorothea would have squinted up under her wax brim then beamed, micro-frost burnt off in an instant. Ivor would have shaken his hand, firm handshakes both. 'A pleasure, sir. A pleasure. What a thing to do.'

Yes, they would have been pleased.

* * * * *

Film finished and put away, Joan talks about her friendship with Hilary and Peter Boardman. It wasn't until she met Peter that she really became involved with the climbing world, she says.

'I'd done one or two radio interviews for Radio Swiss International, the English-language programme at the time, and when, after Dougal Haston had been killed in an avalanche,* Peter Boardman was named as Director of ISM, as we call it – the International School of Mountaineering in

---

* Dougal Haston, born in Edinburgh in 1940, was a Scottish mountaineer who gained international fame following climbs on the Annapurna, the Eiger, Everest and Mount McKinley in Denali. He moved out to Switzerland in 1964. In the 1970s, working with the outdoor equipment firm Karrimor, he designed the iconic and pioneering purple Haston Alpiniste rucksack, the world's first dedicated mountaineering backpack – the sack I've carried with me throughout this book. Haston died in an avalanche while skiing above Leysin in January 1977. His grave in Cimetière de Leysin bears only a numbered wooden cross.

Leysin – somebody rang me to ask if I knew Peter Boardman and I said, "No, but I'll ring Leysin and ask him to ring me back." He didn't ring me back, he appeared on my doorstep,' she laughs, 'and we went over to the cafe here to have a drink. André Georges was there and, though they had never met before, André Georges and Peter Boardman went out on skis. Now, Peter was not a very good skier at that particular time – but they went out to do a first ascent, in the middle of winter.

'When we got round to the following afternoon and they hadn't come back, Dédé's father, Maurice Anzévui, was ready to call out a helicopter to go and look for them but then, just before night fell, we saw somebody who was skiing like that down the glacier –' Joan wiggles a finger in tight zigzags, 'and somebody who was going like that –' wider, shallow, careful zigzags,* 'and we realised that they'd come back. Bad weather had meant that they weren't able to do what they'd been hoping but that was the first time I met Peter and, when Peter and Hilary finally got married, I went over to England to their wedding.'

* * * * *

Peter Boardman was a hero to Tim and a great many other young climbers in the 1970s. Eschewing the siege approach of earlier Himalayan climbs – teams of climbers supported by tens of Sherpas hefting tonnes of gear to mountains, advancing a number of staged base camps up a peak like a military assault – Boardman and his climbing partner Joe

---

* I still have the drawing I made of Joan's description and mime of two sets of zigzag ski tracks.

Tasker became renowned and revered for their application of lightweight Alpine techniques in the Himalaya. In 1977, on their first large-scale climb together, they ascended Changabang (6,864 metres), a graceful bell curve of white granite in Uttarakhand, India. The climb was reported and praised at length in the *Alpine Journal* of that year.*

When he moved out to Leysin, as well as being a highly regarded mountaineer, Boardman was president of the British Mountain Guides, having been elected in 1979. Joan remembers mucking in with Hilary to phone around Swiss Guides and lobby the relevant organisations to try and help get the BMG accepted by the International Federation of Mountain Guide Associations. They had the phone slammed down on them a lot, she recalls, laughing, such was the opposition of the time: 'Of course a lot of the best British climbers were not qualified guides – Chris Bonington has never been

---

* 'In September and early October, Peter Boardman and Joe Tasker made a very difficult new route up the 1700m W Face of Changabang in 25 days. The climb involved extremely difficult rock pitches (Grades V and VI, and A2) including a tension traverse, and the pair were forced to retreat to Base Camp at one stage due to the bitterly cold weather which rendered bivouacs on the face impossible. Tasker compares the route to the E Face of the Grande Jorasses, with the added difficulties of altitude, extreme cold and taxing mixed climbing up icy runnels. This ascent is probably the most outstanding lightweight Himalayan climb so far achieved, and is indicative of the scope that exists for small expeditions in very big mountains.' *Alpine Journal*, 1977, p. 239. The introduction to the account also mentions the 1975 ascent of Dunagiri in the same region of India by Joe Tasker and Dick Renshaw – who we last met climbing as a pair on the Dent Blanche – as a prime example of a 'trend towards lightweight expeditions'. The *Alpine Journal* goes on to say that several 'outstanding climbs have resulted' from this approach, and that 'the ascent of the W face of Changabang by Peter Boardman and Joe Tasker represents one of the more spectacular of these'. Peter Boardman's account of the climb was published a year later in his book *The Shining Mountain: Two Men on Changabang's West Wall* (with material by Joe Tasker), Hodder & Stoughton, London, 1978.

a qualified guide – but I did what was possible for guides around Arolla to meet up with the British over here. I remember I went round to Verbier with Dédé, André Georges and another guide once for raclette with Chris Bonington and Wendy, his wife. Chris was staying in a visitors' chalet which belonged to Arne Næss – the Norwegian shipbuilder who financed and climbed in the 1985 expedition when Chris Bonington finally got to the top of Everest . . .'

* * * * *

'Did you see that Chris Bonington's got up Everest?' Dorothea asks Anthony.

It's 1985, back in the sitting room of Wentworth House in Cambridge.

Anthony says that he did.

'Fifty!* He did it by the ordinary route apparently. He had awfully bad luck and then the last time, the girl who's been so kind, who I like so much, lost her husband, Hilary, she's a wonderful girl I think – beautiful and able, she's teaching English in Switzerland and she helps run the mountaineering school there and she won a first-class skiing prize last year. She was a wonderful hostess to me. I mean I was a sort of PG [paying guest] but she motored me everywhere I wanted to go . . . But the last expedition, three years ago now . . . poor Hilary, her husband, Peter, and, what's the other fellow's name? Tasker – they were both superb and careful climbers and they disappeared. The party thought they disappeared behind the ridge there.' Sounds of Dorothy placing objects on

---

* Chris Bonington was fifty in 1985, the oldest person to have reached the summit at that time.

the table to illustrate what she's saying. 'The party thought that, from below, they'd see them reappear and they never reappeared in the gap *there*, you see. They disappeared in *this* section and nobody knows. Chris and the young doctor, whom I know, they went right round the mountain to see if there was any trace of their ice axes or bodies but there weren't; and Hilary insists, and Peter's mother believes, that they died on the ridge there in their sleeping bags, but I think the majority of people imagine they were swept away by an avalanche. The scale of the avalanches! All the modern mountaineers say they're learning so much about avalanches . . . but they're so gigantic really – fifty houses in size coming down, you know. They're beyond any kind of control.'

'You've seen avalanches, presumably?' Anthony asks.

'Oh, you see them all the time in the Himalayas. You could see them a lot if the conditions are such. You don't go out, but . . . one of my nicest young Swiss friends, forty years ago, he only had two weeks' holiday, you see . . . He was killed at about twenty-four. He shouldn't have gone and he knew he shouldn't have gone – but you do take risks on occasion.

'As I get older, I think the risk is too great. I can't imagine how Chris Bonington with a wife, I think, and a couple of children . . . I think it's rather wicked, if you've got a family. I think you should be a bachelor, or just the two of you's all right really.'

'No,' says Anthony. 'Not with children.'

Listening to the tape again, home now from Switzerland, I picture the North Ridge of Everest mapped out with cutlery and mugs, and I think of Dorothea walking with her sticks around Arolla and Leysin, very interested in the goings-on at the school; taking great pleasure at being in the mix of climbers and climbing talk.

An elder. A link across generations. A bright-eyed old lady who's travelled and lived.

She was nine when Orville Wright flew the first powered aeroplane twenty feet above a beach in North Carolina, thirty when Ivor's college friend George Mallory disappeared on the Second Step of Everest, fifty-nine when Edmund Hillary and Tenzing Norgay succeeded in climbing it, seventy-five when man set foot upon the moon. She'd lived through two world wars, outlived Ivor and all her siblings, and nearly all her climbing friends and peers.

Sat there with Anthony, she lays out the story of another fellow gone, disappeared, in the manner of one acquainted, if not reconciled, to such things. Age or accident had taken them all. Of course it's a wicked waste when people die young but she understands both sides, I sense, she knows what it is to press into the unknown: 'you do take risks on occasion.' She'd never have told them not to go, but the loss is no less for that.

Climbing Days ends with an account of an accident. Leaving for Geneva, Ivor and Dorothy meet four experienced climbers, 'instantly recognisable for the even, tranquil, rhythmic union with which they were walking together up the moraine'. A party elevated above the 'panting spasmodic pedestrians' moiling up the path, notes Dorothea – these were kindred, these were climbers. They stop to talk with them – 'a strong, eager responsible party full of infectious joy at the day ahead'* – and they almost persuade the pair to

---

* Dorothea's use of the word 'eager' is striking and affecting here; inseparable from the image of a face, a keen young face brimming with impetus and hope, and it instantly recalled, to me, Nan Shepherd and her eulogy for those she'd known lost in the Cairngorm National Park: 'A man and a girl are found, months too late, far out of their path, the girl on abraded hands and

extend their holiday by a day and join them, but they reluctantly decide against it and continue on down:

> Next morning, from Geneva, Mont Blanc was gleaming under a clear sky and we thought often and enviously of them as we strolled in its hot streets. The evening papers came out with news of an Alpine accident. Coming down, at the point where all the difficulties were over, at the well-known crossing by the Pierre à l'Echelle, an avalanche of stones had swept down across the path and the leader, with whom we had talked most, had been struck and instantly killed. If we had gone with them? We might all have been ten minutes later, and no accident would have happened. What a toss-penny game at moments mountaineering seemed. Holding the damp printed news-sheet in the Rue de Mont Blanc, it was impossible not to feel. 'There, but for the Grace of God . . .' The best years of our Alpine seasons had come to an end.[28]

Twenty-five pages earlier Joseph Georges is shouting *'Je chouque!'* He was there, the puzzle of the unclimbed North Arête was cracked, the triumph of their climbing lives. Dorothea's account relates how fatigue and failing light made the summit stay brief and the descent fast and faltering but the Dent Blanche triumph was to furnish them with wings. Their distinction was golden and survived them all. Now, powerless and clammy in baking Geneva, they read of the death of a man in a hail of stones, a friend by virtue of passion and chance, and they try to imagine it differently. Here is mountaineering in microcosm – the unparalleled experiences

---

knees as she clawed her way through a drift. I see her living face still (she was one of my students), a sane, eager, happy face. She should have lived to be old.' (Foreword to *The Living Mountain*.)

and acclaim, and the crushingly blunt cost in a few paragraphs – everyone climbs at the mercy of the mountains.

I recall and picture Mallory and Irvine as Noel Odell saw and described them, the last time they were seen alive, as two specks moving up a snow crest, 'two tiny flies on a whitewashed wall', before clouds cloaked them and they disappeared.

* * * * *

I tell Joan about the recording, and she nods sadly.

'We think that Pete just sat down in the snow and went to sleep. No trace whatsoever has been found of Joe. It was a long time before Pete was found . . . and then, when he was, he was recognised because, on his outer clothing, he had the badge for the International School of Mountaineering in Leysin. But of Joe Tasker nothing has ever been found, and amongst the last photographs and film taken of Joe and Pete up in the ice cave, way up on Everest, he was wearing one of the caps which I used to give to the expeditions.'

The caps had a skier on the front, she says, recalling how she hand-stitched patches and the logos of Jardine Matheson, the expedition sponsors, onto every one.

'There must have been about twenty caps – all the team wanted one. There's film and photographs of Peter dipping his head so *Arolla Sport* could be read on the visor. I've got a series of Peter Boardman on different expeditions always with the same insignias.'*

---

* Arolla Sport was the name of the shop Joan and her husband ran in Arolla from 1970/1 to 2006. The photographs mentioned appear in the book

The fact that such identifying markings helped Chris Bonington identify Peter Boardman's body, years later, brings the story home to me there in the room. Small domestic human details, such as Dorothea placing cutlery and condiments to map Everest for Anthony; likewise, Joan's patches, sewn on jackets and caps in Arolla, in this very room perhaps, to be found and rediscovered years later and thousands of miles away in the Himalaya and cited as distinguishing features of one who never returned. The two fronts, home and abroad; those left waiting for news, those in supportive roles, those in harm's way. Chains of command, strategy and communication. We're sitting at the home front now, years later, surrounded by penguins and ghosts – but I think this all later, for Joan is still talking, borne along by the momentum of memory.

'The first expedition that Peter went on when I knew him was to K2, when Nick Estcourt was killed. Just last night, when I was looking for something, I came across a photograph of Pete and Nick Estcourt on K2 just before the accident.'

She breaks off, reframing the conversation slightly at the thought of the avalanche that killed Nick Estcourt.

'Dougal Haston wrote a book, a novel about a skiing instructor who waited for ages to be able to ski down a gully and then got killed in an avalanche, which mirrors what happened to Dougal himself. That's exactly how he went.[29] And strangely enough, at the time when news came through to Switzerland about Peter Boardman and Joe Tasker being missing on Everest, somebody rang the wrong number and

---

which Chris Bonington and Charles Clarke wrote on their return from the expedition, *Everest: The Unclimbed Ridge*, Hodder & Stoughton, 1983.

they rang Annie Haston, Dougal Haston's widow, and she was the person who went and broke the news to Hilary, and put Hilary on a plane to the UK.'

Joan was in Durham at the time, she says. Somebody from Switzerland called her to say that Boardman and Tasker were missing and news would probably break in England later on that day, but not to say anything to anybody.

And obviously it did break later on, she remembers. 'Somebody came in to say, "Have you seen the television?" and I said no, but I did know that they were missing.

'I rang Peter and Hilary's house in Glossop and spoke to Hilary, who asked me to ring her parents in Chester-le-Street because, she said, "They've never been able to understand climbers and you can explain to them better than anybody about Peter being missing."'

* * * * *

'Older pictures have an uncanny ability of suggesting that there is another world where the departed are,' said W. G. Sebald.[30] 'A black-and-white photograph is a document of an absence, and is almost curiously metaphysical. I have always hoarded them. They represent a sense of otherness. The figures in photographs have been muted, and they stare out at you as if they are asking for a chance to say something.'

A black-and-white picture in 2015 is ingrained with the almost comforting knowledge that most of the people within it are of another antique time and likely no longer alive. One knows where one is with such a shot, they are artefacts slightly removed from the living, but colour photographs possess a frisson – the sense that the story they tell is likely ongoing, the same cast still around and able to recognise themselves. As such the slightly queasy washed-out pictures of the 1970s and 80s, be they glossy snaps or matt squares, are 'other' in a different way to Sebald's pictures. They document a world apparently still accessible both in terms of palette and people, whose occupants *should* by rights still be living. The world within such pictures is closer, more tangibly near and so the loss of people – by which I mean strangers or, more precisely, 'those whom we have not known personally', is more instantly affecting than that in older monochrome shots, the emotional pounds-per-square-inch is higher, perhaps.

I know Dorothea and Ivor as black-and-white figures – where they live in photographs, they live with George Mallory, T. S. Eliot and Virginia Woolf, in a world of the departed. An old world now gone. The pictures of Peter Boardman and Joe Tasker in *Everest – The Unclimbed Ridge* which Joan describes are a different matter. The only things which date them are their haircuts and kit.

The caption reads 'At the Second Snow Cave we hit rock',[31] and it shows Peter Boardman knelt inside a low burrowed hollow. Blue light seeps through the ice behind him. To his left, Joe Tasker is turned away, engaged in similar excavations with another man, Dick Renshaw, further back still. All are digging at the rock layer beneath the snow. They've carved out the snow, now they're mining out the rock. Peter has a shovel full of frozen talcy ballast in his right hand, his left is raised to the peak of his blue cap and 'AROLLA *sports*' below a Jardine Matheson thistle logo patch. His face is tanned and puffy under his cap and shaggy hair. All three are dressed in padded red bodysuits with bulky hoods. They look to be lagged against the cold, hands hidden deep in baby-blue oven-glove mitts.

Three men digging in an eerie neon igloo, lit by the flash of Chris Bonington's camera.

The picture above this, on the same page, shows Dick Renshaw crouched outside the hole on a sharp white slope which runs top right to bottom left – puckered and rearing ahead, rocky and sheer behind. The haloed sun has an oddly bluish tinge. Two red marker flags and two birdlike axes guard the cave's entrance: 'Dick outside the Second Snow Cave, with Kartaphu beyond'.

Kartaphu (23,640 feet) sits in the distance, a long way below where Dick is sat. The photograph shows the purple curvature of the earth. Four men arduously digging a hole in the top of the world to sleep inside, thence to climb higher, at an altitude known as 'the death zone' – or the 'regrettable' zone, as Joe Tasker called it[32] – where the body cannot acclimatise, where the air is too thin to sustain human life.*

Everest – The Unclimbed Ridge closes with an epilogue by Charles Clarke written in May 1983:

Now, almost a year later, I can, I think, look back upon death in three ways. I mourn the loss of two close friends. I mourn, too, their great lost talents, singly and combined, their skills of climbing, writing, filming, humour, warmth

---

* Charles Clarke wrote in his diary of 6 May, 'Dick had a strange turn yesterday. Numb face, left tongue, left arm for five or ten minutes whilst on the climb. No headache or visual disturbance. I haven't examined him, other than his eyes, where he has florid papilloedema [swelling of the optic nerve in the retina – a problem which occurs occasionally at extreme altitude] with hemorrhages and ghastly dilated veins. The diagnosis is easy – a small stroke. What's to be done now?' Bonington and Clarke, *Everest: The Unclimbed Ridge*, p. 88.

and drive. Lastly, I question the nature of our journey – to venture with a small team on unknown ground on the highest mountain in the world. The outcome answers the question, 'Was it worth it?' It would not have been had we been able to peer even dimly into what was to happen. Since we are not granted this faculty, I can only look back on the spirit of the venture.

I believe that with the mysteries of our personalities, our curious drives and our self-appointed goals, we could not have turned down this opportunity for fulfillment without denying ourselves a glimpse of the very meaning of exist-ence. In time I expect that we shall do the same again and be lured back . . .'[33]

* * * * *

'Do you understand climbers?' Tim asks Joan.

'No,' she says, immediately. Surprisingly blunt. 'They're a breed apart. You say, "Go away and do what you do but don't expect me to come along and hang about on the end of a rope."'

---

* Whilst I was writing this chapter, the Formula One driver Jules Bianchi crashed at the 2014 Japanese Grand Prix. Whilst I was finishing this book, nine months later, he died of his injuries. It's hard to draw comparisons with any other venture but mountain climbing and motor racing may not be so far apart in their exploration of risk and extremity, and the way they focus and consume those taking part. Listening to the other drivers eulogise and pay their respects, I might have been listening to climbers talk of a fellow mountaineer. Romain Grosjean said, 'You do what you do because you know Jules would like us to put our helmet on, to close our visor and do it one hundred per cent as we have always done. He lived for his passion and he died for his passion.' Sergio Perez: 'As drivers, we shared many moments. We do the same, all of us, and, not to see him ever again, it really shocks you.' Then they got in their cars and raced, again, for him.

But you're forever on the end of the rope, I think, forever on the end of the phone or prisoner in the moment they left. To have known such people, become entangled in their lives and seen them go and waited, you can't loose yourself from that, whatever the outcome. All the testimonies and interviews I've read and recorded suggest that to be around such people, people perpetually focused 'beyond' this world, to the mountains – holding a part of themselves back, seeking something unattainable here, with you, with us – such people will always leave you hanging on.

Perhaps the early astronauts were similarly *other*? Partially abandoned to fate and space; single-minded mystical masochists.

Singular. Different. Other. Apart. Beyond.

'This sort of thing scares the pants off me,' says Tim to the room at large. 'I cannot get beyond a certain point. I can understand going up the Dent Blanche when you can see the route, and it exhausts you, it's a magical experience but . . .' Then he laughs, a dry, tired off-kilter laugh which turns into a cough and softens the atmosphere of the table. I realise I've been growing increasingly edgy and emotionally raw in the past hour, sat round the table tensed as if engaged in a seance; perhaps we've all sensed it – everything and everyone just beneath the surface – but now Tim's simple civilian admission that he doesn't understand the terminal impulse, that *beyond*, has snapped us back together.

There are climbers and *climbers*. None of us understand climbers in the sense of those who seek the extremes of *beyond* – those who seek out the white hells where altitude and cold are anathema to human beings. Perhaps the only way into that world is to meet someone who's been to the edge and come back, but I think of Jonathan Conville and the response of his family to his death on the Matterhorn, establishing the Cairngorm and Alpine courses in his name. They may not have understood his compulsions either but they didn't discourage others from following him. Quite the opposite: their reaction was to encourage and educate in the hope that others would go to the mountains prepared for the dangers and return safely home.

Did Ivor and Dorothea have that *beyond*?

I don't think so.

I think they were adventurers and pioneers with Joseph, but the challenges they set themselves were self-contained. They were drawn to problems which existed within known bounds, elegant solutions to long-considered puzzles, exemplified by the Dent Blanche's North Arête. As with so much of their lives on and off the mountains, their ventures were utilitarian, pared back and well prepared. Recall Ivor with his meticulously sketched, almost academic, plans – hugely fit and up to speed in every sense; recall the formidably muscular development of Dorothea's calves. As such they're better described as focused athletes than shamanic frontiersmen drawn toward oblivion; even reading of their first ascents in China and beyond, I sense that, were the clouds to have enveloped them, they'd have cleared again; they would have turned back. They were practical, solid people, stoic but not self-deceiving. It was a game; a serious game and a considerable undertaking but not worth dying for, not if one could help it. They got to know their mountains as they grew to know themselves and their limits – *Climbing Days* ends with the acknowledgement that, in their mid-thirties (early forties when the book was published), their best climbing was behind them. Having said that, however one frames it, their 1928 breakthrough on the Dent Blanche was an exceptionally brave and dangerous feat, a cutting-edge achievement; something longed for, sought and won; an end for which they'd honed themselves for almost a decade.

But the most affecting thing was that they were still remembered here in Switzerland and celebrated for the climbs they'd made. I remembered Dédé's effusive words of the night before, the fact their names, our name had opened doors – opened a hotel! That didn't happen at Magdalene, I thought; I was charged full whack for that room.

* * * * *

We were both still tired. I felt like a crumpled ball of paper – body and brain. The welcomes we'd received in La Sage and Arolla were deeply affecting and the stories of loss, together with remembrance and talk of Dorothy and Ivor, had caught us out – we were both in tears on the bus back to Les Haudères.

Before leaving we'd laughed with Joan about how the Rossier guardian was correct to berate us. What a shower we must have seemed: not enough cash, hardly any French, no German, eccentric kit – turning up, going out, staying out, bivouacking. When does perceived eccentricity become maddening foolhardiness? There, I suggest. The writer and his amnesiac father. Edward Gorey figures, all we needed were aviator scarves and tennis shoes.

Then, as always seemed to happen here – the land of hubristic ha-ha – Joan told us a story that turned the laughter to ashes in our mouths and made us reconsider. 'To give you a tale which is quite true and happened earlier on this year,' she began, there was a race which was called the Glacier Patrol, *Patrouille des Glaciers*, and in the weeks leading up to it Joan would see groups of three up in the hills above Arolla, marching upwards with climbing skins on the soles of their skis.

The weather was rather mixed in the run-up to the race and on one particular day a guide was out on the Pigne d'Arolla, and as he was coming off the mountain he began collecting groups of other people who had no idea where they were because it had started to snow and blow. So the guide, who had set out with three or four clients, arrived back at the hut with twenty-one! Somewhere on the way, between the summit of the Pigne d'Arolla and the Cabane des Vignettes, he met and talked to a group of three and in the end one of them went with him back to the hut, 'and we still haven't found the bodies of the two others,' ended Joan.

This seemed to be the format of the Alpine story, kindred of the Gorey/Grimm fairy tales – oddly rhythmic, oddly moral, matter-of-fact gravitational fables where the ice always wins. There are rules and warnings and internal logic, and alarm bells ring in the listener's mind when the skiers ignore the guide's advice or the climbers laugh in the face of the weather like sailors whistling at sea. I noted too, Joan's use of 'we' – 'we still haven't found the bodies of the two others' – identifying as one who lived with the mountains, allied with the helicopter pilots, rescue teams, guides and all the others who work and live in the shadow of the Alps. She had become local, married into the community, a resident now for over fifty years. Something about the way she said it, 'we still haven't found . . .' felt uncanny and followed me away from Arolla. Patient, phlegmatic and tough – and I thought of the crevasses up in 'the hills' and Joan in her village at the end of Val d'Hérens, sat at the edge of the ice.

So, yes, we were both rather tired when we left Joan's house, crumpled in body and mind. As the yellow bus sped past the bulk of Hôtel Mont-Collon in the low sun, I looked for Dorothy and I.A. in the grounds and perhaps I saw them in the flash of the trees, dining outside with Joseph and the hotel's patron, talking of the peaks climbed and peaks to come. We were both in tears on the bus, moved and over-whelmed by the histories, stories and scape, inundating us here as nowhere else on my journey because here their story still felt alive.

* * * * *

The bus drove back through the tunnels that run through the mountainside beyond St-Barthélémy; their concrete innards stuttering yellow as we passed through their dusk and on down the slalom hairpins to Les Haudères below. Either side the cliffs and pines, the views across the valley to the scree steeps, crags and snow. The Dent Blanche, appeared, peering round the side of Dent de Veisivi: a white sphinx leant back in its chair, watching us go.

I was still a bit foggy when I got off the bus, fumbling bags to follow Tim. I found him stood with a man who looked to be about ten foot tall. I walked over, small, unsure, though I knew who it was, it could only be one person: André Georges.

T. S. Eliot wrote that genuine poetry can communicate before it's understood. This moment was like that; it bypassed the brain. I knew it was André Georges in my bones, knew it like I knew my own name: there was no way this place would let us go without meeting all the figures in the story. The day had been so filmlike that this encounter

André Georges
and yak. Valais,
2013 (Rosula
Blanc)

was bound to happen, it was part of the narrative arc.

So, as I approached the giant man, I knew it had to be André and the fact that I saw, a second later, that it was written on the door of his truck, parked beside us – '*Construction de chalet – André Georges & fils*' – only tempered my epiphany slightly.

He'd come to take us for dinner.

André does not speak much English so we drove to his home in near silence, occasionally grinning at each other, as if we'd made a getaway. When André was distracted by the road, I studied him sidelong. He was truly built like a bear, not only tall but *big*; his hands on the steering wheel were like wicketkeeper's gloves, his face weathered from a life spent on the roofs of the world, building and climbing in the sun. He looked statuesque in the sense that he seemed to have been chiselled from rock, a mountainous man.

His small cabin house was in a hamlet named La Giette, at the end of a gravel track which snaked along the hillside high above Les Haudères, the windows lit and welcoming in the gathering dark.

Inside we met his partner, Rosula, yak expert and writer, and sat down to a dinner of bread, cheese and wine, in a room of rich woods, on a table with a beautiful patina of age and grain. They built their home together, they tell us, introducing their lives and interests shyly – all of us eager to learn about the others, hushed in the low light and seasoned smells of the house. We told them about our Swiss trip so far, the campsite fox, the Dent Blanche, the day we'd had, and André listened, head inclined, cutting rind from the cheese with a penknife, blade to his beefy thumb.

Rosula acted as interpreter between us for most of the evening since it turned out that André was both naturally taciturn and sheepish about his English, which meant that, when he did speak, it felt like a significant event. His voice was deep but surprisingly soft and his English had childlike grace. Tim and I leant forward to catch his words, and found ourselves nodding – anxious to understand.

'It is a beautiful mountain,' he said of the Dent Blanche at one point early on. And we nodded and waited for the rest of his thought, but that was it; and it's true, of course; a fully formed thought and all that needs to be said when you've climbed it over two hundred times, as he has, alone and with clients. He's scaled the North Arête alone twice in winter, Rosula told us, as well as pioneering a new super-direct route up the sheer north face which he climbed alone, then reclimbed in winter with some young guides.

Such feats lent André's gnomic words a heightened hai-ku quality. He sat in the lamplight carving cheese, listening, smiling gently.

'I make three books,' he said during a lull and took one down from a shelf to show me – André Georges, *Une vie pour la montagne*.[34] His face – red raw, strafed and burnt, beard-iced – gazes from the cover; the smile is the same. Ivor wrote that Joseph Georges had 'piercing eyes which looked through and beyond you'. André's eyes are like that, glacial blue focused beyond.[35] Even a quick flick through showed the truth of the book's title – a life lived *for* the mountains, the sort of life on the sort of mountains that warrant three books and more! Someone who knew *beyond* well and had clearly been a regular visitor.

He could never send a book to your great-aunt because he wrote them too late, explained Rosula, but he'd tried to raise awareness of Joseph's achievements through his writing here, because all the books about him previously were in English so nobody could read them in Valais. Rosula had translated both Dorothy Pilley's and Dorothy E. Thompson's books for André, she said.

Were the family proud of Joseph as a guide? I asked.

Maybe, said Rosula, but André was the twelfth guide in the family. There had been a lot of guides since Joseph, but he was still regarded as the greatest.

What did Joseph do when he wasn't guiding? asked Tim.

André says he worked metal and stone. He built his own house, like everyone here. He had a forge where he made his own pitons and toe-points for climbing boots.

He had a good reputation as a craftsman, the whole Georges family did. Then André stood and got down a clutch of pitons from a hook on the wall, placing them on the table before us. These were made by Joseph, he said, and this one (he pointed to the largest) was in the North Ridge, until the nineties, when somebody pulled it out and brought it to him. Before then André would use it when he climbed.

'He made it and he put it there,' he said simply. 'It was the only one in the route, at a difficult point.'

I looked at the pitons – three short, one long. Black tempered steel. The one from the North Ridge was an eight-inch skewer spike, half an inch in width. The other three, like shear or scissor halves – their blade-shafts drawn and tapering to hard points – were pure, beautifully simple devices, fine-tuned for the mountains. Heavy and hard in the hand. Snug. Solid. I'd take my chances with these, I thought, conscious of the links I was holding, so redolent of the skills of the man who made them. What a thing to survive – artefacts linking the Georges and Richardses; Dorothy, Ivor, Joseph, Antoine with we three here across some eighty years.

André described finding Joseph's name in books, discovering his routes and first ascents with clients that way, because he wasn't much spoken about – the Georges another family who didn't talk.

André, like Tim, went climbing in his great-uncle's footsteps, also starting with the Ferpècle Route, although his climbing career deviated slightly from Tim's thereafter – he worked thirty-five years as a guide and made many visits to the Himalaya, visiting all the eight-thousand-metre peaks, succeeding in climbing nine.* 'I travel in Antarctica, also,' André said softly, in English.

After which, in the slightly stunned pause, he murmured something to Rosula.

---

* There are fourteen eight-thousand-metre peaks on earth.

'He says he thinks it's great that you do this research. In a way he did the same with what he could find about Joseph.'

* * * * *

Dorothy recorded her first meeting with André in her diary on Sunday 1 August 1976. She and Ivor had walked up toward Mont Collon from its eponymous hotel:

Walked up to a huge boulder near glacier where new path goes up to Bertol. Walked down to see André, Joseph Georges' nephew, who had written *most* interested in his uncle's climbs.* V. tall and strong with beard and looking poetic . . . He brought a most beautifully organised volume of Xerox of J.G.'s *Carnet* & wanted to make a copy of it but we declined.†

A letter to André has been drafted across the diary's pages for 23 and 24 May 1976:

André Georges, nephew of J.G.

Congratulations on your ascent of the NR of the DB. What a magnificent climb. We can hardly imagine what it would be under your winter conditions & solo too! Your uncle would certainly have been v. proud of you. Also con-

---

* Great-nephew and great-uncle respectively.
† Dorothy Pilley, Diary, 2 August 1976, RCM. Whilst the refusal of André's offer of a copy of Joseph Georges's *Carnet* – a guide's official record of climbs and achievements – might seem odd, rude even, the obituary of Joseph which I.A.R. wrote for the *Alpine Journal* shows that he had a very thorough and intimate knowledge of his record and possibly already possessed a copy. (See Appendix I, p. 333.) Dorothy omits this detail in her diary, so the episode reads as more brusque than it probably was.

gratulations on your traverse integrale des Bouquetins which my husband climbed for the first time with your uncle. They both felt they would have done it with a much shorter time but it was a v. hot day & they could not find any water! There is unfortunately little I can add to my accounts of him which were published in 'CD' . . . We stayed with her at the Hotel des Hauderés during the Centennial Celebrations – we remember with great delight how kind everyone was to us & what a glorious time we had going by helicopter to the C. Rossier – dear to us because of your other uncle, Antoine – a v. fine climber too, with whom we did many climbs during the old days.

We were somewhat disappointed that the Zermatt Museum did not record the 1st ascent of the NR of the DB. Perhaps because they are mainly interested in their own valley?

Best of luck always in carrying on the reputation of your family but – be careful.

Yours ever, I.A.R. D.E.R.[*]

The first thing I thought when I found this in the Magdalene archive was how much such a letter would have meant to my father, how it would have cut across all the

---

[*] Dorothy Pilley, Diary, RCM: 'André Georges did 1st solo NR of DB in 1975– also climbed it summer of 73. Entire traverse P. Bouquetins 1921' is written at the bottom of the page for Saturday 31 July 1976, the latter a climb described in Chapter 7 of *Climbing Days* – 'Experiments and Discoveries' (1921) – and mentioned in I.A.R.'s *Alpine Journal* obituary of Joseph Georges in 1961: 'Later in the year [1921] (with Dorothy Pilley and I.A.R.) he made the first ascent from the Arolla glacier of the Pte. Sud des Bouquetins, with first descent of its East face . . . In 1925 (with I.A.R.): first south to north traverse of all the peaks of the Bouquetins'. It is the latter climb of 1925 which Dorothy references in her letter to André: the 'traverse integrale des Bouquetins which my husband climbed for the first time with your uncle'.

atmospheres and awkwardness he'd grown up with and allowed him to talk to Dorothea, creating a space where that could happen.

A note on the same spread reveals that it was Joan Pralong who'd written to tell them of André's achievements on 'the NR of the DB'. Did she let Dorothea know about Tim's Ferpècle Ridge climb, I wonder? How this young man, a climber, a relative, had knocked at her door to introduce himself. Perhaps Dorothy knew after all.

And I smiled at the sign-off with its telling dash, 'Best of luck always in carrying on the reputation of your family but – be careful', and thought of Everest on the table of Wentworth House.

* * * * *

I asked André – still 'v. tall', strong, bearded and poetic – about his impressions of Dorothy, that day at the Hôtel Mont-Collon.

A very old lady but she had a lot of character, he said. She was still going for walks and she spoke some French. As a young man, he was very impressed, knowing what she had done. And she really looked at him, translated Rosula, from top to bottom. Scrutinised him, because he's so very tall and Joseph was really small.

Joseph certainly seems small in the pictures I've seen of him; compact and smart in britches, jacket, shirt and tie, often with a beret, though his hands look large and gnarled, and his nose is similar to André's. He looks professional, a businesslike man. The image of the elderly Dorothy peering up uncertainly at bijou Joseph's looming great-nephew is rather comic – most people would be small next to André, but particularly Dorothy in this instance, perhaps, sceptical and fierce with her sticks – a Quentin Blake illustration.

Did she tell you anything about Joseph? asked Tim.

André thought for a moment. She told him about the most difficult part of the North Ridge, he said, and it was so nice to hear.

What did she say about the Dent Blanche?

Just about the detail of how it went. So, Antoine, the brother of Joseph, he was helping with the most difficult parts. There were four people, you know: two Richards and two Georges, and there are twenty metres which are really difficult. It's overhanging at the beginning, so Antoine helped Joseph to get up, lifted him a little so he could climb and then he put an axe in a crack so he could stand on it because there was nothing else to hold on to. So he stood on the axe – and there he put a piton. And then, again, it is overhanging but eventually he said, '*Je chouques!*' He was there.[36]

I asked when he started climbing. He was sixteen, he said. Before then he stayed home to help his mother with the animals on the farm, making hay, then one year a French friend came to stay on holiday and André was allowed to go climbing with him. That was the beginning.

'In the first year I make all the mountains here.'

When he first went out, he didn't have any kit.

'He has never cared about materials,' Rosula said. 'He's still going out with builder's gloves on. At sixteen he was allowed to go to the Climbing School at Arolla for one week to get some teaching.'

He was very young when he started as a guide. The youngest. You were supposed to do military service before becoming a guide and so as soon as he could, he went. But he didn't enjoy it and was always in prison, he says with a rueful shrug. But you have to do it. If you don't do National Service, you're not allowed to be a mountain guide.

Then, for the second time that day, we were shown a film of the Dent Blanche.

This is the super-direct route, explained Rosula, as we watched André and three others setting out and escalading on their crampon points, dawn to dusk, up the plumb glass walls of the north face.

The more I saw of the film, sat watching in that warm wood box, the further away our trudging up the mountain's long snow spine the day before felt – contextualised and paling more with each passing moment of the film into an expedition 'along a mountain' rather than a climb.

Over pictures which looked hard and sheer beyond sense, André narrated how he first went up the route alone, then soloed the same in winter. 'I make six times this route,' he closed, helpfully. *La directissime* – as the crow climbs.

Do you climb alone because you like that best or because nobody else can go with you? I asked.

Rosula translated the question for André and he considered it. Both, he smiled.

* * * * *

Then, a wonderful surprise: they played a film of Joseph from the archives of Swiss Television, filmed at a festival of the guides in 1958.

Joseph: 'When I was eleven, I climbed the Mont Blanc de Cheilon. I was working guarding the cows and, with some tourists, I was allowed to go a little way up – with some English people I went some of the way up – and then I should have gone back, they sent me back, but I hid and then went to the top.'

He said that one of the most important part's of a guide's job is to work in friendship with their clients.

Joseph: 'You become like brothers when you go to the mountains. And you will remember all your life the things you did together. When you're up in the mountains, you don't think what's happening down below – you're in another world, away from everything. You're close to the sky, it's just happiness.'

The man in the film was Joseph Georges, the Joseph Georges of *Climbing Days,* but smaller, diminished by ill-ness and age. He wasn't old, late sixties, but he was tired, I sensed. Worn out. 'By 1942 his health was failing,' wrote Ivor in his *Alpine Journal* obituary. 'And with that he with-drew as firmly as he had advanced, turning to farming and to the building of a model chalet for his sisters.'[37]

Sat in *Yak shu lo ché*, their own model chalet, André and Rosula told us about building their home, their yaks,* their life and climbs together. 'If I can follow, then I climb too,' grinned Rosula, genially.[38] More wine, more cheese – I sus-pected Tim was feeling as sleepy as I in the warmth of the room but we were all too happy in that kirk of Swiss hospi-tality to mention it or make a move either way. So, more wine, more cheese! I began to watch the two of them – André so solid and quiet, a ruminant, and Rosula so bright,

---

* 'At la Giette the smooth, round rock, polished by the glaciers thousands of years ago, emerges everywhere from the land (even in the gardens and cellars of the houses), like the backs of big whales from the sea. That's why our farm is called *Yak shu lo ché* which in the local dialect means 'Yaks on the rocks'. You can often observe our yaks napping on the warm flat rocks in the middle of the pastures.' – An extract from Rosula and André's website, http://www.yakshuloche.ch/

Joseph Georges and Dorothy Pilley, *c*.1926 (I. A. Richards/RCM)

lissome and sharp. Sometimes she'd throw her hand or jut her chin for emphasis – or laugh; they both laughed often, but André's laughter emanated from somewhere tectonic, whilst Rosula kept hers at the back of her throat so it sprung like delighted thunder. 'Ha!'

We marvelled at André's pictures and stories, clarified and coloured by Rosula – here were some photographs from Antarctica where, after an expedition with a group of others, he stayed one month longer and climbed alone. We were shown a picture of the Tabernacle of Ulvetanna – 'a single block of exceptional rock crowned with a white hat', as he describes it in *Une vie pour la montagne*.[39] A monolithic sail of Martian quartz syenite reminiscent of Glasgow's red sandstone only harder and colder and massive and polar.

Then the two of them related climbs in a kind of stereo, Rosula managing to be both impressionistic and pithy, André interjecting facts:

Rosula: 'On Dhaulagiri he went up solo and at that time this was a record; base camp to summit, nineteen hours. By himself, alone. He had just a cook and some staff preparing but he went up alone.'

André: 'Nineteen to go up and six to come down. I started at five o'clock in the afternoon. Climbing all night.'

Rosula (translating André): 'Normally they want to be at the summit at noon so they can come back when there is still some light. On these high mountains, better to go in quick. If you stay and sleep at seven thousand metres you get weaker and weaker just by sleeping. Best to go as quick as possible from low to high, if you can. Be as light as possible.'

Rosula: 'Even if there are two or three of them climbing, there is no rope any more because you can't help anyone. You can't hold anybody. You don't have the strength to secure somebody, so everybody is by himself up on the really high mountains. On Annapurna he also went solo.'

More pictures were shown, tea followed wine. Makalu was mentioned, innumerable peaks and climbs related, explained and underplayed as is the way. Rosula told us that André had an accident. He wanted to do some paragliding whilst in the Himalaya but his paraglider 'didn't really fly' and he fell in the rocks and 'opened his head, broke his ankle and some vertebrae . . .' André grinned and opened a hand in concession that it was not the best day.

Another photograph. André, warming to his subject now: 'The Matterhorn. I make this route. I go alone in September. I make this very difficult ridge.'

He was twenty-five then. He's sixty-one now.

He has been two things, Rosula explained, 'A guide is his profession so they do this every day. Up and down, up and down . . . it's mixed and then he climbs things for himself in between. But for him, the base has always been a guide. He's not like the new sportsmen now who just do for themselves. He has always been a guide and when he had time off, he went to do more difficult things as challenges to himself but his role, his job, like Joseph, has always been about bringing people into the mountains, caring for their security, and making them happy.'

André interjected to say Joseph climbed some very difficult mountains alone.

'You couldn't tell of this at that time,' said Rosula, it wasn't allowed. 'You were only allowed to go into the mountains to earn money but not for your own pleasure.

Sometimes, I think, he was supposed to go with a client but he was really worried about where they were going so, the day before, he'd sneak up to see!'

He never slept outside with a client. Never, Rosula told us. He always brought them to a hut. 'That was his pride . . . because some guides they have a very slow climb and they have to sleep outside.'

Do the Swiss ever bivouac? I asked, hopefully.

Rosula (translating André): 'You would make a bivouac if you're organised and you engaged on something long, but not just because you were too slow. Joseph once walked for thirty-four hours on Mont Blanc because he didn't want to stop with a client.'*

* An account of this marathon can be found in Chapter 15 of Dorothy E. Thompson's *Climbing with Joseph Georges*. A report also appears in Cicely Williams' 1973 book *Women on the Rope*: 'The greatest and most satisfying

At that point, with quite exquisite comic timing, André offered us the use of his car and motorbike to go take a look at the landscape and mountains of Valais during the rest of our stay. I thought about the idea of getting on a motorbike with Tim, then, that evening, tired and wired on wine and cheese, and my attempts to stifle a slightly hysterical fit of giggles turned into a coughing fit. Tim manfully covered for me during this lapse by thanking André and suggesting that, actually, it might be best if we went back to La Sage, and would he mind taking us back in his truck? Which he and Rosula were kind enough to do – apparently untouched by the wine.

* * * * *

The next few days were spent around Dominique's gîte, walking, writing and reading and eating his wonderful food. 'What would you like this evening?' he'd ask us and we soon discovered that the best thing to do was ask him what he'd like to cook. Rösti, baked ham and eggs, cheese dishes, sausages, comfort food to fuel and restore us. We'd hear him humming and clattering in the kitchen and then he'd emerge with rich steaming dishes which smelt of school dinners and mother's love.

During our mornings, we'd walk paths and tracks

---

of all Dorothy Thompson's achievements was the traverse of Mont Blanc from the Refuge Durier over the Aiguille de Bionnassay with the first-ever descent by a woman of the Peuterey Ridge to the Gamba Hut. The Peuterey Ridge is regarded as the finest, longest and most difficult ridge in the Alps – something to which all great climbers aspire but few achieve. With Joseph Georges and Marcel Tommy, she did it in thirty-four hours; almost a record in itself.' Cicely Williams, *Women on the Rope: The Feminine Share of Mountain Adventure*, George Allen & Unwin, 1973, p. 113.

around La Sage, down for coffee in Evolène or up to the woods hanging over the village. In so doing, unbeknownst to us, we were shadowing Dorothy and Ivor's 'Alpine Breather' of 1976, particularly their walk of 26 July, which we made in the same weather and likely at the same speed:

> Took path down to Evolène.
>> Continuously beautiful walk.
>> Flowers beyond credit: wild sweet peas.
>> Wild roses just finished. Acanthus & scabiosa . . .
>> Romantic scenery beyond belief. Raining all the time.
> Glad to have our capes.
>> Found dry shelter under big larch & lunched at leisure.
> Then down (by Col de Torrent path – beautifully zigzag) and set out hard to catch the 16.11 bus at Evolène.
>> Failed, but nice bus conductor let us on in the rain.[40]

Dorothy's diaries of that holiday, whilst scrappier and more notelike than her earlier journals, are filled with wonderfully poetic lines, poignant snapshots of the last time the pair visited the Alps together – spent visiting old friends of flesh and rock:

> Glorious morning. All peaks out. White to the limit.

> Set out to reach a viewpoint from which we hoped the DB would appear up the Col de Tracuit path.
>> DB obliging more and more through these shimmering clouds.
>> Passed a happy afternoon watching the mountains form and North Ridge appearing + disappearing.

Arolla ↓ Sion

Got an excellent pair of boots for I.A.R. – D then wearing his.*

(Fr 84 Repair 35)

Had coffee + took 3.25 up to Evolène again.

A happy moment at Grand Hotel Evolène.

Sat a while in the Hotel garden then to Cemetery.

Found O.G. Jones. Died in 1899, aged 32.†

Sadly failed to find J.G.‡

Dixence.

Clouds still very low. Collected 9.45 + down to Les Haudères where we provisioned. (Joan insisted on paying.)

Drove up with lovely views through the Val d'Hérémence. Turned up the long Dixence Valley + climbed by many zigzags to the telepherique up to tunnels (in which balance was hard to keep) out to a long wide muddy walk with a lovely cirque of partially visible mountains ringing the reservoir – which was ½ full.

Thunder storms a big trouble – interfering with filtering devices and so making the pumping problems more difficult.

At last found a suitable lunch place. Sorry girls were so hobbledehoy. Sun came out, sheltered from wind. Grand to see Aiguilles Rouges, Mont Blanc de Seillon & dimly the Pigne.

Down to Hérémence. There, coffee, raspberry tarts &

---

* That slightly disconcerting habit of suddenly breaking into a third-person narrative, as if the diary is observing events and writing itself. Perhaps it's this 'third person' who tots the tallies of *money spent* in the margins.
† The original diary entry says 'Died 1893, aged 31' but this is not correct so I've amended it above. 'O. G. Jones' is Owen Glynne Jones whom we'll meet again shortly in the 'Lake District' chapter.
‡ Joseph Georges.

view of St. Martin Becs de Bossons.

Looked at new Concrete Church. Enormous.

↓ stairs to pitch-dark entrance. Dramatically most impressive interior.

Auditorium like a theatre. Very lofty with incalculable square openings & high step-like (path to Heaven) forms.

Near us, what might be a pulpit 30ft high with square windows. Home 7.15 Ferpècle.

Day started in beautiful weather but high cirrus clouds like tiger's stripes soon developed.

Met head of guides v. interesting man – but dark glasses. Also man of 87 who made the 2nd ascent of Ferpècle Ridge.

Watched ½ moon set behind the Matterhorn 9.25.[41]

Dorothy Pilley,
the Lake
District *c*.1919
(RCM)

The Lake District

April 2015

Erin lay full length on the rocks above Wastwater, arrowing himself towards the big beasts at its head: Yewbarrow, Great Gable, Lingmell, and half-hidden Scafell, gold-topped in the sunset.

We'd begun to take long-exposure photographs an hour or so before, when the day was turning, and now a blue band of shadow was rising to snuff the fire of the summits. Having helped to carry the kit from the car, I sat on an out-crop milled flat some aeon ago and watched Erin line up and set each shot, then lie or sit statuesque whilst it played out. Click . . . click; the pauses getting longer as the light turned owly and the air grew chill. The lake now bore a glassy calm. Occasionally, a car would whisper along the single-track road over the water to our left – preoccupied as moths chasing torchlight – whilst, to the right, dark screes swept up to Illgill Head. Ahead, Great Gable, sat back broad-shouldered in the valley between Yewbarrow's upturned hull and the skirt of Green How, seemed to recede as the night gathered like a murmuration drawn to the black mirror of the lake.

Then, as a hunter breaking cover, Erin stood and stretched himself, grinning, satisfied, having juiced the last of the afterglow.

'What time is it?' he asked.

Eight twenty, I told him.

'Really!? Blimey, we'd better get a move on.'

So we bundled the camera gear into the car and drove as fast as we dared along the heaving road to the Wasdale Head Inn, headlights pointed toward our supper, dashboard clock counting down to the kitchen's closing, car speakers improbably playing Roxy Music's 'Out of the Blue' – the elements combining in an eerie way which put me in mind of Jonathan Glazer's film *Under the Skin*, the cool sweep of the music seeming to beckon the mist now formed a few centimetres above the surface of the lake onto the road and into the car as we bounced and swerved towards Wasdale Head, battling the clock for stew.

Erin stopped in the car park and I jumped out, ran in and panted to the bar staff, 'Food? Still on? Stew?'

No, said the barman, stew's all gone. Steak and ale pie?

'Done! Yes, please! Thanks.'

* * * * *

The hotel was the hub of our trip to the Lakes; every evening we were drawn back to its lamb stew and dumplings, ales and warmth. It had greeted us, arriving up the valley from Wastwater, with its white walls and painted 'INN', solid and reassuring beneath Kirk Fell. In the days which followed, looking down from Sty Head, seen over the green of Burnthwaite or the path down Lingmell Gill, the inn stood for comfort, our end-of-day reward.

We got to know the staff a bit and once they heard of our jaunts on the fells and peaks around Wasdale – out in all weathers, scrambling iffy routes on snow, photographing at night!? – we began to be greeted as eccentric regulars. 'Hey guys!' said the main barman on about day four, a tall Scandinavian with a winning smile, 'great to see you again. Still not dead!'

Still not dead.

We began to toast it each night like a grace.

* * * * *

Dorothy's Lake District chapter begins with a similar view – the late afternoon sunlight was on Great Gable when she first arrived at Wasdale. Dropped off by the hotel, she's met by C. F. Holland (who we met in Chapter 3), and the pair puzzle over the problem of how to get her old-fashioned tin trunk – brought for 'now unrecoverable reasons' but possibly with the aim of keeping her clothes from damp – up to Burnthwaite Farm, where they were to stay.

> Holland's resources were inexhaustible. He wandered off to return, jubilant, with a tiny wheelbarrow. Somehow we poised the trunk upon it and trundled off towards Burnthwaite. Deafeningly we bumped along the stone-walled narrow lane past the church, destroying the slumbrous afternoon, while sheep lifted their busy noses from the grass in all the neighbouring fields to wonder at us.[1]

Erin and I had crunched up the same lane a few days before in our hire car, for we too were staying at Burnthwaite. Parking in the yard at the very end of the valley road, beneath a cauliflowering sycamore, beside a barn with doves perched on its green gutter, we unpacked our bags from the boot and carried them into the hall of the B & B. Such was the insipid coverage of the mank – a kind of tenacious damp breeze – that I wished I'd worn a jacket for the ten-metre walk between the car and the farm. The first thing Erin did upon arrival was to go and find the owner, introduce himself and sign the visitors' book but I stayed put, surprised and staring, because the first thing I saw at Burnthwaite, framed above the fireplace, was a large photograph of two mountaineers, attired entirely in red, bar big black mitts, hooded with round mirror goggles above iced balaclavas. They're posed at a point high on flinty rocks well above the cloud line which billows to the horizon. The caption read: 'Peter Boardman and Joe Tasker, Resting at 28,000 feet on Kangchenjunga. Photograph by Doug Scott.'

'Friends of yours?' asked Erin, returning with Andrew Race, the farmer, and breaking the picture's spell. A strange coincidence, I told them, shaking Andrew's hand before signing my name, under Erin's, in the heavy leather log-book – another echo of Switzerland.

* * * * *

Erin had arranged the trip in order to take location photographs for the green-screen package he was working on for his company. He'd been travelling around the world shooting different landscapes and now his interest in the Lake District had coincided nicely with my need to visit Wasdale and pick up Dorothy's story post-Switzerland.

Erin is a very personable, likable man; genuinely interested in other people. His social skills are top notch, honed from years spent taking portraits and forging an instant rapport with his subjects – putting them at ease before he steals their souls with his magic boxes.

The fact he'd booked us into Burnthwaite was a happy coincidence, although the accommodation options haven't really broadened since Dorothy first visited in the 1910s; one can stay at the hotel or the farm, or pitch a tent in a field. Whilst camping might have been an attractive choice in summer, Wasdale in April made an actual building with a roof imperative. Such weather seems to take pride in homing in on the back of one's neck, sneaking up cuffs and down socks – everything gets damp, stays damp, becomes wet. And here was a perfectly brilliant B & B! The sensible thing was to stay there so we did. 'No one likes a martyr,' as my mother likes to say to my father when he's being difficult.*

'Mrs. Wilson, of Burnthwaite (enchanted spot) would give you tea, after a wet climb, by the kitchen fireside in the golden lamplight, and make you feel comfortingly at home,' remembered Dorothy in an article she wrote in the Fell & Rock's jubilee journal. 'Of course no bathroom,' she adds, but there was a 'little shed in the garden'.[2] These must have been early memories because, writing in the 1930s, she notes how Burnthwaite has changed since her first visits – 'Baths and modernity have come to it. Then, one sat in a dark, cosy little room and ate in a narrow whitewashed cell, which I believe had once been the dairy. If you were much favoured, old Mrs. Wilson would let you sit and gossip in the kitchen. There one spent delicious long evenings by the open fire.'†

Burnthwaite now has electricity *and* television but no

---

* He'd have cheerfully eschewed comfort and pitched a tent in mank-squared quick as anything.
† Pilley, *Climbing Days*, pp. 58–9. The passage continues, 'The other day an old friend said to me: "The first time I saw you was in Burnthwaite kitchen and you were showing them how high you could kick with climbing boots on. You kicked and you kicked and it was superb; till suddenly your other foot slipped on the stone floor – and then how we laughed!"'

Wilsons. Twenty years after the Lake District National Park was established in 1951, Burnthwaite was bought by the National Trust. Andrew has been tenant farmer since 2003, looking after a flock of around 450 coffee-coloured Herdwick sheep,* which live out for most of the year on the farm's 1,096 acres of fell grazing land which extends around Burnthwaite, over Lingmell and all the way up to Scafell's summit. One of the slightly chastening aspects of our stay was that, however well we thought we'd done, however high, difficult and isolated our route appeared to be, there always seemed to be sheep muck around. The Herdwicks were better mountaineers, the dung said, they'd seen, climbed and defecated over it all before.

* * * * *

Having taken our bags up to our room, we made tea in Burnthwaite's shared sitting room using an electric kettle of which the young Dorothy could only have dreamed. Already in the room was Chris, a fell walker just back from a rainy tromp across Middle Fell. Boots now steaming before the wood burner, he cut a content figure sipping whisky from a hip flask whilst watching a VHS of *The Fugitive*. Any thought that we might be intruding was undercut by the idea that he might be about to tell us a story – sat in the big armchair, I half expected him to get out a big red book à la *Jackanory*, but he showed us his Wainwright Guides instead. Middle Fell was beautiful earlier in the day, he said, describing a walk up from Greendale, the burning

---

* In retrospect they're more often similar in colour to used tea bags but coffee seemed neater and has better connotations.

ache of his calves from the ascent (further than he'd imagined) and, finally, the summit cairn and the view across and up the valley where Lingmell Gill falls, past Brown Tongue to the Scafells.

Erin listened and asked intelligent questions but I, tired from the drive perhaps and forgetting the tea at my elbow, got distracted by Harrison Ford shouting that he hadn't killed his wife and leaping off a dam, and so missed some of it. But when we walked it ourselves, on the morning of our third day in Wasdale, I understood – the buff heather scrub and hummocky grasses underfoot, the long drag up, the bunched gorse and gathering heat in one's legs and chest, the prickly sweat, the view back over Wastwater to the coaly screes and then, eventually, the summit, plinthed in the mizzle. And then, better still, the prospect of Lingmell Gill, white in its flume, the muscular channel around it green rising through tan, bronze and lava dun. Brown Tongue lolling underneath the Scafells' swollen sculpted bulk, reflected in Wastwater's deep deep green shellac.

It was a great feeling to be stood there. Wasdale spoke to a different part of me than Switzerland had, a deeper part; I felt at home. I'd grown up with its literature and art steeped in this landscape, reflecting its wild aspect – Romantics and visionaries. Here were Blake, Coleridge, De Quincey, Walter Scott and Beatrix Potter. I could delve into shared memory here, shared personal and national acquaintance: English class and 'Daffodils', that small hand-me-down of *Peter Rabbit*; journeys up Shap to see university friends in Aberdeen or cousins in Edinburgh – leaving Bristol Temple Meads at dawn, changing at Birmingham, the run of Preston, Lancaster, Oxenholme Lake District, 'change for trains to Windermere,' and Carlisle; motorway dozing in our old Saab for family holidays as a child.

One of my earliest memories, blurred at the edges, a Polaroid third-person vision, is of a holiday to Brathay Hall in Ambleside. I must have been almost three. My mother, Annie, was pregnant with my brother, Joe, and went for a nap after the long drive up the M6 so Tim took me out for a row on the lake. Dragging my small hands in the water, presenting Annie with the flotsam I'd collected when she woke.

'It's really funny, the way you eat like a pig!' I cheerfully told a man with a beard at the dinner table next to me that night, apparently. I followed this up next day, in a loud voice clearly audible to the kitchen staff, with 'Isn't it funny how we've had tomatoes for every meal!?'

'We bundled you out of the room and went for fish and chips,' remembers Annie. 'You were so funny. At one point you said to Tim, "I wonder if people get fed up with all this water?" and he tried to rationalise it and explain that that was the wonderful thing about the place, that it was what all the tourists came for. "Look at the mountains!" he said. "Look at all the mountains." "And the water!" you said. "It's everywhere!"'

I was clearly a very astute child.

With characteristic humour and sincere enthusiasm, Dorothy writes that the landscape around Wasdale allows 'that connoisseurship which finds that the mountains are never on two days alike' to be exercised to the full. 'The relative delights of degrees of wateriness could be tasted! The difference between "A wet day" and "Wet all day" and "*very wet*" properly appreciated.'[3]

Driving over the Hardknott Pass, the vehicular acme of the landscape we'd seen building since the Bowland Fells, we wound down a road which veered and meandered and dropped through the rust and umber bracken like a bored child's finger on a fogged car window – a silver ribbon shining in the rain, soundtracked by an engine in low gear.

Around Cockley Beck, before the incline arrows started massing on the map, we'd stopped beside the River Duddon so Erin could take some shots. The surface of the river was pitted with rain. The patter and swish of water filled our ears. There was nothing I could do to help Erin apart from occasionally holding a camera beneath my jacket whilst he adjusted a tripod, but sitting in the car alone felt daft and ungrateful so we both stood out 'in the weather' whilst he worked – he a chipper picture wizard, me a sodden hunched apprentice – but even sodden it was beautiful; craggy orange slopes rose at our backs, bogs sprung and ticking underfoot, the rich hay of ferns, the shallow rapid river. As so often on the trip, we were the only people there, stood in the streaming air, soaking it up.

* * * * *

The first morning at Burnthwaite was bitter and blowing. We set out towards Great Gable along Moses' Trod, the seventeenth-century packhorse route over Sty Head, which passes through the farm. Walking into the V between Lingmell and Gable, the scale of the slopes became apparent. The Pennine Alps may stand at four times the height but any such comparisons felt misplaced because, whilst those Swiss peaks were thumpers – mounting in the course of several steps each as high as Scafell, hanging valley after valley – Wasdale felt very much akin to Arolla, a 'jumping-off point':[4]

Dan
Richards,
Great Gable,
April 2015
(Erin Patel)

a base within the mountains from which to set about the several-hundred-metre peaks above; and about half a mile from the farm, breath steaming, and over the wooden bridge at Gable Beck, we began to do just that, ascending the grass snoot of Gable's south-west corner, 'the long green grind of Gavel Neese' as Dorothy describes it in the book.

Gavel Neese. I wrote that first as Navel Geese. Such engaging, suggestive names are abundant in the fells – the map says there's a Sour Milk Ghyll somewhere over the way. Our course up Gable ran Gavel Neese, Moses' Finger, White Napes, Beck Head, before a scramble up the back on a lumpen scarp, battered all the while by a freezing wind with gale aspirations.

Gavel Neese: like climbing the spine of a manta ray, wing fins spread left and right. At this aspect the mountain appeared almost squarely pyramidal, summit obscured by the crest of Great Napes and Westmoreland Cairn. I knew that somewhere within the crags of Great Napes stood the famous Needle, but we could not discern it in the dark rocks to the right. The driving sleet we met on the upper reaches of the mountain had begun as wet snow below White Napes and visibility wasn't great, but we trooped up in good spirits, humming the *Jurassic Park* theme tune for 'now unrecoverable reasons'.

On the summit we sat amidst the boulders and cairn blocks, hiding from the wind and snow. Once stopped, we felt the cold begin to wheedle. The sky was clouded low aluminium. On three sides Gable sloped away to short horizons and long drops: a domed swathe of fractured broken rocks and snow. Beyond that, across the valley, the andesite wall of Great End and the Scafells rising as a brute rampart, frosted velveteen in the blunt light, flanks a web of fine white lines.

William Wordsworth, in his 1820 *Guide through the District of the Lakes*, wrote:

> Their forms are endlessly diversified, sweeping easily or boldly in simple majesty, abrupt and precipitous, or soft and elegant. In magnitude and grandeur they are individually inferior to the most celebrated of those in some other parts of this island; but, in the combinations which they make, towering above each other, or lifting themselves in ridges like the waves of a tumultuous sea, and in the beauty and variety of their surfaces and colours, they are surpassed by none.

*　*　*　*　*

We stopped on the summit for half an hour. Erin found a phone signal so he called his wife, Sam, to say we were fine and ask after their newborn daughter – Everything was okay. Yes! he'd love to speak to Beatrice if she was awake . . . from on top of a mountain! Yes, we were being careful.

When he'd rung off, smiling to himself, giddy with his

daughter's voice, I suggested that we make our way down below Gable Crag to a spot named Windy Gap and he agreed. The top of Gable was pocked with small cairns, so numerous as to be useless – like a surfeit of arrows pointing every which way but all saying 'this way'. Gable Crag lay to the north-east but as we started away in light snow the wind rose and a concentrated snowstorm hit and enveloped us in the space of ten seconds. Suddenly the views of Great End were gone, replaced by opaque, loudly buzzing cloud. It wasn't quite a whiteout – I could still see the ground – but in a snap it was on us and visibility was down to a halo of about a metre and a half. I shouted to Erin, we stopped walking and I gripped his arm. We needed to stay put, I told him, so we stumbled back the short distance through the granular murk to the summit's mound, where we crouched in the shelter of the larger rocks and waited the rumpus out. And then it was gone, passing off like a frozen April shower, the sky opening up like a migraine lifting, and we were back where we'd started ten minutes before but dusted and a little bemused.

We walked out through the molehill cairn field, down into the steep fragmented rock descent of the crags, clambering over defrosting ice, slabs and choss, occasionally on our backsides, until we reached 'that strange reddish torrent of rubble' which Dorothy described as curving between Great and Green Gable. It was just as she'd dubbed it: a red spillway so thoroughly harrowed, churned and pulverised by the innumerable feet to have passed between the two fells that it was several metres wide in places and reminded me of green lanes I'd known in Dorset after they'd been 4x4'ed. Footfall has worn the mountain out so much that many must ascend Green Gable by this open-cast path of manmade scree, a mud red scrabble in no way green.

'Something strange seems to have happened,' wrote Dorothy in her essay of 1956.

> I haven't seen in other mountains . . . anything like the disintegration that Styhead has suffered from. There are plenty of paths in the Alps which can carry quite as much traffic over very similar terrain without being turned into such slop and brickyard . . . Some day, perhaps, will the volunteers who so nobly clean up the litter on Great Gable, turn their devoted hands to consolidating a causeway there?[5]

Some things have changed. There is now a hefty stone stairway down Aaron Slack from Windy Gap to Styhead Tarn, and parts of the route beyond had clearly been recently shored up and repaired.

And some things have not changed. Before we descended from the col, I stood in the middle of Windy Gap and leant into the gale funnelled up from Seathwaite as Dorothy and Ivor must have done, as all who stand there must do perhaps: pitched into the wind, testing its strength and ability to hold and push. Erin did the same, seeming to be on the point of lift, a fraction away from rising to ride the air like a bird, hawks in the rain – by then it was torrential. We were so drenched by the time we reached Styhead that we joked about climbing into the mountain rescue stretcher box there to hole up out of whatever the Cumbrian equivalent was for 'old women with sticks'.*

---

* It should be stressed that climbing into a stretcher box is a BAD IDEA except in the most extreme emergency. I am not advocating such action. Should the reader ever need to do so, please put everything back exactly the way you found it. Such boxes and their contents are there for a reason and save numerous lives each year.

But no, down the track to Wasdale we sloshed, imagining packhorses steaming and creaking, bemused by the distance still to go; it already felt a long day. I amused Erin en route with the story of trooping to the Idwal Slabs with Emily Benton and the Pinnacle ladies. 'The fish in Cwm Idwal were drier than we four, come the end,' I told him, and he laughed and grimaced, half to me, half to himself, for his knee, damaged in a car accident years ago, was beginning to cause him pain.

* * * * *

Later, in the Wasdale Head Inn, having bathed and changed – thankful for Burnthwaite's 'Baths and modernity' after a slow home stretch, amiably limped – we spoke about chance and ghosts. I explained who the two men were in the photograph hanging in the lobby of the farm and how they were just the latest apparitions in the travelling coincidence of *Climbing Days*.

Take this inn, I told him – once our dishes had been cleared and the bar begun to empty for the night – outside you have the stable and the Barn Door Traverse, where, arguably, buildering began. Up on Gable there's the Napes Needle which Walter Parry Haskett-Smith first scaled for its own sake and, in so doing, arguably, invented a sport.* There is a strong case that when Coleridge ascended Scafell

---

* 'Haskett-Smith climbed the Needle when climbs and climbers were few indeed. But even in my early days you could, after a year or two, know, or know about, almost all the mountaineers you seemed ever likely to meet, and Haskett-Smith could tell you in polished and witty phrase the most uproarious stories about most of them.' Pilley Richards, 'The Good Young Days'.

Pike in 1802, he was the first tourist to do so.* This really is a rock climbing pilgrimage site. And then there are the ghosts particular to me, the Dorothean traces, accrued coincidence and reverberation. Take the fact we're based at Burnthwaite, as Dorothy was so many times; the walk down here to the inn, beside the church there, the same walk – that's a tangible memory to me. It tallies with her book and that idea, that doubling up, following in her footsteps, seeing what she saw . . . I find it fascinating, you know? It's palpably *there* . . . and then there's the odd bit of déjà vu, like the fact my climbing partners always seem to have bad knees! I broke off, laughing – wondering how Anthony was at that moment in Barcelona.

It was after closing now and the staff were tidying up, wiping down the bar and putting chairs on tables. If we liked, we were welcome to finish our drinks in the hotel lounge, they said; it was warmer, there was Wi-Fi and the room was old. If we were interested in the history of the place, we'd like it.

The room beyond the connecting door was familiar to me, it was indeed old: wood-lined, dark-panelled and snug

---

* Pilley, *Climbing Days*, p. 69. Dorothy notes a few lines before on the same page that Ivor was just finishing a book about Coleridge as she was writing her Lake District chapter. A diary entry from 3 December 1934 consists of a series of short Christmas messages to be copied out into specific photo-cards and letters at a later date – such drafts being a feature of Dorothy's journals. The first such, unaddressed, paragraph reads: 'Christmas Card: "This was taken on our return from the Alps this summer. We're in Magdalene garden, just outside Ivor's study & the College can be seen behind the holly hocks. The last month has been a dreadful time as my mother had a stroke. We thought she would pull through but she had a relapse & died. So now I am looking after Father – in London with too much on my hands to write the Christmas letters I would like to do. My climbing book is to come out in Jan and Ivor's *Coleridge on Imagination* is just out."'

– the crucible of the Easter climbing meets at Wasdale, as described in *Climbing Days*: 'Through a cloud of smoke, when the clamour of that extraordinary game, billiard fives (now, alas! a thing of the past since the table has been mistakenly banished), died down, strained figures could be seen – hands on the edge of the table, feet up on the wall – working their way round it.'[6]

I saw the room through the ninety-year-old smoke. Though I could see no trace of feet on the walls, I knew that they were there. Later in the week I discovered a photograph in the hotel hall of the same spot some century before, heaped with tens of hobnail boots on the still extant tiled floor with ropes and coats hung up besides. So we ended the night on benches where the billiard table once sat, Erin editing pictures on his laptop, whilst I read through my notes on Wasdale Head – still thinking of happenstance, endings and beginnings; wondering if my discoveries might be more due to a lack of research than a surfeit, or perhaps a poor memory.

The last book I wrote was about the creative process and one of the most interesting discoveries was the way that artists surround themselves with 'stuff' to fire and inspire their work. The painter Jenny Saville talked about the way that she, inspired by Francis Bacon before her, had a mulch of material on the walls and floor of her studio. Such resource continually changed as she worked and moved through it, turning pictures and texts up anew, cycling through ideas thereby. I think my notebooks for this book have worked in a similar way, the loose sheets of notes and quotations in my desk drawers, the photographs and postcards I've collected, the bookmarks and stickers in my several copies of *Climbing Days* whose purpose I've long since forgotten; haphazard and completely disorganised perhaps, but sometimes words and images fall into place.

Here, for example, is a wonderfully vivid fragment from Janet Adam Smith's *Alpine Journal* obituary of Dorothy, an image from the end of her life: 'In June she joined in the celebration of the centenary of Haskett-Smith's ascent of the Needle. One climber remembers her holding court in front of the Wastwater Hotel, arrestingly handsome in a green dress of Chinese silk, black hair centre-parted like raven's wings, youthfully alert despite her sticks.'[7]

And then there are Dorothy's descriptions of her early climbing inspiration and idol, Owen Glynne Jones, 'hero of innumerable unemulatable acrobatic feats' – O. G. Jones whose grave at Evolène Dorothea and Ivor visited together in 1976. Writing of Jones in 1956, Dorothy's wide-eyed reverence is still evident in remembrance of a man who died when she herself was only five years old. For her, he was a saintly figure and an icon in several senses – a great man due his full name, written out like a benediction – synonymous with Wasdale and the Lake District:

> How the clear-cut, rather ascetic face of Owen Glynne Jones used to gaze out of its frame, as it were over our heads; how I used to admire the power of those fingers that lay across the ice axe. C. W. Patchell, who gave me tea once from a kettle he had hidden in the Honister slate quarry, told me how he had noticed, as Owen Glynne Jones' second, that he would often use only one finger on a hold, drawing himself up on it as securely as if he had used his whole hand.[8]

Another slight piece of serendipity, my coming here next, after my Swiss trip with Tim, for Owen Glynne Jones was killed with three guides in a climbing accident on the

Ferpècle Ridge of Dent Blanche, buried at Evolène.

The English equivalent of those Alpine cemeteries –
Cimetière de Leysin, Evolène, Grindelwald, Zermatt – can
be found in the enclosure of yews around St Olaf's which
we daily passed on our way to the Wasdale Head Inn from
Burnthwaite.* A tiny humble ancient church said to have
beams of Viking ship timbers surrounded by the graves of
fell farmers and fallen climbers.

Next day, I spoke to Andrew about the churchyard down
the lane. Not for him, he said, all the farmers underground
arguing eternally. He'd like his ashes scattered on the daffodils beneath the sycamore outside his front door.

We were up early to get a good start on a walk up Piers
Ghyll. The weather was not promising but nor was it pour-
ing so we walked out in good cheer – along Moses' Trod as
before. At the wooden bridge we kept right and followed
the main flow up the Lingmell Beck, stopping so that Erin
could shoot black blown-ink trees against the hessian hills.
He carried a large rucksack full of camera kit which, though
heavy, wasn't onerous, he said. My purple bag had a thermos, a tealoaf, spare gloves and the map.[9]

We crossed the stream just beyond the convergence of
Lingmell Beck and Spouthead Gill in 'a beautiful waters-

---

* Until 1977 the church was unnamed. It's referred to in *Climbing Days*
(p. 62) as 'the yew-shadowed churchyard at Wasdale where Frankland, that
superlative climber, is buried:

> Here he lies where he loved to be

and the 1903 pioneers of 'The Pinnacle Face of Skafell':

> 'One moment stood they
> High in the stainless imminence of air,
> The next they were not.'

meet' as Wainwright wrote in his guide to the route we were taking. Losing a foot on slick boulders, I slipped so one leg met the waters until just below my knee. For the next hour I could feel the beck-damp wicking through my trousers, sock and boot as we climbed Lingmell – but my knee was fine, and so was Erin's, having mended itself overnight . . . until it wasn't and announced itself worse and by that point we were up above Piers Ghyll on a mountain in the whistling snow.

Looking from Gable the day before, I'd seen the banks of Lingmell rise from its base taupe to frosted top. We'd tramped up the matted slopes below Stand Crag and Criscliffe Knotts – tussocks and quag, clothes wring-wet, huffing, Piers Ghyll deepening, 'that vast cleft, which seems in some light a baby Grand Cañon tilted up,'* down to our left. Over the nascent canyon, sheep stood chewing, perched on outcrops, indifferent and blank. I thought of Bristol Council's plan to stock the Avon Gorge with goats to keep the grass and shrubs in check. Teetering on a precipice clearly didn't put the Herdwick off their lunch. We ate a piece of teabread in solidarity and shortly after crossed an invisible line where rain became sleet.

Dorothy wrote of Piers Ghyll that:

Climbers avoid it because of a chilly stream that disputes the use of the holds with them. But in the midst of the drought of 1921, on July 10, a party of three[†] thought that

---

* Dorothy was obviously referring to the Grand Canyon here. I'm not sure why she's used a name halfway between the English and Spanish – *Grand Canyon / Gran Cañón* – an authorial quirk or an editorial aberration, perhaps.

[†] A. R. Thompson, W. A. Wilson, A. Walters. (Original footnote to *Climbing Days*, p. 78.)

their chance had come to make the first descent. The whole Lake District had been ransacked for weeks for a Mr Crump. Such was their astonishment to see him on the gorge sitting sideways on a ledge and gazing down the Ghyll. He had been marooned there twenty days with an injured leg, without food, maintaining life on an intermittent drop of water! Happily, he was still able to walk and was nursed down to survive unharmed.[10]

Now I was nursing Erin up it instead. After a time walking on the edge of the Ghyll's chasm drop, we reached a scramble of scree beneath some obnoxious-looking crags. I could make out the path as a crease beneath slush. It stopped at a streaming soapy rock wall with onward passage possible by a kind of alternating-tread stair crack.

This was not climbing. It should not have been a problem. On a dry day it would have been a moment's scramble, a fun clamber, a means to an end, but that afternoon, in the sleet with only three knees between us . . . why had we gone on? I think I thought it would be easier to keep on up than turn around and start back down what was now a fairly dicey icy path. I remembered the pained stumping of the day before and how Anthony had laboured down Montserrat – the *out* often seemed less fraught than the *return*. Perhaps I thought a slog up Piers Ghyll might act as a respite for Erin's knee in the long run, images of an easier trail down Brown Tongue. In any case, I was wrong and the reality was that we were stood at the foot of rocks up which Erin said he could not go. In snow. Under a sky like lead.

Now was not the time to tell Erin that the only reason we were here, this route specifically, was that I'd been taken with Dorothy's story of the chasm and Mr Crump, and it seemed a fine atypical path up to Scafell Pike but *atypical*, *little visited* and *quirky* were now unwelcome words.

Everything was dark and slick. The thought occurred that we'd been animating and enlivening a hard indifferent soaking stretch of mountainside. Shorn of momentum and humour, everything suddenly loomed. We were alone with our three working knees below Middleboot Knotts, above the black hole of Piers Ghyll. All striking and starkly beautiful if one had that hat on, none of it kind.*

I was angry at the situation, fiercely cross and worried. As we stood there, I could feel my wet toes in my saturated boots, skin suddenly prickling itchy. Water dripped off my hood and face onto the map as I looked for a flatter alternative route which didn't exist, whilst reassuring Erin it was fine. It *would* be fine. We both had plenty in the locker to get out of this – and with that I thought back to the Conville course and assessed the situation. Erin was in pain but was able to walk. We had food and drink. I knew where we were on the map. We were warm and alert. The weather was bad but not terrible. We had phones to call out in an emergency, but I was damned if this was going to turn into a problem.

Stay here, I told him, drink some tea, and I moved to scout about for a solution. I found one, I thought, a bit more scree, a scramble and a crawl and we'd rejoin our route. Rock was out, he couldn't do rock, but scree was okay. Scree had give. Scree was fine.

Erin disagreed.

'I hate this. I bloody hate it,' he called to me a few minutes later, midway up a loose slope. 'Everything's telling me not to go on.'

---

* An accident black spot, I was later to learn.

Apart from me, I told him, cheerfully. (Cheer with an edge of coax and threat.) I'm telling you it'll be fine. If you slip back, I'm here. It really isn't as scary as you think. Put your foot there.

Shortly after this I was following him up a shallow chute full of slop and moss dreck, explaining that, should he begin to slide, I was his backstop. He was scrabbling, pained and miserable, I knew. After a while he announced that there was no grip, no holds and he was coming back down. He wasn't, I told him. Then, having made sure he was braced and solid in his stance, I climbed out and round him so that I was at the top of the trough, braced myself, took hold of his hand and reached over his back for the straps of his rucksack. Right, I said, you're going nowhere but up. Come on.

We obviously had no rope. There was no belay but I was well set and had a good strong grip. It was awkward and stupid, probably more dangerous and certainly more painful than if I'd pushed or cajoled him up the original stone-ladder route, but there it was.

E. E. Cummings wrote that 'all ignorance toboggans into know'; I don't know if Erin realised how real the possibility of his tobogganing down into Piers Ghyll on top of me was, had he just let go of everything and pulled. I assume not at all.

'I hate this,' he repeated into the rock, once we were ready, but his feet began to search for holds again and slowly, slowly as I began to haul in support, he ascended in wincing increments until we were both splayed in the snow on top of the crag.

'That thing with the bag straps was good!' he laughed a few minutes later. 'You've done that before.' Yes, I lied. Classic strap hauling, there . . . you can't move in *Climbing Days* for reading about it; although most people seem to have favoured ropes.

At some point we had swapped rucksacks so that I was carrying Erin's bag of camera kit, a bag of amazing weight. What were his cameras made of? I wondered, as I shouldered it on Lingmell – aren't such things meant to get smaller, faster and lighter as technology improves?* I imagined the contents as cast from iron, but it provided great ballast whilst I pulled him from the chimney onto Middleboot's upper, into the thickening snow.

Half an hour later, towards the top of Scafell, the wind was blowing hard and oblique snow sped across us. The cloud was low, the ground underfoot was a mix of iced rocks and powder, and visibility was down to 'bathroom mirror after a shower'. Much as we narrowed our eyes and peered, the paths remained obscure. Occasionally we'd stumble or be blown over. The general scud and din was loud. After a few minutes of what might charitably be called 'getting our bearings' – tapping each other on the shoulder, shouting muffled inaudibles, whilst shaking our heads and pointing at the map – we spied a large cairn to huddle behind so we could disagree out of the wind. Cairns meant paths, we agreed, and indeed once there we found ourselves in the midst of several. I was just looking at my compass when a family of five trudged past. The white sea parted for a moment and two parents appeared, leading three intrepid children – the two youngest raw-faced and screaming, whilst the third seemed to have entered a fugue state of sorts and just stared blankly ahead.

'Let's follow them,' said Erin, wisely. Then, bounding

---

* I think this is known as the fourth tenet of Moore's Law.

over, suddenly buoyant and *inexplicably* jaunty, shouted
'Hello! You alright?' at the surprised, somewhat teary quin-
tet. I stood up and followed, embarrassed, for some reason
waving, the awkwardness stemming from the fact that I
knew our air of helpful benevolence was a ridiculous sham.
'Hello, we're tired, he's lame, the weather's abysmal, but
you seem to know what you're doing. Can we trail down in
your wake?' is what an honest pair would have said; instead
of which, Erin stood there hale and hearty, grinning, and
we asked, 'You alright?' and 'How are you getting on?' as if
we were competent adults.

I think I even offered them soggy cake, which they
politely declined.

* * * * *

The snow became rain below Scafell Crags, the whole sky
emptying out so their massive forms were veiled. Only their
heft impressed to our left, the great mouth and face I knew to
be there, obscured by teeming soup. Deep Ghyll, Lord's Rake,
Broad Stand were beyond, somewhere – the stuff of *Climbing
Days*; the things that I was technically here to see – but there
were no views up nor down until Brown Tongue when we
emerged from beneath Scafell's fug hat, the valley opened
and we traipsed home down another set of well-worn stairs.

When we arrived back at the inn that night we must have
looked like two drowned rats. Erin had hobbled the long
drag in stoic silence, pausing only to sigh, thrash and scream.

When we took off our jackets the dark patches beneath
resembled low-visibility tabards of damp – dark down from
our necks, up our arms, down our backs . . . our trousers

slurped when we sat – and the puddles which formed around our table were cause for glances, jokes and asides behind hands from fellow drinkers. The staff grinned delighted grins at our appearance. 'Hey guys!'

Hey.

They asked where we'd been. We told them.

'I think it's so great you do these things. Nobody does these things in this weather. It's crazy!'

Thanks chaps. Got any stew?*

* * * * *

As we warmed up we began to talk again. I apologised to Erin for making him go through all that and he said he'd enjoyed it really, now; in retrospect: 'Bloody awful at the time, mind.'

I unpacked my pockets, which were full of chocolate wrappers and other rubbish found during the day. The collection of trash I found on the path had become an angry mania as the trip went on. The foil papers formed part of a larger haul of energy drink cans, crisp packets, banana skins, glass, plastic bottles, screw caps – some from Scafell, some

---

* The staff were all young, an even mix of boys and girls; walkers, climbers, some fell runners too, who either grew up nearby or were drawn from afar by the prospect of work in Wasdale and the chance to explore the district on their days off. This was the inn at the end of the road, after all. Everyone was either there for a reason or lost. The third or fourth morning, walking out past St Olaf's with Erin, I saw one of the girls setting off straight up the seeming forty-five-degree slope of Kirk Fell alone, powering up through the bracken and red ferns, head down, set. I could still make her out when we reached Mosedale Bridge – high on the fell, stopped and looking back over Wastwater toward the sea – and I thought what an amazing place this must be to live, work and wake within each day. Perhaps she was thinking the same that moment before she turned away and disappeared into the clouds.

Climbers on Napes Needle, 1978 (Tim Richards)

from the churchyard, some from the farm approach. Walking with Erin provided the time to litter-pick, swearing under my breath. It felt an almost personal attack. I might not climb as Dorothy and Ivor climbed, or write as they wrote, but I could at least help keep the fells from being spoilt by idiots.

Pilgrimage is personal and often ambiguous. Memories are abstract, in constant flux. It's easier to store and organise paper archives than moments in landscape long ago. It's comforting to think of documents and records as facts, but in Dorothy and Ivor's case they often seem more invitations to explore elsewhere. Sitting and reading of climbing in Cambridge or Bath bordered on cognitive dissonance since so many of the documents were means to an end – a record of life lived with a view to climbing rocks. Without physical interaction with rocks, half the story is denied – they are writing towards corporeality or, at least, to inspire the curious and outgoing. And so here I was.

One of the reasons I love 'The Good Young Days' – Dorothy's article to mark the Fell & Rock's 1956 jubilee – is the sense that she is unpacking her memories of the Lakes. Half the recollection is a roll-call of climbers, famous and half-forgotten, heroes and heroines, names which must be mentioned (in no particular order). Throughout there is the sense of kinship in landscape – a generous celebration of people and place and that magical third thing, the shared joy of climbing.

Names and anecdotes tumble over the page, her writing is brimful of smiles and fraternity – 'I am approaching later years (I am trying to stop by 1926),' she writes 'and there is a chance . . . that I may accidentally leave out some well-loved name. The minute I let this go – from the Almagell Alp – a string of deeply remembered figures frequenting Wasdale will stalk across my memory's screen.' Deeply remembered, deeply felt – 'It went down into the very form and fabric of myself.'

She quotes part of a letter written by Pat Kelly – 'to whom I owe so much' – about a solo climb she made from Deep Ghyll, as an example of what climbing meant to 'this remarkable personality who was the chief inspirer of the Pinnacle Club'.

A bite of lunch in Deep Ghyll, some moderate climbing to get warm and to gain confidence, and then a delight which only a rock-climber can appreciate – to stand on a mere inch or so of rock and look down an almost sheer 200 feet: the awesome exhilaration of a delicate, airy, upward step to a toehold on which to balance before grasping a firm bit of rock securely with both hands and so raising oneself on and up to the land of pure delight – out in the sunshine to sit on top of Pisgah and have a view to satisfy all hill lovers. Just across the way was the Pike, with its summit cairn and new War Memorial. Gable, Kirkfell, Yewbarrow, the Screes: the very names will call up the picture to one who knows.[11]

There may have been no view that day, when Erin and I struggled up, climbed round, passed by, got rained on, but we gleaned more of the world, came closer to knowing.

Climbs are invisible, people pass away, but rocks and stories endure. We'd had adventures, looked after each other, engaged with the mountain in the same spirit as Dorothy, Ivor and their circle delighted in the mountains – and in such acts of care and adventure we honour them and add to the ongoing story.

* * * * *

On our last morning, Erin woke early to photograph the farm. I found him set up in the stables with the gentle-faced cattle, and left him taking pictures of the doves in the barn.

The day was clear and warming as I walked out along Moses' Trod for the third and last time. Up Gavel Neese, above the swollen becks, feet on the sprung turf, winding up the manta ray, the dull dun world of the day before had given way to saffrons, mustards, green-golds and sap. The white noise of water, the drum of my heart, footfall, hard breath, skylark and a yellowhammer, climbing in a volley of sun and song.

At the improbable upright of Moses' Finger, I branched right onto the scree towards the Needle. Looking down Gable now, I found the shimmer of a heat haze, and the warmth was such that I took my jacket off, unthinkable the day before. What a change in the fells the blue sky brought, everything available and there to be seen. There was the sea, over Wastwater, the fells stood around, spread out as the wonderfully named Bentley Beetham put it, 'like goods in a shop window . . . you make your choice and up you go.'*

Dorothy begins her Lake District chapter with an account of how, that first evening in Wasdale, C. F. Holland – having sorted out her tin trunk debacle –

> with an energy as unfailing as a mountain torrent, dragged us off – my brother Will and I – to climb all the Napes ridges then and there. The rose red of a perfect July sunset was creeping up the rocks as we tore at Holland's 'slow pace' . . . Round the slopes we contoured on the tiny path; then, suddenly, the Needle was there! In that breathless moment it surpassed I don't know how many dreams.[12]

I now saw it too, a steepling finger of rock about twenty metres tall standing out from the crags around it. I reached it up some car-sized blocks – buffed and polished by many thousand hands and feet.

'When I first climbed the Napes Needle, its holds felt smooth enough. And that was in the pre-triconni era!'

---

* 'You go to Pillar or the Napes, to Scafell or Dow, and there are the climbs all spread out before you, like goods in a shop window; and having paid due regard to the price – the standard of difficulty of each – you make your choice and up you go.' Bentley Beetham, 'An Interim Report from Borrowdale', *Journal of the Fell and Rock Climbing Club*, no. 40, vol. 14 (III), 1946, p. 180.

remembered Dorothy decades later, in reference to the metal boot nails or 'Trikes' which had 'sawn away a good deal of valuable rock since then'.[13] I can report that there is still a lot of the Needle left; it hasn't been completely milled to dust. Seen from below it still looks grand but the thought of climbing it alone didn't appeal – more due to the descent than the scrambling up. I wondered how many times the rescue teams had been called out to find a climber sat like Symeon the Stylite, alone at the top of the pillar. Haskett-Smith must have been a brave man, that first time, all on his own.

I sat in the sun of the Needle's plinth for about an hour or so, 'just being with it' as Nan Shepherd might have said.

* * * * *

Back at Burnthwaite, Erin was packing the car.

Andrew the farmer was sat in his tractor forklifting, shifting and doling out bales of hay to feed his sheep. The fields at the rear of the farm were full of new sheep set for the fells. It was spring and he was busy but he stopped his engine to climb down and talk to us. Had we enjoyed our stay? He told us about his regular and annual bookings, the feisty people he sometimes had to deal with at breakfast, and the trouble with Wastwater being voted Britain's favourite view – the *difficult* year that followed 'until it blew over and was forgotten': people turning up in taxis – men in thin shirts, women with high heels asking where the shops were . . . 'Normally the only taxis are the ones we have to call for the folk who've climbed down the wrong side of Scafell!' he laughed. 'I tell them it's cheaper to stay the night here, have breakfast and then walk back. A taxi all the way round's about £50 but some people do it . . .' He smiled and shook his head.

Then we settled up in his kitchen, the kitchen where Dorothy sat so many evenings with old Mrs Wilson. At the back there was a beautiful old Aga range, warm cream and chrome. I wondered if Dorothy sat by that, if they'd recognise each other.

Andrew agreed it was harder getting down the Needle than getting up, yes, there were rescues, people got stuck, but he was glad we'd got up Piers Ghyll alright, that was one of his favourite routes. Then he told us a story about walking up there with his dogs, having left before dawn the winter before. They'd reached Middleboot as the sun was rising, hard frost everywhere, silent and pristine. Then one dog, excited, knocked into another and that dog fell down, down into the ghyll. Andrew climbed after it, watched by the other dogs, found it, cradled and carried it home. It survived but it's fragile, he told us. It's got no more lives left.

Then the card machine beeped and broke the spell and we set off back past the church, the hotel – leaving the same way the glacier left, down the road towards Stanton Bridge. Erin turned on the radio once on the road round Wastwater, and we ended up departing to the sound of Boney M. But maybe it's better that I close this chapter with a word from E. E. Cummings – with the proviso that the last line might run on 'to "Ra Ra Rasputin"'.

> when faces called flowers float out of the ground
> and breathing is wishing and wishing is having –
> but keeping is downward and doubting and never
> – it's april(yes,april;my darling)it's spring!
> yes the pretty birds frolic as spry as can fly
> yes the little fish gambol as glad as can be
> (yes the mountains are dancing together)[14]

The Dent Blanche

July 2015

As time passed and I was able to consider my Swiss trip with Tim at a distance, I began to think that I actually had an opportunity to revisit the Dent Blanche and attempt it again in a different way. This time, I would climb with a guide, experience that professional relationship from within, do everything properly – in the Swiss style – and finish the book on a high.

On 1 March 2015, I wrote to André to ask if we might climb the Dent Blanche together. I thought about the email for a couple of months before sending it because it felt so risky; a big thing to ask, important not to seem presumptuous – 'It would be a great privilege for me if you'd consider it, I hope you don't mind me asking' – what if André said no? What if he said, 'Ha! You're joking!? No.' What if he said nothing at all?

Rosula responded next day with the news that André had recently undergone an operation on his ankle. He'd broken it four times during his life, she said, most recently in the Himalaya, after which he'd had to walk ten days on it to reach help. He would still be recuperating during my visit in early July and so be unable to climb the Dent Blanche, she concluded.

I emailed back, offering my best wishes to André for a speedy recovery from what sounded like a series of grievously painful injuries and asking if they could recommend a local guide who could accompany me in his stead.

Rosula replied the same day; it *was* painful after the operation but had improved a great deal since. André had been in plaster for eight weeks and, though out of that now, could not work and so was resting, painting and reading at home. They could recommend a local guide, a good friend named Jean-Noël Bovier. Also, I was welcome to stay at La Giette or André's workshop in Les Haudères or, if I was looking for solitude, André's hut at Alpage de Tsaté – although this might be too far from a village if I had plans which involved seeing or meeting other people (*ever again?* A slightly concerned voice in my head puzzled. Just how remote was it?)

That night I wrote to introduce myself to Jean-Noël and ask if he'd be prepared to climb with me. An email next morning, in French: he'd spoken to André, he knew who I was. 'I know about the legacy of your ancestors who climbed the North Ridge with Joseph Georges. I will be happy and proud to take you to the Dent Blanche.' I'd only need minimum kit – shoes, crampons, a harness, rucksack, ice axe, helmet, gloves, etc. – he'd bring the rest.

He explained his fee, which I agreed to pay. I didn't quibble, I wrote it off as what the adventure cost, asked Faber for some more money, booked a flight to Geneva, made a cup of tea and marvelled at the modern world. The whole thing had taken four days – I'd found somewhere to stay (several places!), engaged a guide, arranged travel – there was something both comforting and unsettling in the ease with which one could lock down such a trip. Where Dorothy and Ivor arranged trips through telegrams, letters, travel agents and trunk telephone calls, I'd fired off a couple of emails and bounced around the internet. I hadn't spoken to anybody directly yet everything was set. Four months hence, in the first week of July, I would be back in Valais.

*****

On the morning of departure I left Bath in a plaid shirt and old jeans. My Haston pack stuffed, Chouinard axe and helmet strapped on the back.

No box! The ice axe went in the hold with the sack. My only hand luggage was a satchel and a book. I wore my mountain boots.

Once arrived at Geneva Airport, I made my way down to the station, bought a coffee and the same baguette of cheese and ham and tart of *crumble fruits rouges* as I had the September before and boarded the train to Sion.

Sion – pronounced like a fast car passing, or a bee past the ear, '*Siyon!*' I remembered how we couldn't discern the name in the train announcements the first time, awaiting an announcement for 'Sea-on' which never came.

A clear blue hot day. I knew what was ahead and what to look out for, which side of the carriage to sit. Mont Blanc looming like a giant albino kraken beyond Lake Geneva.

The lack of stress to be by oneself and returning somewhere, *going back* – cognisant of the world to come – a happy lazy traveller; pondering the apparently insoluble mystery of Swiss plug sockets; watching distracted people smoke on shaded station platforms, eyes fixed on destination boards; the stern searching faces of children, the train skimming like a stone over the lake like the swish of the word Sion, '*Siyon,*

siyon, siyon . . .' The reassurance and momentum of the train. The blink and rhythmic flick of shadows – trackside trees and pylons, stations, the flashing linear blur of passing trains. Fresh-cut grass embankments, a winning lack of fences, fields of toasting corn, the heat of noon sun. A bright orange villa. A frog-faced turret on the way out of Lausanne.

Round the crescent fish-shaped lake we ran – Geneva, Lausanne, Montreux – onto the green tongue of the Rhône valley and down to Martigny. Striped red-and-white factory chimneys, roads swinging off on sculptural chevron concrete legs. Lines and lines of vines grown wherever they'd take, a hardworking landscape and, always beneath the soil, breaking out above the upswing of the forest slopes, the escalating rock.

* * * * *

Sat on a bench outside Sion Post Office, I watched people and buses come and go beneath the wooden canopy of the bus station, honeycomb above the bumblebees. I ate some teabread, baked and wrapped in foil by my mother – a cousin of the cakes she used to make for my father when he went on expeditions to Svalbard and the like: a brown-paper parcel of teabread wrapped in foil and newspaper (for the team to eat and read), a letter and a tin of Fortnum's Earl Grey. It also echoed Joseph Georges's tin of pears, and Ivor's bottles of champagne – comestibles carried and proffered at the top. I had the idea that Jean-Noël and I would eat teabread from home on the summit of the Dent Blanche . . . however, it was too big to take as was, so I ate a great chunk sat there in Sion bus station, thinking of the summit, to help.

On the bus I deployed my trademark terrible French to

ask if I could be dropped off near La Giette, please. Luckily
I had my map, which helped the confused driver a lot. Yes,
he said, once we found it on the page, then pushed a lot of
seemingly random buttons and printed me a ticket which
said somewhere else.

The Dent Blanche reared immediately the bus climbed
into Val d'Hérens. I was stunned by its glaring blatancy.
Where had we been looking on the journey up the first
time? And so white. It hung there and we drove towards it,
up the approach toward the North Arête.

The bus set me down at Grandpra, beyond and above
Les Haudères. The day was still and baking and the soles of
my boots grew hot on the small road doubling back toward
La Giette. I could hear the three-tone horn of the bus sound
as it approached an unseen hairpin bend en route to Arolla.

The track which ran beyond the road was dusty, snaking
on a contour beneath blue pines. There ahead was *Yak shu lo
ché*, set up above the road, and the figure of André sat outside his house, waving, great arm aloft.

When I arrived, André was standing, enormous as ever,
with the aid of crutches. He shook my hand, slapped my back
and poured me a glass of wine. We sat together at the table
outside his front door, looking across at the mountain which
dominated everything else, compelling the eye. The
Mountain. Apex of the book and so many climbing lives – or
'life' as a climber might say. Funny to be back but also perfectly natural, this is what people do with the Dent Blanche:
they see it, in books or photographs perhaps, they visit to see
for themselves, perhaps look from neighbouring peaks, and
then they return time and again to attend and attempt it however they can. It absorbs and preoccupies, lives in the mind,
whether, like André, one has grown up in its shadow or, like

Dorothy and Ivor, become enchanted from afar. Such feelings are normal because the object is so extraordinary – an Alpine monarch, a unique and beautiful mountain. All of this was in André's cool gaze that afternoon as he looked across the gulf of air between La Giette and the Dent Blanche. Of course I was back, the happy silence said. It was understood. A Georges and a Richards sat together regarding the Dent Blanche for the first time in forty years.

* * * * *

When I'd asked André where I should pitch my tent, he'd explained that La Giette was too steep for tents so I'd best stay in the house. He showed me to a bed in the corner of the main room, a cushioned nook beside an open window where Rosula had set up a telescope so she could watch her yaks above Alpage de Tsaté. André turned the telescope to scan the hillside beyond La Sage – there's Rosula, he said after a moment, motioning me to look. Across the valley I saw a single figure in a rectangle of steep meadow, working to cut the grass with a machine which looked like a hammer-head trimmer or a lobster mower; slowly walking it side to side, leaving a pale green wake. She'll be home soon for lunch, said André, so I put my bags on the bed, changed my shoes and shirt and returned outside to find him preparing food. Cheese, cured meat and bread, apricots, wine and juice – rinds and skins dropped onto the flagstones to feed attentive Anuun, an Australian shepherd–border collie cross, and two peacocks who strutted around La Giette, imperious and highly strung.

Rosula arrived a few minutes later, driving along the track towards us in a small utility jeep like a 4x4 golf cart. She was brown as a nut in a floppy sun hat and singlet, shorts, rolled-down socks and hiking boots. The back of the jeep was full of rakes, pitchforks and ratchet straps.

Would I mind helping since I was staying during harvest, I was asked. Of course, I said, absolutely. André noted it would build me up for the Dent Blanche – a phrase that recurred throughout the week ahead; whatever I was doing was 'good practice for the mountain.' That ever-present mountain over there; like jogging within sight of the Olympic torch or preparing for a driving test round the village streets of Silverstone.

That night, at supper, I met Jean-Noël. He arrived bearing wine, a kiss for Rosula, a smiling solemn handshake with André and an enthusiastic greeting for me. It was obvious that he held André in the highest esteem. A few days later, driving towards La Sage to begin the walk to Rossier, he told me how honoured he felt to have climbed with André – a legendary figure, now a friend. In fact, the first time I met Jean-Noël was in the pages of *Une vie pour la montagne*, photographed on the Dent Blanche's precipitous north face as one of the young guides who reclimbed André's super-direct route with him in winter conditions.

Jean-Noël was about my height, five foot ten. He was tanned, swarthy, lean, tough, sharp-featured, his hands strong and calloused. His smile, when he deployed it, was engaging and bright. His eyes had laughter lines, a wry face; he had a habit of holding one's gaze whilst talking – speaking excellent English in short bursts, intercut with encouraging instructional noises and cartoon sound effects.

'We go up like this, *zzzp zzzp zzzp*,' he buzzed at one point on the Dent Blanche, moving his pointed finger in a zigzag, 'there there there,' up the rocks. He also possessed, I was to learn, a seemingly infinite stock of expletives, snorts of contempt, exasperated gestures, pitying looks and myriad ways of rolling his eyes which cut me to the quick. But I liked him immediately, that first night at dinner, and hoped he liked me too. We spoke about the weather forecast for the coming week and how fit I was feeling, resolving to climb the Dent Blanche over the weekend, walking up to Rossier from Ferpècle on Friday morning, ascending the mountain and returning to La Giette on the Saturday.

* * * * *

For the next few days I spent my mornings writing, sat with a notebook at the table in the main room, helping to bring in the harvest in the afternoons. Waking shortly after dawn – Rosula and André already having left to begin the day's work – I'd make tea and stand by the window and watch the shadows of the opposite hillside cut diagonal and dark across Les Haudères. As the sun gained height above Pointe du Prélet and Pointe du Tsaté, the valley was revealed and all the tiny cabins, barns, chalets and shingle-roofed boxes picked out. The patches of bright green meadow amongst woodland and swathes of forest below the couloirs, cliffs and scree, all freshly minted and clearly defined in the early morning light; and above, radiant and dominating all, was the Dent Blanche.

The week as a whole was beautifully clear, still and hot, perfect for harvesting the various small precipitous meadows Rosula and André were responsible for. First, the grass was cut with the special mechanical bug hedge-trimmer machine – which Rosula told me cost more than her car – then left to dry in lines on the ground known as swaths, turned once or twice as necessary. On the second or third day, the swaths were collected together with long rakes like school brooms and tarpaulins before being dragged and forked onto trailers and trucks. As the dry grass mounted, piled up unfeasibly high, the ratchet straps which held it down created two bulging hemispheres so it looked like André was towing a series of hay brains back to La Giette.

The harvesting was strenuous work and reminded me once again how physically fit and energetic Rosula and André were. Even convalescing and half-hobbled, André was abler than I, forking grass up into the barn more swiftly than I could get it to his feet. One of the side effects of his lack of English and my lack of French was that any complaints or instructions went via Rosula. Hence, whilst it had at first seemed that he was shouting rather a lot at Rosula whilst waving a rake about on the hillside earlier in the day, his frustration was actually directed at me and was translated and passed on (in a slightly sugar-coated form, possibly) – could I please rake everything together better and quicker, please?

'Dan, you need to be faster,' Rosula now called down from her position in the attic. 'André's complaining that he's having to collect his own grass.' But eventually it was done and we'd walked up to the house for dinner. Each day several neighbours or friends would turn out to help cut or gather in the hay and Rosula would furnish them with food and drink to thank them for their labour. In this way the evening meals became the time to relax and talk, sat outside on the flagstone terrace, bathing in the last of the sun, cheerfully tired and content with the sense of a job well done.

These were the times when I spoke to André most during my stay. It was over such a meal that he told me about the only time he'd seen his great-uncle Joseph. André was in

La Forclaz with his father, he remembered, about seven years old. Joseph was sitting in front of a barn and, although not exactly sure who he was, André felt that Joseph must be an important person because his father spoke to him with such respect. That was the only time.

Another night we drove down to Les Haudères for pizza, sat beneath the sheer pine prow of Petit Dent de Veisivi which towered bottle-green in the dusk. Over food I was told how André had once been called out to climb up there to find an injured party of mountaineers. There were two of them, said Rosula – it was really bad weather, they'd got lost, one had fallen and broken his leg. When André found them *they* were worried he was on his own, she laughed. He'd been out in a thunderstorm climbing and scouring the mountain all night – 'All night,' chipped in André for emphasis – and the first thing they said was 'Why is the helicopter not coming!?' André carried the hurt man down across his shoulders, guiding the other, until they met fellow guides out on the search and, together, got everyone to this very pizzeria, where the man with the broken leg was treated, splinted and dosed on analgesia to such a degree that he insisted on staying and buying everyone drinks for several hours before going to hospital.

I picture André, climbing alone, picking his way up the vertiginous streaming woods above us in the dark, *all night in a thunderstorm*, to be met by people upset he wasn't a helicopter. Maybe they had to shout the question several times to be heard above the thunder, 'Why is the helicopter not coming!?' As if the miraculous appearance of a man, the spearhead of rescue effort emerging out of the darkness, were somehow disappointing. Listening to the story I felt bad for my urge to thump the pillock Catalonians my last time in the Alps. This was so much worse; these two had been in serious trouble, got lost, fallen, broken, stuck, and then objected to the type of rescue party sent out.

Standing there, saturated and tired, perhaps André too considered boxing their ears, but no, he probably shrugged, told them it was too wet for helicopters, patched them up as best he could, carried and led them down. In short, rescued them, just as Joseph did repeatedly in both *Climbing Days* and Dorothy Thompson's *Climbing with Joseph Georges*.

* * * * *

The next morning broke with the scream of fighter jets. The Swiss army must be on manoeuvres in the area, André explained, and it must be a big deal because they'd got *both* jets out flying. The two flew low over us, up to Arolla, banking round behind the Dent Blanche and on towards Brig. They did this several times like wasps in a greenhouse. Switzerland is such a small country their jets never hit top speed for fear of overshooting the boarders, observed André, before driving off down to Les Haudères to see a mechanic about one of his harvesting machines, which had broken and was currently marooned precariously in a meadow high above La Giette. I went back inside to my writing. The Dent Blanche, I noted, was noticeably darker than at the start of the week. Only the north wall was fully white now, the top and right-hand side looked shadowed and foily, although snow still shrouded the long run south to the Ferpècle glacier, the route I'd be climbing in two days time. I thought back to the conditions on the mountain the last time I'd been there – the overcast cloud, the snow, the benighting, the dark, the cold – the warmth of the day seemed to deny such things were possible. Seen from the window of *Yak shu lo ché* through rising air and sheer summer sun, it was strange to think it was the same beast. I half wondered if there'd be any snow left come Saturday at all or whether it would all have evaporated in the soupy heat.

* * * * *

Jean-Noël collected me from La Giette shortly after breakfast on the Friday, which dawned fresh and clear as ever. The rumour of a thunderstorm had not come to pass. On the steps outside the cabin we gravely inspected my kit, the crampons that I'd borrowed from a friend in London, axe, leather boots – no, the boots were causing concern. 'You see this,' Jean-Noël said, twisting them this way and that, 'this is no good. Your sole isn't rigid. Your crampons will fall off.'

André disappeared into the cellar and returned with a pair of his own boots which fitted the bill and, remarkably, my feet. Rosula then insisted that I take a pair of yak-hair socks since my wool ones were old and had holes. Helmet, harness, all were nodded through and then we were sat in Jean-Noël's Volvo, waving goodbye and driving down to get provisions from the Les Haudères stores.

We purchased protein (cheese, sausages), salts (mixed nuts), some bread, some chocolate too. Jean-Noël bought an energy drink so I did too; it seemed good practice to follow his lead.

On the drive to Ferpècle Jean-Noël told me about his family and the way the life of the mountain guides had clashed with the strongly conservative Catholic sensibilities of the region. Guides were exposed to new, foreign, liberal influences through their work, he explained. They were independent and travelled more, sometimes abroad. They met outsiders, learnt foreign languages, had their eyes opened to different ways of living and thinking, so they were always viewed with slight suspicion, like peculiar exotic cousins. His mother had not been happy *at all* at the thought of her son becoming a Swiss Guide, even though there had been mountain guides in the family for generations. But he *had* become a guide, he told me, smiling as he drove, the winter season was just over and he'd been out skiing with clients all over the region, driving several hours each day sometimes – some new, some returning, all sorts of nationalities, ages and abilities. Hard work, I said. 'Oh yes!' he told me. 'Oh yes, hard work but that's good. You have to take the work when it's there because here the snows go and then,' he drums his hand on the steering wheel for emphasis, 'then we have to do other things.'

This year they didn't open the ski lift at La Forclaz for the first time since it was built in the 1960s, Jean-Noël told me. Not enough snow. Then he described how he and Dédé skied down to Les Haudères from Rossier a couple of winters ago – off-piste, off the glacier and down the valley, fizzing over meadows, along roads, through fields, mile after mile – it sounded fantastic, close to flight, the sort of run where everything needs to align, the weather, the landscape and the people. 'You need to be tip-top,' Jean-Noël told me in the car, 'tip-top to do such things.'

We parked above Ferpècle at the end of the road and kitted up to walk the several hours to Rossier. I saw that Jean-Noël had a compact rucksack into which he packed the ropes and other bits we'd need, together with his crampons, food, jacket and the rest. Lastly, he strung his axe neatly on the back.

The day was hot. We were both dressed in T-shirts. I'd

slathered up all week in Sherpa Tensing suncream and borrowed Rosula's sun hat to shield my head and neck.

On the steepening path below Bricolla, discussing the madness of Fifa, we bumped into two dozen chamois goats on the path. We waded through them, cheerfully, as they nibbled and peered at us with their yellow keyhole eyes, but then they started following. At first it was fine, a sort of awkward skittering herd of rubbernecks, but after a mile or so Jean-Noël was losing patience and lobbing the occasional warning rock. 'Go away!' we shouted. '*Allez-vous en!*' This seemed to encourage them. 'I just cannot bring myself to beat them,' Jean-Noël confided in a embarrassed tone – as if this was both a moral failing on his part and the obvious answer to our predicament – but the curious goats eventually lost interest and trailed off towards the shuttered Bricolla hotel to find somebody else to pester.

Next came the crazed glaucoma of the Ferpècle Glacier, rising splayed and shattered like a stoved-in windscreen, and I asked Jean-Noël if we could stop so I could look and he acquiesced slightly reluctantly – because he wanted to get up to Rossier *today*, I sensed, '*Zzzp zzzp zzzp*', direct and fast, but I, having never been this way before except in wired retreat, wanted to take it all in. So I did, I sat and had a drink and took it in a minute, aware of Jean-Noël's itch to move and the proximity of the summit, that metal cross unseen, up there, the fulcrum of the book.

A month later, working to finish the manuscript in London, I went to an evening of readings organised by English PEN. The poet Jack Underwood stood up and read a series of poems from his recent book, *Happiness*, and one of them transported me back to that moment overlooking the Ferpècle Glacier with the imminence of the Dent Blanche hanging above us, caught between these two elemental vaults of rock and ice:

Sometimes your sadness is a yacht

huge, white and expensive, like an anvil
dropped from heaven: how will we get onboard,
up there, when it hurts our necks to look?[1]

* * * * *

The Rossier guardian was lovely. All my fears proved unfounded. Jean-Noël had sorted everything out by the time I arrived at the cabin, having arrived some fifteen minutes ahead of me, since the altitude had bitten on the upper reaches of the glacier and my final drag took a long time for panting and blundering, feeling the familiar drunk jet-lag fatigue descend.

But when I arrived up the rock pile and icy steps to the prayer-flagged platform he was already settled in, asking if I'd like a drink and something hot to eat. We sat outside on a bench overlooking the scarred and pitted icefall, and ate hot rösti with sausage and eggs whilst discussing the dorsal range stood behind Mont Miné, which features the pinnacle of Aiguille de la Za and culminates in Dent de Veisivi.

Signing in, Jean-Noël kept repeating my name aloud to be mischievous, knowing my chagrin about the events of the previous year. 'Stop it, Jean-Noël!' I hissed out the corner of my mouth, but the guardian just smiled. All was well – I had a guide! She clearly assumed I'd turned over a new leaf and was now a responsible and viable mountaineer, if she thought anything at all.

After the rösti I went upstairs for a nap. This too was standard practice, Jean-Noël told me: first rösti, then a nap. Eating well and sleeping to let the body acclimatise and manufacture more red blood cells, these were key things to do. So I crawled under rugs in the dormitory atop Rossier, vaguely aware of the opalescent light shifting across the pale wood walls and ceiling, and other residents arriving, unpacking and settling down to nap around me, sated with rösti, bone marrow whirring.

Then, a few hours later, we all stomped down to dinner – bouillon soup, lasagna, a whole peach for pudding. I was quiet, thinking of the next day. Jean-Noël seemed similarly pensive although he made an effort to include me in his conversations with the other guides and clients, translating the French and referring kindly to me and my family's past on the mountain. I felt strangely muted and apart from it all – tensed like I used to be as a child at home on Sunday nights, after tea and *Antiques Roadshow*, faced with another school week, filled with a kind of sickly dread, knowing I'd homework due.

After the meal I went to sit in the corner where Dorothea and Ivor had been photographed after the centenary celebrations of 1966 – the picture that made it onto postcards, Ivor writing of a cosy restorative meal followed by a snooze 'after a long cold spell of standing at ceremonies in a Blizzard'.[2]

I smiled to think of them. Almost there, I thought. Tomorrow we'll see.

Then almost everyone went to bed, having checked and laid out their gear in the boot room for the morning; the dormitory settling down from whispers and rustling to regular breathing, soft snoring and the silence of people staring at the dark ceiling, waiting.

* * * * *

The first people left at about 2 a.m. I was aware of their movements and leaving but did not stir myself, although could not regain sleep thereafter. When the call came it was the main call with torches at 3.30. I sat up, steeled. The last hour had been a rehearsal of everything to come as best I could envision it, calling back the breakfast, kit room, feel of walking with crampon points on stone and snow, the prickle of the cold around one's face, ears and neck – that frisson of elation at the unique crystal day, yet to start. I felt the thrill of being up out and doing whilst everyone else was asleep and recalled the sound of boots on hard snow, that fulsome crunch, the feel of wrists in strapped jacket cuffs, the tacky tactile feel of gloves.

Dressed and restless, I went down to breakfast, having hardly the patience to butter the dry toast and apply the thick jam but we all did it, huddled over the trestles in the low light, layering on the cheeses, hunched gulping sugared coffee in taut silence as, outside, the deep sky still set darkest indigo.

Then, having eaten, we pulled on our boots and stepped into harnesses. In a strange way it reminded me of playing cricket – the concrete-floored pavilions, the rubbery smell of the kit, the feel and shape of it all, elasticated strapping, the bulkiness; having to alter my gait to work around it all. The sense of expectation and unspoken pressure, the certainty of having to walk out and be attacked, tested and judged . . . the knowledge that I actually wasn't very good at cricket but now it was too late.

Climbing above the Grand Gendarme, the Dent Blanche, July 2015 (Jean-Noël Bovier)

* * * * *

Jean-Noël was waiting for me on the terrace. He seemed on edge, testy. He inspected my fastenings and yanked my harness a couple of times to check its strength, then tied us together and led the way past the hut and behind to start the ascent.

My memory of the next hour is of climbing in the blue dark, the way lit hard-white by our head torches, the hypnotic crunching of our feet on hard snow and the charged total silence of the mountain. We left Rossier by the same route as I had before, round the back to the rock buttress, over the rock outcrop and up to the snow, but the snows felt

Near the top of the Dent Blanche, July 2015 (Jean-Noël Bovier)

harder, seemed to work for us this time, and we strode on and seemed to move higher, faster than the first time, without belays, reaching the easing snowfield in quick time, keeping left; zagging up the triangle of the main ridge direct rather than looping around the back to the loose rock junkyard. Up, as the sky began to ghost pink at the edges; I remember being out of breath and asking to stop a moment and Jean-Noël telling me no, we'd stop later, this was nothing, this was a mushroom pasture, an old woman's donder. So we didn't stop, and we didn't stop much all day. I gasped in the higher altitude – 'Breathe more, fill your lungs,' instructed Jean-Noël. We put our crampons on for the first time high on the western flank as the day began to break, and I found the hard ice tricky, unable to match Jean-Noël's economy of movement and thought, missing my footing several times, spikes catching in gaiters, fumbling with my axe – failing to tuck it back into my bag straps, muttering – feeling his annoyance through the rope, redoubling my efforts to be better, listening to the rhythm of our spiked feet scraping, punching on.

At some point Jean-Noël took umbrage at my ineptitude in crampons. High on the mountain, when the light was well up, he announced that he thought we should probably go back because I wasn't good enough and this was no place to learn. He said it flatly, as if it was rhetorical. I was aghast and stunned. I refused, apologised, promised to try harder – possibly not in that order. We weren't going back, I said; he was not taking me back down now. We went on.

At times he seemed to be purposefully cranking up the pressure, stood silent scornful or criticising: this was ridiculous, Dan, he had thought I was competent. More to the point, this was not even tough! 'One could take a donkey up here . . .' he said at one point; that remains to be seen, I thought. Then he began to refer to me as 'Mr Richards':

'This is a forking serious mountain, Mr Richards.'

'You are not really good enough to be here, Mr Richards.'

'This is no place to learn, Mr Richards.'

'You are walking like a drunk man, Mr Richards, surely you cannot be forking tired!?'

I moved through a range of responses – desperation, angst, stubborn silence, anger – Jean-Noël seemed to positively invite my hostility, or perhaps he didn't care and it didn't touch him? Whilst I'd been keen to explore the guide–client dynamic this wasn't really what I'd had in mind. Was it a regular tactic he employed with inexperienced clients, I brooded? Tough love honed to make me redouble my efforts?

Dan Richards and Jean-Noël Bovier, Cabane de la Dent Blanche (Rossier), July 2015 (Marlyse Vuadens)

I felt like correcting him: 'Actually, Mr Richards is my dad. If you want to chastise me, use my full name, Daniel. No one ever calls me *Daniel* unless I'm in trouble.'

I climbed the dry rock sections well, he was happy with that. I got a slap on the back and a 'Yes, Dan!' at the top of one hard section but then, straight away, why wasn't I watching him closer? I should be putting my feet where he was putting his feet. Concentrate, Mr Richards! And so I spent the climb in a heightened state of tension – keen to please, deferential, pushing myself to keep his high pace, scrambling and following, doing as I was told until, day fully dawned, stood on a cornice, he pointed and said, 'There you are.'

The cross. God, I thought, that was quick! That was bloody fast. *Zzzp zzzp zzzp!* I shook Jean-Noël's hand. 'This

is what you get with a Swiss Guide,' he told me, grinning
for the first time all day. 'We get you there, *zzzp.*'

* * * * *

En route down, we passed other parties, including some
who'd woken up at two. A German group, a French woman
climbing with two guides, a couple of others, but the mountain was quiet, wind low, sky clear.

Below the steepling Grand Gendarme, a helicopter
whumped overhead, circling round from the west. A minute later it was back, curving away before returning again.
Jean-Noël stopped to watch it. Something must have happened up top, he said. Then we carried on down, rappelling
about fixed points below the main spine ridge, Jean-Noël
anchoring and lowering me first before turning and bouncing down himself. The snows had softened in the warming
day and the route back felt unsettled underfoot. Now my
boots sank deeper, first to the ankle, then to the knee, later
up to my waist, so the descent became harder going as it
went on and felt far longer than the climb – but half of that
had taken place in a kind of dreamy darkness, when the air
was freezing cold and the ground set hard as the rocks to
come.

It transpired that Jean-Noël had not slept since we'd arrived
at Rossier. Without sleep he's a monster. Without sleep, he's
a grizzly bear. In retrospect I wonder if the fact we went up
without helmets was actually because he was sure we
wouldn't need them or because bleak insomnia had made
him lose the will to live and me with him by default.

Later, back at Rossier, other guides marvelled at the

treatment he'd doled out to me – they laughed. No, it wasn't normal, they said. He'd been cruel if anything, at the very least! But by then the Stockholm Syndrome had taken root: I defended all of it – no, he'd been quite right, I wasn't good enough but he'd got me up there, in spite of myself.

When Jean-Noël said I should have climbed the smaller mountains *around* the Dent Blanche for a couple of seasons before tackling something so serious, he wasn't wrong, that's what people used to do. Indeed that's what Dorothy and Ivor did, climbing everything, climbing the Dent Blanche several times by several routes over several seasons, always circling it with an eye on that North Arête. André might have shinned up the Ferpècle Ridge at sixteen but he was special, a prodigy. Tim's climb of the Ferpècle Ridge in 1981, aged thirty, on his first visit to the Dent Blanche, working from his route book, had impressed Jean-Noël when I'd told him, but such things were obviously only impressive if they came off!

André later told me that, in times past, a guide would put a client through their paces to ascertain their level, see if they were good enough for, say, the Dent Blanche. Jean-Noël hadn't done that. He'd taken it on trust, and I had been good enough, as it turned out: up the normal route with a good kicking.

Once back at Rossier, Jean-Noël told me that I'd done well, and how he'd failed to climb a certain route on the Matterhorn five times before achieving success, thwarted each time by combinations of bad weather and poor conditions on the mountain. 'Sometimes it just doesn't go,' he told me over rösti, squeezing mustard from a large toothpaste-style tube – the sausage, eggs and fried potatoes arranged to form a smiling face on his plate. He was pleased we'd been two of the last climbers away in the morning but the first to reach the top and the first back for lunch. He also praised me for my efforts and noted that I hadn't seemed too badly shaken when I fell through a cornice shortly after we began the descent. No, I told him, I knew you'd be annoyed, having to brace and save my life like that, so I put it out my head and set about trying not to fall through any more . . .

The guardian told us that the helicopter had been for a couple of the climbers we'd passed on the way up, one of whom had lost a crampon on the summit and been unable to descend. Jean-Noël was not impressed. I imagined his reaction to a client of his losing a crampon down a mountain and grinned into my rösti. They wouldn't dare, I thought.

* * * * *

After eating, photographs, shaking hands and settling up with the guardian, Jean-Noël walked down on his own. I had decided to stay another night, to write and rest before descending next morning, making the most of my time on the mountain because, perhaps strangely, we hadn't stopped at the top very long at all. It hadn't turned out to be the end, only a moment halfway. We hit the summit like swimmers turning at the end of a length, head full of the return, a great gulp of air and then away. There was no celebratory tea-bread, it hadn't occurred or been missed. Instead, the small foil parcel was carried up and returned, untouched. I ate some now, with a coffee from the still-smiling guardian, brewed on the steaming machine behind her wooden bar. I sat alone in the corner with the postcard ghosts of Ivor and

Dorothea and drank it watching the figure of Jean-Noël disappear over the brim of the glacier, back through the bruised translucent ice and pit-pocked snow to the smooth rock piles and meadows, the waiting chamois on the slalom earth paths, down through the woods to his Volvo parked on the Ferpècle road.

He'd climbed the Dent Blanche over fifty times, he'd said. André reckoned he'd been up well over two hundred, alone and guiding, although he never kept a proper tally. Such a strange job. As Joseph said in that film I'd been shown in *Yak shu lo ché*: 'You become like brothers when you go to the mountains. And you will remember all your life the things you did together. When you're up in the mountains you don't think what's happening down below – you're in another world, away from everything. You're close to the sky, it's just happiness.'

It had been, I thought. That rang so true. Jean-Noël: the tormenting older brother I'd never known, the moments of the climb emblazoned on my mind now, for ever perhaps. That instant when he said, 'There you are.' The deadpan fact of it, the top, the cross, 'There you are.' My '*Je chouques!*' – I'd always remember that, the shock, the happiness, a split-second moment of transcendence, all else forgotten, a small taste of *beyond*, perhaps.

Epilogue

I walked down to Ferpècle next day after breakfast, leaving Rossier in bright sunshine, setting off down the glacier, alone. Long shadows sped ahead of me, over the snow, the only noise the crunch of my boots.

Later in the meadows, past the moonland boulder cirque and the glacial streams spilling lines through fluorescent ice, I rested by the shut Bricolla Alp Hotel and waited for a party on the path behind me to catch up. The group were a guide, his porter and their client – Rémi, Samuel and Gisèle – whom I'd met over dinner at the hut the night before. The four of us descended to Ferpècle together with the sun high and baking at our backs. An hour or so later, at the head of the road, I phoned André and he agreed to pick us all up in his truck. We trooped to the Hôtel du Col d'Hérens to wait there with a beer – 'My friend, André, is a great man, a great great climber!' I told them. 'Our families go back a long way . . .'

Twenty minutes later I experienced the impact of my friend André *turning up* – impressive even on crutches, charismatic and massive. And later, on the drive, I listened to the climbing chat between Rémi and André, the shy way the former asked the big man questions, aware that he was in the presence of a master. And André answering the younger man in his deep soft voice, the smiles and pauses, and the hush in the back seat as Samuel and Gisèle leant in to overhear.

'My friend, André.'

An hour later, back at *Yak shu lo ché*, André slapped my leg and congratulated me on my climb, as a fellow mountaineer. As a few days before, we ate bread and cheese and looked across to the Dent Blanche, but now *both* of us had scaled it – André, over two hundred times; me, one and a half.

I'd ache for a couple of days, he warned me, with a grin. All of me. If I didn't feel it yet, I would soon.

The next evening, Jean-Noël visited for raclette. He was all smiles (which was a relief) and it was a wonderful night. We all sat out under the stars to eat and talk about mountains and climbing. Later, after the cooking fire had died down, André got out his iPad and we watched the films he'd made of his expeditions and climbs on the Eiger and Makalu. He told us about the different members of his teams, some of whom had not come back. The Makalu pictures cut from André wearing branded shirts, tight eighties jeans and trainers, walking into the foyers of big Swiss banks to talk about sponsorship, to airports and tearful farewells, to lorries of supplies being unloaded by porters in tundric steeps. There are lots of shots of people smiling and giving thumbs-ups whilst snow blows horizontally across them – huddled in tents, braced on glacier, roped on sheer ice and rocks. A Russian man dances about a battered-looking stove in a sooty yurt, clapped by porters – he was a great guy, smiled André. He did not come back.

Towards the end, over aerial pictures of Makalu's broken serrate range, a French voiceover summed up the trip – at which point Jean-Noël turned around to me, excited, 'Did you hear it, Dan? She said, "Because it's there."'

Because it's there. Mallory's ontological piton on which so much, so many people hang.

'I notice that nowadays many retiring climbers take up painting as a means perhaps sometimes of still pursuing the old elusive question: What the hold that mountains have on people may be? Just as some try to analyse it in Diaries!' wrote Dorothy in 1956. 'I have sometimes felt that some people may climb as a way of dodging this question, not exploring it. And, maybe, to some climbers there is no such question at all, any more than there would be on a race track.'[1]

André had taken up painting whilst convalescing, I noted next day whilst packing my bags to return home. The Matterhorn, in rumpled worked oils, hung on the wall of *Yak shu lo ché*. A red web crisscrossed the picture, marking the routes he'd climbed in his prime.

* * * * *

On my return to England, I met up with Robert Macfarlane in the grounds of Emmanuel College, Cambridge. We discussed 'Because it's there' and the idea of *beyond*, both subjects he'd tackled in his book *Mountains of the Mind*. '"Because it's there" does the job,' he told me. 'The urge to climb is an ineffable, maddeningly strange impulse – or knot of impulses, I should say. Having written *Mountains*, I now tell people: there are three hundred pages which attempt to explain that phrase "Because it's there", but I'm not sure any of the reasons I give is better or more valid than any other!'

In his 1927 essay 'The Lure of High Mountaineering', Ivor has a go at unpicking the knot of the *why* but admits the difficulties early on. The average non-climber – *civilian*, I'm tempted to say – is hard put indeed to explain why any reasonable soul should wish to climb, 'or what anyone gets out of it so that he should keep at it with such stupid pertinacity': 'To go up one mountain would probably be an interesting experience, especially if it were the highest; to keep on climbing mountains seems to be mere silliness. To describe a passion to those who do not share it is a difficult enough task, let alone explaining it.'[2]

Mountaineering must seem, to the outside eye, 'particularly pointless', he notes; so much so that 'In this it perhaps stands alone.' Perhaps I felt this too, unconsciously, when I began on the adventure that became this book – following in the wake of people and a passion I did not fully comprehend. But I was to discover that, whilst the mountains stand alone, challenging and beguiling, the climbers and their stories form a strong and animate web – threads my father began to trace as a young man in the seventies and eighties and I, becoming engaged and venturing out and up, took up. Gradually, by talking to the Pinnacle Club ladies in their Snowdonian hut, revisiting Burnthwaite and the Fell & Rock meets in the Lakes, meeting my second cousins, Anthony and Chris, and reconnecting with the Swiss Guides of Valais, I followed *Climbing Days* back to source. The discovery of the fondness and esteem with which Dorothy and Ivor are still regarded in the valleys around Les Haudères will remain with me always. I don't think Tim or I have ever been so moved or delighted as in the two days which followed our night spent *à la belle étoile* on the Dent Blanche.

~

I came to appreciate the importance of Joseph Georges le Skieur in Dorothy and Ivor's story. One of my favourite

Joseph Georges,
c.1926 (RCM)

finds in the Magdalene archives was a very smart framed portrait of Joseph which Dorothy and Ivor apparently kept on their bureau in Wentworth House. They never forgot him, respected and held him dear always, the deepest of friendships forged in the mountains. Their adventures formed the apex of all their climbing lives. Without his help, knowledge and trust – together with his brother, Antoine – the Dent Blanche's North Arête would surely have remained forever out of reach, a dream.

I remember André's description of that climb, as told to him by Dorothy – four people: two Richards and two Georges on the crux twenty metres of the north face, the rock overhanging, the mesmeric drop. Antoine helping Joseph up, lifting him so he could climb and wedge an axe in a crack and stand upon its wooden shaft 'because there was nothing else to hold on to'. I imagine him stood there, framed against the sky, watched from below – stood on the handle of an axe! – banging in a piton for protection . . . the fulcrum of *Climbing Days* perhaps. And then '*Je chouques!*' He was there.

The reconnection with Joan Pralong, and the magical friendship I found with André and Rosula; the final climb with Jean-Noël: all these people transformed my mountain odyssey into a warm journey of discovery, making this book something more than a flat recapitulation of Dorothy's memoir; hopefully I've written a companion piece – a slightly mad, tangential adventure that sought to meet them in their element and, in so doing, developed a deeper love of both the mountain world and the pair themselves. So it seems apt to end here, in Cambridge, at the beginning; with Dorothy's final words from her preface to *Climbing Days*:

'Those of my fellow climbers who share a need to analyse our common passion will understand that this long attempt to explain a love of mountains yet ends with – Why?'

Ivor, Joseph and Dorothy. Bertol Hut, 1928 (Antoine Georges/RCM)

Appendix I: Obituaries

Joseph Georges (1892–1960)

Joseph Georges de Pierre, of La Forclaz above Les Haudères, was known as *Le Skieur*, because as a young boy he had made himself a pair of skis from a magazine picture – and was for some time the only ski-runner in the Val d'Hérens. There was a gay originality and initiative about his climbing and a mastery which impressed all who went with him. He had a modest but justified confidence in his powers and his judgment, which enabled him often to make ascents no one else would start for – and this without any rashness.

He was a compact, lightly-built man who on a path gave little sign of his inexhaustible strength. A simple-seeming, friendly face; but with piercing eyes which looked through and beyond you. On rock or ice, if they became exacting, he was suddenly released or possessed but always with the shrewdest professional care for the safety of the party.

His *Carnet* opens with two premonitory entries. The first (1919) is an ascent with Cornelis Tromp of the Dent Blanche, his neighbour peak, the scene of his chief triumph. The second is an admiring account by high officers in the Diablerets Section of the S.A.C. of a swift *solitary* ascent of the Za *par devant* which, they happened, from the Douves Blanches, to catch Joseph making. He was highly reticent about them, but there is little doubt that Joseph – like Klucker – was fond of lonely reconnaissances. At 11, he nipped off (he confessed to this) leaving Canon Girdlestone, his employer, sketching at the Pas de Chèvres, and traversed the Mt. Blanc de Seilon. A few years later, having been taken over the Col d'Hérens and told to go home via Sion, he filled in the time by a solitary high level exploration of the Zermatt glaciers, leading him somehow back to Bricolla. These were the errors of ignorant youth; he came to have the gravest suspicion of crevasses. The itch to see 'how it might go' could catch him out. On the North-east ridge of the Jungfrau in 1923, a rotten gendarme (since fallen) pushed him on to a solitary second ascent. Ours, next day, was the third. On the Boussine arête of the Comb in de Chessette (1925), to quote from his *Carnet*, 'Joseph left me to reconnoitre and found the rocks so difficult that he had no option but to continue to the summit. When he got back to me, from the first ascent across the South flank, a rainstorm drove us down to our bivouac.'* A similar threat probably explains his ascent with W. G. Standring of the North-west face of the Scheidegg Wetterhorn. Starting at 10.30 a.m. for a look at ground neither had seen, Joseph decided at a certain height that it would be safer to go on than to climb down that limestone in a rainstorm.

Looking through his *Carnet* one is struck by the return of certain themes: climbs seized between storms, infectious enthusiasm, cheerfulness, skill as a teacher, thoughtfulness, companionship, an amateur readiness to linger on summits to sundown, quickness and imperturbability in crises, mounting good humour through times of stress. Of a descent (with night out) of the Ferpècle ridge (1921) G. M. Bell recounts:

* *Alpine Journal* Vol. 37, p. 369. (Original footnote.)

'During the whole time of 32 hours he was unfailing in helpfulness and good humour.' Jean Gaspoz, as leading guide, had been disabled and Joseph had taken command: 'His quickness and attention prevented an accident caused by a stone from assuming fatal proportions.' In the night Bell fancied he saw a guardian angel taking care of Gaspoz. The idea of Gaspoz having '*un ange gardien*' was somehow ever after a source of inextinguishable mirth in Joseph.

The fifth entry (1919) is already prophetic: '*Il possède, entre de qualités qui en font le plus agréable camarade de course, une connaissance de la montagne (tant en ce qui concerne la neige que pour le rocher) qui lui acquerrait bientôt la réputation d'un des meilleurs guides Valaisannes. Puisse cette prophétie se réaliser au plus vite.*' (G. Colladon, ingr.) It was to be. In 1921 he made (with Myrtil Schwartz) the first ascent of the North-north-east arête of Mt. Collon, '*24 heures d'efforts ininterrompus*'. Joseph had a low opinion of this as a reasonable route. Later in the year (with Dorothy Pilley and I.A.R.) he made the first ascent from the Arolla glacier of the Pte. Sud des Bouquetins, with first descent of its East face. Next year (with R. B. Graham, R. S. T. Chorley and M. H. Wilson) the traverse of the Dent d'Hérens with descent to Breuil by the Col des Grandes Murailles to the Mont Tabor glacier. Joseph used to recall, wonderingly, how, in the steep couloir, seeing a stone coming straight for him '*J'ai sauté en pleine pente*' – to alight on one foot on a pebble stuck in the ice slope.

They returned over the Matterhorn (no other parties that snowy day) and back by the Quatre Ânes to the Bertol.

He was happiest on ground he had never seen before, and the Montanvert peaks and glaciers that year (1922) were as often as not in cloud. It was characteristic of him that when his party was taking a needed poor weather rest-day, he could not resist taking John Pilley over the Grépon with 'a stiff storm on the summit'. Thenceforward he was to range widely, visiting most parts of the Alps.

In 1924, the Graians: the North ridge of the Grivola, then all ice, gave him perhaps his biggest feat in step-cutting, 6½ hours.

In 1925 (with I.A.R.): first south to north traverse of all the peaks of the Bouquetins; (with Dorothy Thompson) down from Mt. Blanc via Mt. Maudit and Mt. Blanc du Tacul to the Torino after bad weather – 'no other party on that day'. At the Aiguille du Goûter Cabane the night before: 'at 9.30 p.m. Joseph descended alone to search for 3 people calling for help – About 1.30 a.m. he returned, laden with rucksacks, having brought a chilled and exhausted party up on the rope in complete darkness, the lantern being blown out ten minutes after he left the hut.'

In 1926: the Dent Blanche with a novice he was teaching (J. H. Hannah) – 'in spite of the opinion of the local guides that it would not be possible for a week' – and the Zmutt arête under similar conditions . . . 'When his own client is settled in Club huts, he lends his help to any caravan present.'

In 1927 (with R. Ogier Ward): first ascent of the Mer de Glace face of the Aiguille de Leschaux with descent to the glacier de Frébouzie and Col des Hirondelles. In 1928 (with his brother Antoine Georges, Dorothy Richards and I.A.R.): first ascent of North arête of the Dent Blanche. 'Bricolla, 1.00 a.m. Col du Grand Cornier, 5 a.m. Surplomb, 10.30–1.30 p.m. Summit, 5–5.20 p.m. Foot of S. Arête, 7.15 p.m.'

With this 'a hope shared with J.G. for many years was realised and his genius found its full expression'.

In 1929 (with Dorothy Thompson and Meyseiller Marcel as porter): Brouillard arête, Mont Blanc; untracked, unknown ground, 'arêtes on Mt. Blanc de Courmayeur covered with iniquitous snow'. Later, a big sampling of Dolomite climbing with Winifred Murray, Joseph going off by himself to do the Kleine Zinne by the Zsigmondy Kamin, Winkler Thurm by Winklerreis traverse (in 30 minutes), Fünffingerspitze No. 3 by Sudwand, in between neighbouring climbs. In 1930 (with the same): spring climbing in Corsica. July (with Ella Mann): Bregaglia; Il Galla direct from South col Ago di Sciora in much snow.

August (with W. G. Standring): North-west face of the Scheidegg Wetterhorn. August 24 (with J. M. K. Vyvyan): 'Charmoz-Grépon, including the first ascent (as an experiment) without artificial aids of the Grand Gendarme on the Grépon, by a chimney and flake on the Nantillons side'. 26th: 'starting from the Tour Rouge (with porter Junien of Chamonix) we traversed the Grépon from the Mer de Glace side to the Nantillons, descending by the couloir Charmoz-Grépon, climbing the Grand Gendarme and passing on to the summit by the Cheminée Knubel.' Sept. 5 (with J. M. K. Vyvyan and A. E. Foot): Mont Blanc *via* Dames Anglaises, Aiguille Blanche, Grand Pilier d'Angle, left Gamba at midnight, reached Grands Mulets 7 p.m.

Then come gaps in his *Carnet*. Entries are filled in later and many ascents are no doubt missing. He cared little about it. In 1932 he was triumphing with the Comte de Grunne and the Mission Scientifique Beige on the Ruwenzori peaks from the Belgian Congo side. In 1933 (with Molly FitzGibbon) he did the first complete traverse of the Hornli ridge of the Eiger, from Bonern to the Mittellegi and repeated the North-west face of the

Wetterhorn. In 1934 (with Molly FitzGibbon) he repeated the Bouquetins traverse. In 1935 (with Molly FitzGibbon and G. R. Speaker); the Ryan route on the Plan. In 1933 (with Dorothy Thompson and Meyseiller Marcel); Mt. Blanc by the Bionnassay, descent by the Peuterey (first combination of these arêtes) 'nearly 34 hours' climbing – delayed by the treacherous condition – unexpected recent snowfall at the Grand Pilier d'Angle and the icy condition of the rocks above the Col de Peuterey which involved abandoning the ordinary route.') 1935 (the same); Mt. Blanc by the Innominata; icy conditions, Grands Mulets 9 p.m.

In the following years Joseph's detachment from his *Carnet*, and perhaps his shyness of it shows. His friends can testify that it was rarely available. By 1942 his health was failing. And with that he withdrew as firmly as he had advanced, turning to farming and to the building of a model chalet for his sisters, for whom he would seek in Aosta the choicest of traditional ribbons. He never married.

Three more notes from the *Carnet*: 'Joseph Georges being not only a model instructor but a perfect companion with whom one would wish to climb indefinitely' (H. W. A. Freese-Pennefather, J. M. K. Vyvyan, Quintin Hogg). 'I have never enjoyed any two days of my life more than these last two; and this is entirely due to him' (Godfrey Nicholson), from an absolute beginner, after the Petite Dent de Veisivi and the Za *en face*. The last entry: '*Tout le long de ces journées, la joie et la bonne humeur et la jouissance de la montagne ont formé un lien solide entre nous*' (E. and E. Aebi, La Forclaz, Sept. 1942).

I. A. RICHARDS, *Alpine Journal*, 1961

Ivor Armstrong Richards, CH (1893–1979)

Ivor Armstrong Richards was born at Sandbach in Cheshire in 1893, not a great distance from the Welsh hills which he learned to know and love in boyhood. As a Cambridge undergraduate and young don, he lost his heart to the crags. He was an inveterate designer of new routes. Many remained theoretical but not all. The Holly Tree Wall on Idwal Slabs was worked out by him with C. F. Holland. Dorothea Pilley, later to become his wife, was with them. It was a typical perfectionist enterprise discarding and incorporating variants until at a later date it was finalized to Ivor's satisfaction. Dorothea remarks: 'He had great pleasure in telling his second (me) how to do an awkward move as though he were analysing a mathematical problem'. Good craftsmanship was at the heart of his delight in mountaineering, particularly in the Alps where so many different skills combine. It is the underlying theme of his superb essay 'The Lure of High Mountaineering'. I still recall his displeasure when I clumsily destroyed the outer edge of a snowstep on some traverse. Objectively, it did not much matter in that particular place. He minded the clumsiness. A well-made snowstep deserved to be respected like a well-made poem.

Though not perhaps one of the handful of great guideless leaders of the 20s and 30s, his talent for planning expeditions was of a high order and he and Dorothea made a remarkable team, picking up peak after peak, often traverses, as the seasons went by, mostly alone but sometimes with friends. Once or twice they had the rare pleasure of making a new route from some little frequented quarter. Such was the ascent of the rock spire of the Becca Rayette by the big unclimbed ridge running up from the Val Sassa. It cost them a fearsome descent in the dark of the Upper Chardonney glacier followed by a night out and a dawn descent into the Valpelline.

1921 found them at Arolla. They climbed the Aiguille de la Za carrying on with a traverse of the extended crest of the Douves Blanches dropping down to the N Col de Bertol. Here, they were met by a young guide who explained that he had seen them on the long ridge, guessed they might be thirsty and had brought them a flask of hot tea. This was Joseph Georges le Skieur. They made friends at once and engaged Joseph for a week which finished with the Ferpècle Ridge of the Dent Blanche and a new route up the Petit Bouquetin from the Arolla glacier. So began one of the great guide-client partnerships. In succeeding seasons they did many fine expeditions with Joseph. I name 3 for their difficulty and/or diversity. The NE ridge of the Jungfrau, a second ascent. The summits of Monte Rosa to the SignalKuppe, followed after a rest-day at the Cabane Margherita by the traverse of the Lyskamm and over Castor down to the Schwarzhorn. The N ridge of the Grivola, that year (1924) a shining curve of ice which entailed more than 6 hours continuous step-cutting for Joseph. In 1928 came the climax, the longed-for unclimbed N ridge of the Dent Blanche, an achievement splendidly described in Dorothea's book *Climbing Days*.

Ivor's professional career began brilliantly at Cambridge in the 1920s. He became a Fellow of Magdalene in 1926 and was one of the key figures in building up the English School and in a revolutionary approach to literary criticism. He was also deeply involved with C. K. Ogden in the invention and use of Basic English.

But, all told, Richards spent many years away from Europe. Ivor held a chair at Peking 1929–1930 and from 1936–38 he was director of the Orthological Institute of China.

Wherever they went they sought out mountains and in Yunnan they made first ascents of Gymaloko (6100m) and Haba Sham (5790m) in the Soweto range. Returning home via America they visited the Bugaboo chain and made 2 first ascents. They were in Canada twice in the 30s and made a first ascent of the highest point in the Bobbie Burns range with C. Kain.

I pick only a few examples and have not even enumerated all their 'firsts'. A complete catalogue of the ranges they visited would double my already over-running space. Ivor was still climbing small peaks in the Alps in his 85th year and in his 87th year he joyfully accepted for himself and Dorothea an invitation from the Chinese Government to return to the University of Peking for an extensive lecture tour, taking up once more the problems of Basic English. It was a gallant finale but more than his now frail strength could bear. He was taken gravely ill, flown home to hospital in England and died in Addenbrooke's some weeks later.

At the outbreak of war, Ivor was due to go to Harvard where he was appointed to a chair in 1944. He was loath to leave England but the Foreign Office was insistent. Some war years were spent in New England. As always every possible opportunity took the Richards to mountains. Working with the Canadian Alpine Club Ivor trained Commando units in mountaineering. In winter, he and Dorothea, with the famous Bemis Crew of the Appalachian Mountain Club, climbed all the main summits of the Mt Washington range on snowshoes.

Snowshoe travel appealed to them specially and they made many trips à deux in the White Mountains.

In 1935, 7 of us met to ski in the Oetzthal; Philip and Margot Bowden, Paul Sinker, Ivor and Dorothea, Theo Chorley and myself. All but the Bowdens were novices, but after a few days they suggested a glacier tour: 'You'll be alright' said Philip: 'You're all mountaineers'.

During the war, when we were scattered, I recalled those days, specially perhaps the evenings in some Austrian hut when with legs luxuriously stretched out and tongues loosened by 'thee mit' or kirsch, talk began – real talk. It was dominated though never domineered by Ivor. He began to talk only when he had sensed the mood of the company, moving through depth, brilliance, irony, wit that could blast away any sham position but at other times could be puckish in its play. During those privileged evenings I caught glimpses into one of the finest minds of my generation.

He was surely the most distinguished writer-cum-climber member of the Club since Leslie Stephen and it was good to hear of his pleasure when he knew just before he fell ill in China that he had been made an Honorary Member. He wrote a number of brilliant books but unlike Stephen he wrote little specifically about mountains. I think of the essay already mentioned, 'Mountains and Mountaineering as Symbols', an exciting adventure with ideas (*AJ* 8235), a few poems, among them the entrancing 'Building Fires in Snow'.

KATHARINE CHORLEY, *Alpine Journal*, 1980

Dorothea Richards (1894–1986)

Dorothea Richards's love-affair with the mountains started in her teens, with a reading of A E W Mason's *Running Water*; and after a family holiday in North Wales, culminating in an ascent of Snowdon, she knew that her greatest pleasure in life was to be among the hills. And so, when long after they could be climbed in memory only, 'my own fanatic passion' still burned bright.

Dorothy Pilley was born in 1894, daughter of an industrial chemist. She early made it clear that her energies and ambitions were not to be confined by the conventions of a comfortable middle-class home in Blackheath. She did various kinds of war-work, then turned to journalism, first as a reporter for the *Daily Express* (resigning in 1922 after a clash over the paper's line on the Irish troubles), then as a freelance. She had scant formal education; her university, she said, was the Cliffs of Wales. There – in thick tweed knickerbockers, under a full tweed skirt put in the sack at the foot of the climb – she learned to test and stretch herself, to face danger and discomfort; and there she made friendships that lasted a lifetime. In 1917 and 1918 with Herbert Carr, R A Frazer, I A Richards (and his spaniel Sancho Panza), C F Holland and others, she explored Tryfan, Lliwedd, the Devil's Kitchen, Cwm Idwal – and was one of the first party up Holly Tree Wall. Then came the Lakes (with Eagle's Nest Direct) and the Cuillin (a new climb on the West Wall of the Cioch); and in 1920 her first Alpine season, under the wing of the Carr family. Ascents of Charmoz, Grepon (in a snowstorm), Geant, the traverse of the Drus, led to membership of the LAC (because of the last war years, one alpine season backed by a notable list of British climbs was enough to qualify). These climbs were guided; she had also led the Aiguille de l'M and the Petit Charmoz. Her conviction that women must learn to lead if they were to become true mountaineers led her and like-minded friends – Pat Kelly, Len Winthrop Young, Lilian Bray, the three Wells sisters – to form the Pinnacle Club in 1921; for 20 years she edited the Club's Journal. Her second alpine season started with a guideless party of women at Saas Fee, who traversed the Egginergrat and the Portjengrat. Then came the Zmutt Ridge of the Matterhorn, climbs round Arolla with I A Richards, and their fortunate meeting with Joseph Georges le Skieur: a guide whose enthusiasm matched their own.

This happy partnership over many years included the second ascent of the NE ridge of the Jungfrau (1923), the N ridge of the Grivola (1924, where Joseph cut steps for six hours) and – a long-cherished ambition – the first ascent of the N ridge of the Dent Blanche (1928). This was perhaps the high point of her climbing career, and it is fittingly the climax of her splendid *Climbing Days*.

There, helped by the diaries which she kept from girlhood till her death, she recorded, along with the rocks and ridges, summits gained and new routes made, the climber's sensations and emotions: the miseries, discomforts and apprehensions, as well as the exhilarations and delights. Lively, laced with apt quotations (IAR helping?), *Climbing Days* remains one of the very best of mountain books.

Two years before the Dent Blanche climb, Dorothy Pilley had become Dorothea Richards. She had been in Canada, IAR in the States; they met again and married, improbably in Honolulu. Henceforth, with Ivor's appointments at Peking (1929 and 1936–8) and at Harvard (from 1939), they spent most of their days outside Europe. Wherever they went they found something to climb – the Great Wall of China, the peaks of Yunnan, the Japanese Alps, the Diamond Mountains of Korea, the Selkirks and Bugaboos of the Canadian Rockies – where, in the war, Ivor did some training of commando troops.

Whenever possible, they were back in the Alps in the summer – always preferring to cross a peak or pass and come down into another valley, always ingenious at finding good climbs that the crowd had passed by.

In their Harvard years they were off to the White Mountains most weekends – snow-shoeing and 'lighting fires in snow' as Ivor described in a poem of that title. At the end of one such weekend in 1958 they were involved in a car crash which left Dorothea with a badly damaged hip. Lameness severely restricted her mountain activity, but by no means ended it. Teleferiques and chair-lifts helped with high-level walks in the Alps and hut-to-hut wanderings in Austria; a donkey and driver made possible a camping holiday in Peru; a helicopter took the Richards to the Cabane Rossier in 1966 to celebrate the centenary of the ascent of the Dent Blanche (and correct some myths about their N ridge ascent!); a snow-mobile on the lower slopes allowed Dorothea to climb Mount Hood in Oregon in 1968, her last big mountain.

In 1974 the Richards moved back from the American Cambridge to the English, and were soon again in the swim of Alpine Club affairs. After the merger with the LAC Dorothea became the first woman Vice-President of the Club, in 1975. After Ivor died in 1979 – taken ill during a heroic educational mission to China at the age of 86 – Dorothea gave £4000 in his memory to the Alpine Club Library. She loved the meetings and dinners, the sociabilities of club life – at the Alpine, Fell and Rock, Pinnacle – and was a tireless recruiting sergeant for them. She was avid for the latest climbing news, as eager to hear of the doings of her contemporaries' children and grandchildren as to recall her own golden days.

After IAR's death she lived on in the house which Magdalene College had made available for them, next to the Fellows' Garden, and looking down to the Cam. There she welcomed friends, and sallied forth to lectures, concerts, plays, exhibitions, dinners – 'an excuse for a splendid party was irresistible', as Henry Chadwick said at her funeral. She resented growing old, and worried her friends by behaving as if she were not: trains and buses when she could well afford taxis, a rucksack for her luggage, a liking for very late nights, a reluctance to abandon 'my gipsy ways'. It was no use arguing with her on grounds of comfort, common-sense or the convenience of others. Like her friend T S Eliot's Rum Tum Tugger she would do as she did do, 'and there's no doing anything about it'.

'I never guessed age might keep me sur place,' she complained to me in 1984, after poor health forced her to cancel her cherished annual holiday in New England. But it didn't! In the early 20s she and Ivor had seen the New Year in on the top of Snowdon. In 1986 she saw in her last New Year at the climbers' hut in Glen Brittle where she sat up happily with a party of Scottish climbers till 3 am, drinking whisky and talking mountains. In June she joined in the celebration of the centenary of Haskett-Smith's ascent of the Needle. One climber remembers her holding court in front of the

Wastwater Hotel, arrestingly handsome in a green dress of Chinese silk, black hair centre-parted like raven's wings, youthfully alert despite her sticks. My last sight of her was on the afternoon of Prince Andrew's wedding which (despite her disapproval of TV) she had watched on a friend's set. What she'd most enjoyed were the shots at the Palace: 'You know that Victoria Memorial in front of it – I climbed it on Armistice Day in 1918 with the help of a soldier and a sailor'. There was no one like her.

Let IAR's lines be her epitaph, written to cheer her after the hip accident, recalling a late descent from the Epicoun:

> 'Leaping crevasses in the dark,
> That's how to live!' you said.

JANET ADAM SMITH (JANET CARLETON),
Alpine Journal, 1987

Appendix II

The Lure of High Mountaineering

'Red with cutaneous eruption of conceit and voluble with compulsive hiccough of self-satisfaction,' the mountaineer strides into his hotel, back from his peak or his pass, no doubt jostling Ruskin in the doorway and so stirring him to this little masterpiece of descriptive vituperation. Today Ruskin is almost forgotten; in his place (no more welcome in his eyes than the climber with his axe and rope and uncouth footwear) now stands the tourist, very often an American, who, if he has not the same feelings about the figure that shambles noisily by, is usually as hard put to it to explain why any reasonable soul should want to do just this, or what anyone gets out of it so that he should keep at it with such stupid pertinacity. To go up one mountain would probably be an interesting experience, especially if it were the highest; to keep on climbing mountains seems to be mere silliness.

To describe a passion to those who do not share it is a difficult enough task, let alone explaining it. The passion I write of is eminently respectable. The pope and the new conservative member of Parliament for Cambridge – not to mention several kings and queens – have been among its devotees. It is a powerful passion, enthralling many until long past their sixtieth year. It is a serious passion, judged by the test that a considerable number of people have cheerfully lost their lives in its pursuit. They did not know, of course, that they would lose them, but they were perfectly well aware of the possibility, and had decided upon the question of 'Worthwhile?' And their fellow fanatics, when one of these calamities occurs, commonly treat it quite as a matter of course without raising questions of justification, unless carelessness or recklessness is suspected. Yet somehow this passion, more than most, does need some explanation. It is surprisingly new, having come in only about seventy-five years ago; and its activities are to the outside eye particularly pointless. In this it perhaps stands alone. Games, though no psychologist will claim that he can completely explain them, have at least a good historical standing. We are never really puzzled as to why people play them even when we feel no inclination to do likewise. Hunting, fishing, yachting, gardening, camping, and the rest of the sports can plausibly be regarded as survivals, although of course this is not the whole story. Immemorial antiquity lends them sanction; though I doubt whether many yachtsmen or amateur camping parties were about in the sixteenth century.

To enjoy unnecessary discomfort or insecurity we must first be bored by comfort. These two sports in part appeal through their contrast with ordinary existence, and to some degree mountaineering shares this attraction. But while the positive lure of yachting and camping – that is to say, the part over and above contrast – links on to ancient and very widespread pursuits, the positive lure of mountaineering, including the impulse to go up to the top of the hill when the way is difficult, has a very meagre history. Unless hunting takes them there, the natives never climb their mountains. Genuine mountaineering – Alpinism, for example – is an entirely new development, appealing only to a moderately sophisticated mind. It is, in fact, a strangely professional pastime. What blend of what desires and delights will account for it, or what obscure needs and tendencies must we invoke?

Like other passions, this one has stages. And again, like other passions, it has degrees of impurity. We can study it here only at its ripest and purest. The novice, thrilling with anticipatory tremors at the largely erroneous picture which he makes for himself of his first serious climb, mixes in too much that is imaginary and has nothing to do with the matter. I have known one such novice afterward to confess that he 'got the wind up' far more on his first big mountain than ever on the battlefield – and this was a man who saw a good deal of nasty fighting.

We must set aside also the confirmed habitué of the mountains, whose early ardour has declined – the man who goes on climbing moderately difficult ordinary mountains by the best-known routes in the company of guides who have such a reserve of mountaineering ability that only what the insurance companies style as an 'act of God' could prevent the caravan from returning in safety at the appointed time. Let me try to describe instead what happens in the mind of the guideless climber, experienced enough to know what he is doing, when he is engaged upon an ascent which is just within his powers as the leader of his party.

He probably knows a good deal about his proposed climb. The idea of it may have been in his mind for a long while. He will have read about it, studied it, surveyed it from neighbouring summits, perhaps. One of the incidental charms of mountaineering is the unexampled opportunity for detailed, intricate, concrete planning which it allows. The mountaineering fanatic spends hours, whole long winter evenings, gazing at maps and photographs and talking to the other members of his climbing party about the expedition. This planning as the day approaches grows more and more responsible. Here is another attraction. There are very few pursuits in which the question of competence comes more sharply to a head. A great ascent shares the glamour of an Arctic journey – a point will come when the climber will need his strength and skill to extricate himself. The factors upon which success depends are varied enough to need careful thought, yet not too numerous or too uncertain to be estimated. In this a big climb resembles a miniature campaign. It is a concentrated form of exploration, with the tedium cut out and the dramatic intensity heightened. The man whose mountain career begins and ends with scrambling up the Matterhorn or treadmilling up Mont Blanc under professional guidance misses so much of all this that he may well conclude that climbing is an overestimated pastime. Mountaineering is a craft which requires years to master, and the sense of increased competence is no small part of its attraction.

Some of the branches of this craft are never mastered and have therefore an inexhaustible fascination. Weather lore, for example. The condition of the mountain and the difficulty of the ascent vary with the weather and the season in ways which may baffle the utmost sagacity. A stretch of glacier which early in a snowy year would be easy and would take but an hour to cross may a month later, after hot weather, be nearly impossible. Its ice is always cracked here and there, split by fissures which may be no more than a few inches or a few feet in width though hundreds of yards in length. When narrow, these 'crevasses' are covered by the carpet of the surface snow and can be crossed if the snow is hard, as it is in the early morning, without anyone's being able to detect that the apparently innocent white expanse is actually stretched across what are in effect bottomless abysses of ice-walled darkness. These crevasses widen as the summer wears on. The snow that roofs them grows thinner; first a ripplelike hollow shows, then the ripple splits open; then the crevasse walls appear, smooth, shiny, black blue, overhung with treacherous bulges of unsupported snow. Here and there the snow roof is more solid, and a bridge is left across which a climbing party can pass, if need be, at certain hours and under certain conditions. But sometimes the crevasse can widen out without clearly revealing its presence, and only the sudden collapse of the snow roof under the weight of one of the party will show that it is there. The crevasse may be several hundred feet deep. Picture yourself walking on a snow blanket stretched across an opening in the dome of Saint Peter's and you will be able to understand one of the possibilities of glacial travel. This is why the party will be walking in single file as far apart as they conveniently can, and why they will be keeping the rope which links them to one another reasonably taut. Should anyone fall into a crevasse far enough for his head to disappear, it is no easy matter to pull him out again.

The quality of the snow, as much when it was lying upon open gentle glacier slopes as when it is draped about the wild upper ridges, or is clinging in seemingly precarious fashion to the steep mountain walls, changes with the hour of the day, the angle at which the sun strikes it, the wind, the weather of the last few days. To plan an interesting expedition wisely, all this must be reckoned with. Early enough in the morning the snow will generally be good. This is why the climber usually starts with the first daylight. But there are other reasons. In the Alps, unless he has slept in one of the many Swiss Alpine Club cabins that are perched for his convenience high up, often upon tiny outcrops of rock surrounded by glacier, he will have two or three hours of steady preliminary walking, on a path if he is lucky, before the difficulties and the high mountaineering proper begin. He has to start early to economise time and to make use of the cool of the day, for he will have from four to eight thousand feet to ascend, and time is precious. Every big climb, and above all every new climb, is a race against the sun.

The weather affects the rocks of the mountain as much as the glaciers. A light sprinkle of snow overnight will give the peaks a fairylike silvery glitter, but will put serious climbing out of the question – not so much because it makes the rocks slippery as because it makes them so cold to the fingers. Only the easiest rocks can be climbed with fresh snow upon them. The slipperiness comes a day later when the snow has melted and the moisture has refrozen to invisible ice – *Verglas*, as it is called – an abominable substance very difficult to deal with.

Often the descent will need special consideration. It will be late in the day, the snow will be soft, stones which in the morning are firmly bound by frost will be loosened by the sun and ready to begin their awful, hopping, bounding, whirring flight to the valley. Anyone who has loafed away an afternoon in the high Alps will have heard that faint growling, sometimes rising to a roar and rarely quiet for more than a few moments, which means that miscellaneous debris from the mountains is slipping from them. A stone fall on a great slope is a horrible spectacle whether seen from above or from below, but especially when seen from below. Some mountainsides are death traps for this reason in the afternoon.

A prudent climber will rarely get too close to falling stones, but through bad luck or misinformation he may see more than he cares of them. He will be working down a ridge which stands up in low relief upon a great tilting side of the mountain. To right and left a wide, shallow, dusty gully, floored with worn slabs of rock and broken with zig-zagging scree-littered shelves, may offer easier progress. A little rivulet of water staining the recesses of the rocks and sending a faint tinkle up to his thirsty soul may add to the temptation. He continues down the ridge. Suddenly from far above, where the upper cliffs lean forward and domi-nate the lower glacis, a single sharp report will sound. He looks up, every fibre tense and quivering. For a moment nothing will be visible; then exactly like a bursting shrap-nel, a tiny cloud will flash out which looks like smoke but actually is dust. The falling missile has struck some scree-covered ledge. Usually the climber will see little more; he will have his head, and as much more of himself as he can, well and safely tucked away in the shelter of some over-hanging boulder or cranny. But he will hear the whole slope, as it seems, leap to life for the falling stone sets a myr-iad others in motion. Down they come, whirring and hum-ming, taking enormous bounds and ricocheting across the whole width of the gully. By the time they pass him, they will often be flying too fast to be visible. Only the screams of the air or, if a large boulder is fairly launched, a rumble not unlike that of an express train will tell him that they are past, and he can look down to see them splash into the snows below or leap into the open mouth of the crevasse which is nearly always there to catch them.

The prudent climber, I repeat, keeps well away from falling stones. Occasionally, however, circumstances may force him to run the risk of crossing such dangerous ground. He may be late in leaving the summit; hard pressed for time to work out the intricacies of the glacier before night falls, he may have no other way of avoiding a night spent *à la belle étoile,* an experience which is nearly always miserable and sometimes dangerous in itself. For a tired man may not be in a state to resist the great cold of the night high up without shelter, and the weather may be changing or the wind rising.

When for any such reason dangerous ground has to be crossed, the climber may hurry, but hurrying is otherwise something which he sedulously avoids. From one point of view he is the most leisurely of sportsmen; he takes a great deal of exercise, but he takes it as gently as he can. He cannot afford to hurry in an expedition which will probably take fifteen hours to complete and may take twenty. On the other hand, he cannot afford to waste any odd minutes. All successful parties develop an elaborate technique for saving seconds — at first a conscious effort, later an unconscious habit. The beginner gives himself away by the time he squanders. He wants to stop to fix his puttee, or to put cream on his face, or to get out his gloves, or to put them away. A dozen little jobs arise and half a dozen little calamities befall him which the more experienced man foresaw the last time the whole party stopped to feel or to put on the rope.

But there is more in time-saving than this, difficult though this trick of not stopping seems to be to acquire. Consider the management of the rope alone. We are tied on, if there are three of us, one at each end and the third in the middle. There will be thirty or forty feet of loose rope between us. Most of the time we shall be all moving together. The rope must be kept moderately taut whenever there is any possibility of a mishap to any of the party. This is not so difficult when we are walking in the leader's footprints across a snowfield. But suppose we are working up a fairly steep face of rock. Fairly steep means an angle of about fifty degrees. This looks like sixty-five degrees until one measures it, and is usually talked of as eighty degrees. This face will not be smooth – few faces are. If it were, we should be moving one at a time, gathering the rope in and letting it out as required. More probably, like most big precipices that get climbed, it will be built up of a chaos of jammed blocks of all sizes at all angles, held in place by the weight of the rocks above. Over such ground experienced climbers can pass with great safety and speed, but the loose rope must be kept from catching among the innumerable spikes which jut out everywhere. To keep it free while himself moving with special care to avoid dislodging any of the rubbish with which all such faces are strewn, the climber must give a continual series of nicely adjusted flicks. In time this becomes automatic. Usually he can carry a few coils – enough to control it – in one hand, the same hand also holding his ice axe; he climbs with the other hand and with his feet and with a knee now and then.

This sounds like one of the dreariest and least inviting of imaginable exercises, and so it is until the knack has become second nature. But when everything is going as it should, the very fact that all this tiresome detail is being dealt with without effort, by the mere sweet-running mechanisms of the nervous system, yields a peculiar exhilaration. I should ascribe a great deal of the fascination of mountaineering to this sense of successful technique. The good effect of doing anything that one can do well radiates throughout the whole personality. One's other faculties benefit, one is at peace with oneself, and the illusion of a complete mastery of existence grows strong. Add to this the slight tension which the situation, the drop below, and the constant need to care impose, and it is not hard to see how this routine part of climbing can acquire a charm.

More difficult rocks have another fascination. The technique of overcoming them without delay and without undue fatigue has much in common with the technique of the arts. Mediocre performers, for example, resemble one another in their procedure, but the masters of the craft develop individual styles. The difference between a breathless muscular struggle and an easy, balanced movement is often too subtle to be analysed, but every golfer will understand how powerful the appeal of success here may become. And because the movements called for in rock-climbing are perhaps more varied and their nicety not less than those of any other sport, the spell cast is the stronger. To go lightly up a rock wall when the only hold is the friction of the fore-arm pressing against the sides of a vertical crack while the feet push gently yet firmly upon roughness not much bigger than a thumbnail is an achievement which allows a good deal of innocent self-flattery to develop. And if meanwhile the glance which is seeking for suitable roughnesses can travel past the poised foot and see nothing beneath but the glacier some hundreds of feet below, there is nothing in this to impair the pleasure, provided that equanimity is maintained. Calm control and alert, deliberate choice of pose are the essence of good rock-climbing; the exhilaration which accompanies it is as much made up of a sense that one's judgement is trustworthy and one's intelligence clear and unflurried as it is of any physical delights. And the final movement of such a passage, when the climber reaches handholds like the rungs of a ladder (no higher praise is possible), a roomy ledge to stand upon and a spike of rock round which he can 'belay' the rope, and so guarantee both his own safety and that of his companions who will now follow him, brings a quiet glow of triumph which is much more than a mere relief of tension or a sense of escape. A good cragsman, it may be remarked, can almost always retrace his steps and return to his companions if the passage should prove more difficult than he anticipated. It is, in fact, only on this condition that he is justified in assuming the responsibility of leading his party. There are plenty of borderline cases, of course, in which a climber may not be perfectly certain whether he should proceed or return, and it is just here that his judgement is tested.

Intelligence, not of a low order, is exercised at many points in any interesting ascent. The choice of route constantly demands it. A fine mountain is a succession of problems to be solved on the spot. Few who have not climbed can realise how very intricate a mountain face may be. Rocks by themselves can require varied enough evolutions, for most cliffs are more like highly tilted labyrinths, when you come close to them, than the solid walls which from a distance they appear to be. And often the choice of one fissure rather than another, of one shelf or shoulder or buttress rather than its neighbour, will make a difference in time to be counted in hours and spell success or failure for the whole expedition.

But the complexities of rock-climbing are matched by those of ice and snow. A broken glacier can present a maze which only a mixture of good luck and happy opportunism will unravel. It is a strange experience of coming down in the late afternoon, one's heels sinking deep into a vast bulge of snow – like a swelling sail, but more dazzlingly white – to survey, as the slope curves over and what is below is revealed, the wild, contorted chaos of waves and chasms into which the glacier ice is riven as it descends. Through this chaos, often by a series of carefully planned leaps interspersed with thoughtful performances on bridges of snow – an all-fours position which distributes one's weight over the fragile structure is not unusual – and as a rule by much chopping of steps along the slopes of the ice waves, an intricate way is forced. It is astonishing how often the way followed will seem the only one that is possible, and how rare it is for no way to be found.

I have lingered somewhat over the technical attractions of mountaineering because this side of the sport is the one least easy for the layman to imagine, though some knowledge of it is necessary if the climber's passion is to be understood. If I have said enough to show that a great climb is not a rash adventure but a campaign in which a prudent strategy and skillful tactics have both been required, I shall have gained my purpose. I have said nothing about the view from the summit – the excuse which the non-climber usually provides for the climber, who is often lazy enough to accept it. The view from the summit is as a rule no more interesting than the other views. And I have said nothing yet about the beauty of the high peaks. Before attempting to say what little can be said about this there is another fact, less often mentioned, which must be indicated.

Few climbers are for long exempt from a certain modicum of anxiety – a watchful apprehension which rarely rises to the point of distress, but remains as a background of consciousness giving a special *dramatic* quality to each incident. It is tempting to speculate further upon this feeling, for it may have an intimate connection with the beauty which the climber sometimes sees. With fatigue or indisposition this sombre tinge easily develops into a clouding dread, more or less well controlled. When this happens the whole expedition changes from a joy to a nightmare. For some climbers this is not an infrequent occurrence, though it may be but for a moment. With the unloosing of anxiety the whole character of the landscape is transformed. 'The eye altering alters all.'* There are always plenty of sights in the high mountains which are capable of taking on a hideous aspect. Gaunt, disintegrating black cliffs that can be contemplated without horror only by a mind which is perfectly in possession of itself; obscure convolutions of grimy glacier which stir nothing but nausea unless one is able to hold oneself in check; sinister grey curtains of ice, furrowed by stone falls, that hold no hope for any living thing for thousands of feet; monstrous gaping jaws of crevasses fanged above with sharp blue icicles and lipped with treacherous bulges of soft snow. Even the transcendental sparkle of the snow on the upper ridges turns easily to a mere grim glitter. The instant this anxiety slips loose, beauty vanishes. Naturally it does, for this holding down of tremors, this serenity amid stress, was its very source and being. Perhaps even the man who deeply feels the beauty of a great mountain from the valley is doing something similar. He is holding in control a set of feelings which if they broke loose would distress him. Let his equanimity be sufficiently destroyed, let some grief or

* Blake, 'The Mental Traveller.' (Original footnote.)

harshness throw him off his balance, and he will not find peace among the hills, he will not see beauty in them, but only a hateful, discomforting presentation of that side of the universe which is least the concern of man.

The climber is not less susceptible to the ordinary beauty of the mountains, if I may call it such – this power they have to stir such subtly mingled feelings when they are seen from below; and his privileged enjoyment of their extraordinary beauty, the still more mingled thrill which they awaken in him when he is actually upon their ridges, does not, in spite of all that Ruskin had to say, betoken a lack of sensibility. In the best instances the closer, the more intimate, experience is an amplification of the other. It is possible, of course, to climb for a whole day, or for a week, or for a lifetime, with scarcely a moment of the genuine awareness; just as it is possible to perambulate miles of galleries or listen to the best orchestras in the world without any result which is worth mentioning. But it is the claim of the mountaineer that the very conditions of his sport do tend to make a more fully awakened response likely. The passion, like others, can go astray, and bogus forms are not uncommon. There are collectors of peaks, for example, who know as little of the genuine worship as mere collectors of pictures. Fortunately, perhaps, they rarely know what they are missing.

I. A. Richards, *Atlantic Monthly*, January 1927

Agua

Agua is the huge and graceful volcano that towers up in perfect symmetry over Guatemala City. You don't, from here, at all realize how far off it is or how high, 12,393 feet. Nor do you from Antigua – thirty miles nearer – nor from Santa Maria, the jumping off village to which motors can climb. You only realize all these things high up on the peak itself – when the lights of Santa Maria and Antigua and Guatemala are floating, as in a nether sky, beneath you as you start wondering if the night is yet half-way worked through.

Santa Maria is a compact little village with a large central square in which a brisk game of *futbol* was scuffing up the dust when we arrived to bargain for a guide and two horses. The local Indians feel that the volcano is their possession and that to hire a guide for it is only a visitor's duty. The horses were: one for the provisions and blankets, the other for me. Since my broken hip-joint disqualified me, through a motor smash three years ago, I have been experimenting with ascent-descent devices. Once despised wire ropeways of all varieties now find in me a *connoisseuse*. Carrying chairs too, as in ancient China, would appeal could I find them. I even read a bit enviously in the *Chronicles of Bernal Diaz del Castillo* of the way Cortez' Indian *cargadores* could bundle you up in a hammock and porter you off thirty miles or so a night. Imagination has played happily also with the Rope Trick of the Other India – herewith depicted by that rising artist of New Delhi, Krishen Khanna; the more so since an indignant correspondent protested that 'this superstitious trickery has long since been exploded!' Krishen's adepts don't seem however to be letting that bother them a bit. And a contrary minded correspondent exclaimed, 'Well, we have been messing about with ropes for long enough, it's time somebody got onto the Indian method.'

In comparison, use of a mere horse seems commonplace. However, he can take you up the continuously steep path to tree line — more than 3,000 feet of lift — leaving you rather more of a rather steeper path to amble up yourself in the dawning. That was the plan; the bargain was struck and six-thirty, half an hour after dark, was very deliberately selected as the exactly right moment for departure.

Futbol died out as dusk fell and neat little fires under cooking pots glowed out in the corner of the square where soup awaited passers by. Pilgrims preparing for the nation-wide thronging to Esquipulas on the morrow, 15th January, were expected. Lads of the village loafed and gazed. The girls gathered in a group, poised their burdens on their heads and departed. The great open church door brightened with candlelight, while brats played an indecent kind of tag on the platform before it. Just in the doorway — neither inside nor out — a three-man band: drum, pipe and 'cello, established itself to play distorted versions of juke-box favourites while devout men dodged in past them to their prayers. We watched through clouds of copal incense burnt rather in the doorway than within. Beyond, the long pavement of the nave was strewn with pine needles and flower petals and ablaze with candles. The drum beat mechanically, the tunes jigged on; nobody however seemed much interested; they have a dogged capacity for just going on endlessly. But where were those horses?

It seemed they could not be found. The Alcalde or village mayor – to whom we had brought a persuasive letter – tired of assuring us that they would soon appear and went off with a powerfully built young crony. Another hour wore by. Then he reappeared. Alas ! The time had been spent on *aguar diente* in a pilgrimage spirit. Alcohol, so high Guatemalan authorities are quoted, 'carries prayers aloft by its volatility'. It certainly had added wings to the Alcalde's tongue – and to the crony's. He posted himself up against us and harangued us fiercely – with formidable gestures – on, we gathered, Guatemala's wrong at the hands of British Honduras. (On local maps this is a province of Guatemala, Belize, and the President had just been voicing his recurrent threats of violent action.)

Somehow local violent action didn't seem too impossible. I wasn't sure that the Alcalde's badge of office, which he kept slapping, would do us much good. We began to feel that a Rope Trick might be exactly what we would want to waft us skywards away from a somewhat frightening situation, since the strong young man was getting to the ugly stage. But the Alcalde's wife, a slight, firm-featured, barefooted woman with an understanding look, now appeared and said a few effective Mayan words from time to time while keeping a watchful eye on the fiery one. None the less it was a relief to hear a clatter of hoofs on the cobbles.

Our guide was a tall, thin, pleasant-faced lad with a two-foot long machete on his belt, and the horses were nimble-footed little idle-bones, both of them. Not having been on horseback since my accident, I suddenly realized that I might not be able to mount. However, a score of onlookers and would-be helpers settled that. They were just longing for a good laugh and burst out as I gave a howl of disjointure on swinging into place. I.A.R. had duly warned me! I rode off proudly, but as soon as we were out of sight of the audience, I had to have the stirrup replaced by a high loop from the saddle-bow. So perched, I could just take the jerking of my horse, who would charge up six strides and then pause to puff and blow, timing his spurts, it seemed to me, to meet overhanging boughs and spiny bushes which, he hoped, might sweep me off his back.

Before long we began to realize that the half moon we had counted upon was due soon to vanish behind Agua's vast black mass. Heavy clouds too were clinging to the cone and scudding across the great sky-lantern. To supplement it we had only a pocket flashlight, which our guide soon borrowed to help him locate the path. It zigzagged and twisted among terraces and steep planted slopes of peas and beans and corn. When we halted, cornstalks rustling in the wind backed up the panting horses. Fusilades of fire crackers from Santa Maria reminded us of the pilgrimage. Enormous kapoc trees overhung at intervals, casting impenetrable shade, lit only by glowing fire-flies. In gullies the path sucked and gurgled underfoot from unusual, recent rain. There was not another soul on the mountain. Out on the open ridges, cold struck, and the remote galaxy of Guatemala City shone up at Orion.

At last, the moon set. We had started about 9.0 p.m. and were a bit surprised to find it was near one o'clock. Time to repose. We were on a hummocky slope of big grass tussocks dotted with conifers – not too bad for a blanket-wrapped perch. As we tossed and wriggled under a cluster of pines, plop! the cloud cap on the mountain was coating the pine needles with glistening drops. Our tossings and the passing gusts brought these down on us in showers. So did tugs of the horses tethered to these trees – munching, redolent presences dragging pack ropes across our blankets. We felt it very clever and kindly of them not to step on our toes. Why they had to be tethered so near we did not make out fully.

You most of you know such nights *à la belle etoile* with not a star shining, how the lumps are in the wrong places, how you cannot find the very thing you have brought for your comfort, how the rain (it turned to that) keeps your face under the cover and you stifle, how you wonder why you do such things, how dawn seems plainly Joshua'd – and then suddenly it is there.

A blazing fire (7.0 a.m.) was soon cheering up the thick white mists. It was interesting to watch local woodsmanship. Guatemala has a pine that is incredibly fat in gums – so much so that slivers of it can be burnt as candles. In a soaked forest – as now – a Mayan hacks out some of it with his machete, builds a little shelter of boughs and bark, and lights up his fat pine under this to dry his fuel out. We had tea going in quick time and before we had drunk it a cloud shifted and there shone the ghost of the sun. Before we had packed and set off on our walk up (8.30 a.m.), the only too actual sun was blazing and we were getting ready to reverse recent judgements on the pleasures of travelling in the night.

Crumbling coffee grounds (volcanic ash) lay underfoot thence to the crater.

Imagine a pine-dotted basin with a level floor about the size of Trafalgar Square. There is one entrance to it, the rest of the lip being thin and made of firm red rock offering mild climbing. You wander round this rim looking out over Central America searching for the Oceans it divides. Down one long twisting gully in the slope below you can see the site of the first capital of Central America. In 1541 an exceptionally atrocious earthquake followed by a water-carried landslide from high on Agua (whence the name) utterly wiped it out. Refounded a few miles away, at Antigua (the ancient), it became the most important city in the Americas and then in the 18th Century, after many damaging shakes, on 29th June 1773 came a sharp jolt sending everybody out into the streets.

Ten minutes of perfect calm. Then such a minute as has rarely happened anywhere. The capital was shifted again.

Antigua became a ghost town and is now a national monument.

Oddly enough it has not had a bad shake since. From the summit you see it laid out below you dreaming idly in the sunshine.

Good to perch in the Spring-like air by the cairn and review some of one's night thoughts. Why do such things still? Why not defer to one's disabilities and desist? The answer then and there seems too plain for any words. It is not merely that you are tuned back by it into how much else of your mountain life. That is true, but the real answer is far simpler than that: too simple indeed for me to say, but – to borrow from A. D. Godley –

'Yours is a spice of the Ultimate Good.'

Dorothy Pilley Richards, *Journal of the Fell and Rock Climbing Club*, no. 56, vol. 19 (III), 1962

Lighting Fires in Snow

Tread out a marble hollow
  Then lay the twigs athwart,
    Teepee-wise or wigwam,
So that the air can follow
  The match-flame from the start:
    As we begin a poem
And some may win a heart.

For twig to twig will beckon
  If lightly laid above
Better than you can reckon.
    Waste no time devising.
  No, no, it is not love,
    But the drying fume arising
If the draft be free enough.

As the under cavern reddens
  Leave well alone!
Cold fuel only deadens.
    But pile across the smoke
  And give a dog a bone.
    For its life's sake, don't poke!
The wise fire knows its own.

The wise poem knows its father
    And treats him not amiss;
        But Language is its mother
To burn where it would rather
    Choose that and by-pass this
        Only afraid of smother
    Though the thickening snow-flakes hiss.

I. A. RICHARDS, 1958[1]

Richard de la Mare, Chairman. P. F. du Sautoy, Vice-Chairman

Lady Faber, T. S. Eliot, Morley Kennerley (U.S.A.), Alan Pringle, David Bland, Charles Monteith, Peter Crawley

FABER AND FABER LTD

PUBLISHERS

24 Russell Square London WC1

Fabbaf London W.C.1. Museum 9543

Mrs. I. A. Richards,
c/o Miss Joyce Penny,
46a Belsize Square,
Swiss Cottage, N.W.3.

30th September, 1964.

Dear Dorothea,

Thank you for your chocolate cherries, which I shall share with Valerie who will enjoy them as much as I shall.

I wish indeed that I could give you a quotation from something that I have written to help the blurb of CLIMBING DAYS. But mountaineering is the last subject that I am capable of writing about, since it is well known that I do not like uphill movement and have no head for heights. People who know me would ridicule and those who do not would wonder, while I doubt whether mountain climbers include in their number many of my admirers!

Yours affectionately,

Tom Eliot

Letter from T. S. Eliot to Dorothea Richards, 30 September 1964 (RCM)

Acknowledgements

This book is dedicated to my family, my inspiring and vital father, Tim, my tireless loving mother, Annie, and my audacious creative brother, Joe – thank you all for your love and the inspiration to write and travel.

My grandfather Bob's great constancy and love was a huge support and comfort – my thanks to him.

Thanks also to the extended Richards family for their encouragement and assistance, particularly my cousin, Celia, who put me up in Edinburgh before and after the Cairngorm trip, and my great-uncle, David, for his time, support and memories of Dorothea and Ivor.

I am hugely grateful to the thoughtful generosity of my great-aunt, Elizabeth Thomson, and her son, Anthony Thomson.

One of the great gifts and joys of writing this book has been the discovery of Dorothea's nephews, Anthony and Christopher Pilley, my second cousins. Their friendship, hospitality and contribution cannot be over-emphasised. I thank them both with all my heart.

The other great delight and discovery, of course, was the rekindling of my family's relationship with that of Joseph Georges le Skieur. André Georges and Rosula Blanc could not have been more welcoming, kind or inspiring. I offer both my sincere gratitude and the hope that we remain in touch for many years to come.

To Jean-Noël Bovier, my thanks and admiration for all your help and guidance.

Thanks to my editor, Walter Donohue, who, together with Samantha Matthews, my copy-editor, Eleanor Rees, and my proofreader, Jim Caunter, shaped and honed this book; and thanks to Sarah Ereira for creating the index. Indeed, thanks to all at Faber for their help and wise counsel.

To my agent, Carrie Plitt, my thanks and esteem for your friendship, advice, reassurance, editorial care and expertise. You're wonderful.

Thanks to all at Conville & Walsh, and Clare Conville particularly for her faith, support and silver shoes.

I am indebted to Magdalene College, Cambridge, for their help and generosity. Dr Richard Luckett and Dr Jane Hughes were gracious, knowledgeable and accommodating throughout the writing of this book – my thanks and best wishes to them and all at the Pepys Library.

Thanks also to John Constable for kindly allowing me to reproduce elements of his brilliant introductions to *I. A. Richards: Selected Works 1919–1938*.

I am hugely grateful to Karen Stockham for her contribution and encouragement. Your knowledge and analysis of Dorothy's diaries, the notes and research so kindly shared, not to mention your thesis *Women's Mountaineering Life-Writing 1808–1960*, were invaluable over the past couple of years.

I owe the adamantine ladies of the Pinnacle Club much. Thanks to Margaret Clennett and Hazel Jones for their help and forbearance and permission to use materials from the club's amazing archive.

Thanks also to Lucy Killen and all at the Jonathan Conville Mountaineering Trust.

Jonathan Preston and Mark Samuels taught us well and were excellent sports; my grateful thanks to them and my fellow mountaineers: Freddie Dunmore, Ella Sadler-Andrews, Louie Smith, Sam Stocks, Baiba Sustere, Samantha Trevitt, James Walsh and Patrick Walsh.

To Emily Benton and David Cochrane, thank you for your energy, friendship, advice and crampons. Also, to Erin Patel, for his company, camaraderie and good humour – my thanks and best wishes to you, Sam and Bea.

Thanks to Andrew Race and family for their hospitality and warmth at Burnthwaite.

I am very grateful to Caroline Teesdale for her kindness and translation skills, and Rory Hill for his editing nous and general literary moxie.

Thanks to David Potter in particular, great friend and supporter, for his unfailing generosity and encouragement. We talked, drank, ate, walked and argued this book into being. All my love to you.

To Rob Howe and Jess Carey – and all the Careys of Rookery Farm – my gratitude and appreciation. Thank you for the space to write.

I am very grateful to Will Conner, James and Havva Bulley, Roz and Clare Coleman, Louise Dennison, Mark Dishman, Julie Hutchinson, Alex Lingford, Andy Pointer and Katie Tutt, Lucy and Tim Snelson, and everyone else who lent me a sofa or bed whilst I wrote, climbed or researched. Thank you all.

I am very lucky to benefit from the kindness and skill of the artist Stanley Donwood, who has furnished this book with a most wonderful cover. Thank you, Dan.

I read from an inchoate version of this book at several events during its writing and was heartened and thankful for the warm reception and encouragement I received from both audiences and fellow writers.

My thanks to Lee Brackstone and Dan Papps for having me along to their ever excellent Faber Social nights, Catherine Woodward for putting me on the bill of Live Lit Lounge, and Chris Gribble and Writers' Centre Norwich for inviting me to their brilliant Worlds Festival. I am much obliged to you all.

With specific reference to Switzerland, my thanks to Joan Pralong, André 'Dédé' Anzévui, Dominique Anzévui, Mme Rosemary, Mme Laurence at Camping Arolla, and the guardians of the Bertol and Rossier Huts.

Among friends too kind and numerous to mention – Jeff Barratt, Andrew Walsh, Robin Turner and all at Caught by the River, Robert Macfarlane, Richard Lawrence, Damian Porter at Ogwen Cottage YHA, Sandra Chandler and family, Giles and Caroline Mercer, Charlotte Smith, Alec Cumming, Sir Quentin Blake, Dr Charles Clarke, Kevin Parker and Sophie Utting, Deborah Smith, Emma Jane Unsworth, Horatio Clare, Melissa Harrison, Kirsty Gunn, Bill Drummond, Jonty Driver, George Szirtes, Susan

Acknowledgements

Barker, Jan Morris, Harry Parker, Lucy Hughes-Hallett, Vaughan Oliver, Erica Jarnes, Jen Calleja, Stewart Lee, Helen Mort, Liz Berry, Jon Greenaway, Rob St John, Marcus O'Dair, Tatjana Smith, Geoff Dyer, Kim Sherwood, Catherine Sutherland, Jack Underwood, Adrian Cooper and Little Toller Press, Chris Sherwin, Kenneth Blackwell, Stephen Reid, Ged Martin, Philip Langeskov, Emma Naomi Smith, Nina Hervé and Will Burns, Milly Hirst, Megan Bradbury, Ron Butlin, Chris Joyner and Nou Laniado, Amy Sumner, Louisa Yates and all at Gladstone's Library, all at *Lighthouse Journal*, Jon Baker, Karen Reilly, Sal Pittman, Steve Gullick, Mel Kidd, Tom Killingbeck, Scott Pack, Patrick Hargadon, David and Sandra Lees, Leah Hamilton, Erica Horton, Theo Lecrinier, Sara McGavin, Will Jennings, Robert Hyde at Galileo Publishers, the Bicycle Shop, the Playhouse Bar, Mr B.'s Emporium of Reading Delights, the Book Hive, the Brathay Trust, the British Mountaineering Council, the Alpine Club, the *London Review of Books*, Starzec's Shoe Repairs, EasyJet for their great kindness, patience and restraint, and Pete Healey – wherever he may be. Thank you all.

Notes and Abbreviations

In the picture credits and notes, 'RCM' refers to material in the Richards Collection, Magdalene College, Cambridge.

Archival documents and photographs of I. A. Richards and D. E. Pilley are published with the permission of the Estate of Ivor and Dorothea Richards.

A. C. Benson's diaries are published with permission of the Master and Fellows of Magdalene College, Cambridge.

All *FRCC Journal* extracts are published by kind permission of the Fell and Rock Climbing Club of the English Lake District Archives.

Hope

1 I. A. Richards, 'Hope – to D.E.P. in hospital for a broken hip', in *The Screens and Other Poems*, 1960; *New and Selected Poems*, Carcanet, Manchester, 1978.

2 Dorothy E. Thompson, *Climbing with Joseph Georges*, Titus Wilson and Son, Kendal, 1962. The book is dedicated to 'Dr. and Mrs I. A. Richards, with whom I first climbed the Alps, and to all my Friends of Days among the Hills.'

Cambridge

1 I. A. Richards, *Selected Letters of I. A. Richards*, ed. John Constable, Clarendon, Oxford, 1990.

2 Author interview with Dr Richard Luckett, Rye, June 2013.

3 John Paul Russo, *I. A. Richards: His Life and Work*, Johns Hopkins University Press, Baltimore, 1989, p. 35.

4 In the biographical register which fronts *Selected Letters of I. A. Richards* (Clarendon, Oxford, 1990), editor John Constable introduces Russo as the author of 'the standard account of

Richards' intellectual development'.

5 'On her birth certificate and her publications, her name is given as Dorothy. She preferred Dorothea and Richards called her by that name.' Russo, *I. A. Richards*, p. 700, endnote 59.

6 Russo, *I. A. Richards*, p. 48.

7 K. E. Garay, 'The Search for the Meaning of Meaning', *Russell: The Journal of Bertrand Russell Studies*, Winter 1990–1 (Reviews), McMaster University, Ontario, Canada. Reprinted with permission.

8 Russo, *I. A. Richards*, p. 17.

9 John Haffenden, *William Empson, Vol. I: Among the Mandarins*, OUP, Oxford, 2005

10 Dorothy Pilley, Diary, 13 September 1912, RCM.

11 Dr Richard Luckett's introduction to *Selected Letters of I. A. Richards*, p. xv.

12 James Roxburgh (1892–1974) was Richards' 'closest friend at Magdalene' (see Russo, *I. A. Richards*, p. xx). In 1954 Roxburgh was knighted for distinguished service as judge on the Calcutta bench. In an unpublished obituary (1974) Richards wrote that Plato's remark that the only good reason for a person's holding office was to prevent a less capable one from holding it, and Socrates' belief that the Good holds everything together, often reminded him of Roxburgh. – Russo, *I. A. Richards*, p. 692. A. C. Benson, Diary, 28 February, 4 and 15 March 1915, Magdalene College, Cambridge.

13 I.A.R. and D.E.P. in the Rockies, 1926 (Photo by Ray-Bell Films, Minneapolis). Dorothy Pilley, *Climbing Days*, G. Bell & Sons, London, 1935, facing p. 82.

14 A letter from Sir James Roxburgh to Dorothea in the Magdalene archive, dated 15 September 1964, reveals that the photographs of the imp's recovery in *Magdalene College Roofs & Climbs* 'were taken by one Matlock, since deceased'. In his essay 'Magdalene College Cambridge and the First World War', historian Ged Martin recalls a conversation with Roxburgh at Magdalene a few years later, around 1970, within earshot of the famous belfry: 'Some dons regarded the earliest cohort in the reunion cycle, informally known as "1485 to 1923", as hard work, and junior Fellows were brought in to make up a home team. Thus I found myself, on a summer evening, drinking sherry in the College

Garden and talking to Sir James Roxburgh. Upon discovering that he had been a judge in India, I tried a conversational ranging shot and asked if he had ever come across Gandhi. "Come across him?" came the reply. "I fined him one rupee!" This had been part of a Raj strategy to make light of the 1931 civil disobedience campaign.' Cf. *The Times*, 16 February 1974.

Martin's essay is enlightening in many ways but particularly regarding A. C. Benson and the individual stories of the college men who served. Ivor's name appears as a surprise inclusion in a paragraph discussing the *Magdalene College Magazine*'s 'war list': 'The College list was eclectic in its definition of service, for instance including two old members who worked with the YMCA. "Somewhere in Flanders" was a YMCA centre called, with the permission of the Master, "Magdalene". Located in a cellar – everything above ground in the village had been destroyed – "Magdalene" provided free hot cocoa, a warm fire and reading matter. Second Lieutenant Arthur S. Macpherson of the Labour Corps appealed for reading matter – cheap editions of the classics, novels and magazines. Also included in the Magdalene list was I. A. Richards, later one of the College's most notable intellectuals, who suffered from tuberculosis, but qualified thanks to his service in the Inquiry Bureau at a military hospital [in Bristol] – an episode omitted from standard accounts of his life.' Ged Martin, 'Magdalene College Cambridge and the First World War', April 2014, gedmartin.net. Reprinted with permission.

15 Supplement to the *London Gazette*, 22 September 1916. I later discovered from my great uncle, David Richards, that Kenneth was also awarded the MC, indeed the MC with Bar, for his service on the Western Front: 'T./Capt. (A./Maj.) William Kenneth Armstrong Richards, M.C., R.A.M.C., attend. 55th Fd. Amb. For conspicuous gallantry and devotion to duty. He followed up an attack under very heavy fire and organised and carried out the evacuation of the wounded during several days' operations with the greatest courage and skill. (M.C. gazetted 4th June, 1917.)' (Supplement to the *London Gazette*, 2 December 1918.)

'Father told me that the King awarded him the first MC at Buckingham Palace – "May I congratulate you?" he asked – and the Duke of Gloucester the second, which took place in Bratton marketplace, Westbury.' (David Richards, speaking to the author, November 2016). Bars were awarded to the MC in recognition of the performance of further acts of gallantry meriting the award.

16 A liberal reformer, Benson had signed a Cambridge neutrality manifesto in the days before war was declared as well as being an early supporter of suffrage and Votes for Women. See *The Times*, 23 March 1909. Again, I'm grateful to Ged Martin for his research and scholarship: 'The European crisis seemed caught in a curiously slow-motion phase throughout July [1914]. It was not until the beginning of August that the German intention to invade Belgium became apparent, and Britain faced the decision whether to go to war. Two days earlier, Benson had privately deplored the "awful fatality" about the process: "it seems as if we might be plunged in war for simply nothing at all". He signed his name to a manifesto from Cambridge dons, published on 3 August, which expressed "their conviction of the supreme importance of preserving England's neutrality in the existing situation, considering that at the present juncture no vital interest of this country is endangered, such as would justify our participation in a war". This is a startling declaration, all the more so coming from the author of "Land of Hope and Glory", with its imperialistic invocation: 'Wider still and wider / Shall thy bounds be set.' . . . It can be surprising to realise that, within his admittedly narrow world, Benson was a radical reformer, for instance sardonic in his lampooning of the merits of forcing schoolboys to learn Greek. Even so, Benson as pacifist comes as something of a shock . . . [and] it remains remarkable that Magdalene was not swept by the bellicose patriotism that historical caricature might have predicted . . . In most cases, principled pacifism collapsed under the pressure of events. Even before the Cambridge neutrality manifesto appeared in the newspapers, Benson reflected, "we can't avoid war if France is invaded – it would be neither honourable nor prudent". "I'm not a Pacifist any more," he wrote after war was declared on 4 August – receiving the news after an afternoon cycle ride. "I think our intervention now more a police intervention, to preserve and unprovoking nation against gross bullying."' Ged Martin, 'Magdalene College

Cambridge and the First World War', April 2014, gedmartin.net.

17 A. C. Benson, Diary, 13 October 1923, Magdalene College, Cambridge.

18 I. A. Richards, *Selected Works 1919–1938 – Volume 4. Practical Criticism (1929)*, ed. John Constable, Routledge, London, 2001.

19 I.A.R. to D.E.P., 19 November 1923, RCM.

20 Russo, *I. A. Richards*, pp. 65–6.

21 I. A. Richards, *Selected Works 1919–1938*, ed. John Constable, Routledge, 10 vols.

22 Author interview with Dr Richard Luckett, Rye, June 2013.

23 I.A.R. to D.E.P., 20 November 1923, RCM.

24 Richards: *Selected Works, Volume 4. Practical Criticism (1929)*, p. xi.

25 W. R. Neate, *Mountaineering and Its Literature*, Cicerone, Cumbria, 1978, p. 43.

26 Katherine Rundell, 'Diary', *LRB*, vol. 37, no. 8 (23 April 2015).

27 Pilley, *Climbing Days*, p. 79.

28 A. Harry Griffin, *The Coniston Tigers*, Sigma Leisure, Wilmslow, 1999. We'll meet this scene again in the 'Lake District' chapter.

29 Pilley, *Climbing Days*, p. 79.

The Pinnacle Club

1 C. Baker, Snowdonia, London Midland & Scottish Railway, 1933, in Beverley Cole and Richard Durack, *Railway Posters, 1923–1947: From the Collection of the National Railway*, York, England, Laurence King, London, 2000.

2 Pilley, *Climbing Days*, pp. 5–6.

3 Dorothy Pilley Richards, 'The Good Young Days', *Journal of the Fell and Rock Climbing Club*, no. 50, vol. 17 (III), 1956.

4 Ann C. Colley, *Victorians in the Mountains: Sinking the Sublime*, Ashgate, Farnham, 2010, p. 116. See also David Mazel, *Mountaineering Women: Stories by Early Climbers*, Texas A&M University Press, 1994.

5 Pilley, *Climbing Days*, p. 84.

6 'The Opening of the Emily Kelly Hut, 5th November, 1932', *Pinnacle Club Journal* 1932–4.

7 Dorothy Pilley, Diary, 18 May 1934, RCM. Names as listed on 19 May: A. Wilson, N. and E. Wells, E. Feibnoch, K. Fairfield, R. M.

Watson, J. M. Cobham, E. Jennings, B. M. Deed, B. Eden-Smith, R. P. Allaun, M. Taylor, D. and P. Seth Hughes, C. Carter, R. Hale, E. Lowe, M. Barnard, S. Harper, Dr P.-R.

8 Dylan Thomas, 'I Fellowed Sleep', *18 Poems*, Fortune Press, London, 1934.

9 Emily Kelly, 27 November 1920, Pinnacle Club archive.

10 The letters Emily Kelly wrote by hand are dynamic, swirling, free-flowing affairs – aesthetic as well as effusive and humane – see 15 February 1921, Pinnacle Club archive.

11 From Sue Clifford and Angela King (eds), *Local Distinctiveness: Place, Particularity and Identity*, Common Ground, London, 1993, p. 19.

12 Pilley, *Climbing Days*, p. 131.

13 I am indebted to Dr Karen Stockham for her help and research regarding the Pinnacle Club. See Karen Stockham, *Women's Mountaineering Life-Writing 1808–1960*, University of Exeter, 2012.

14 Pilley, *Climbing Days*, pp. 56–7.

The Cairngorms

1 Janet Adam Smith wrote about her climbing adventures in the Highlands and Grampian Alps in her 1946 book *Mountain Holidays*. As with *Climbing Days,* the book features beautiful photographic plates – Smith's shots of Scotland and the Cairngorm range are remarkably vivid and handsome.

2 Pilley, *Climbing Days*, p. 92. See also I.A.R.'s 1927 article 'The Lure of High Mountaineering' in *Complementarities: Uncollected Essays of I. A. Richards*, ed. John Paul Russo, Harvard University Press, 1976, p. 237 (originally published in *Atlantic Monthly*, 1927; a shorter version of the piece was published as 'Mountaineering' the following year in *Cambridge Review*). See Appendix II, p. 348.

3 A fragment from 'Summit of Corrie Etchachan' by Nan Shepherd, *In the Cairngorms*, Moray Press, 1934, repr. Galileo, Cambridge, 2015

4 Nan Shepherd, *The Living Mountain*, Aberdeen University Press, 1977; Canongate, Edinburgh, 2011. Extracts reprinted by permission of Canongate Books Ltd.

5 Richard Brautigan, *Sombrero Fallout: A Japanese Novel*, Simon &

Schuster, New York, 1976; Canongate, Edinburgh, 2012. Copyright © 1976 by Richard Brautigan. Reprinted with the permission of the Estate of Richard Brautigan; all rights reserved.

6 'Death in the snow: why have five climbers been killed on one peak?', *Guardian*, 3 February 2007.

7 Pilley, *Climbing Days*, p. 245. For more on François Bernard Salles see the 'Barcelona and Catalonia' chapter of this book, p. 115.

8 Pilley, *Climbing Days*, p. 245.

9 Dr Seuss, *The Cat in the Hat*, Random House, New York, 1957.

10 *ibid.*, p. 105.

Barcelona and Catalonia

1 Charles Bukowski, 'I am with the Roots of Flowers', *The Roominghouse Madrigals: Early Selected Poems, 1946–1966*, Ecco, New York, 1992.

2 Dorothy Pilley, Diary, 10 July 1919, RCM. 'Despite this pact, Pilley continued to leave off her diary for days at a time throughout her life, probably chafing at the ingrained discipline of diary writing from childhood. However, she never succeeded in rebelling completely against the habit of diary writing, writing a diary each year until her death in 1986. "I am singularly disinclined to write this diary, and make my first entry, with a sense of duty to obey." (3 February 1920).' Stockham, *Women's Mountaineering Life-Writing*, p. 130.

3 Bryher, *The Heart to Artemis – A Writer's Memoirs*, Collins, London, 1963, p. 123.

4 *ibid.*, p. 126.

5 *ibid.*, p. 149.

6 Dorothy Pilley, Diary, 27 September 1913, RCM.

7 Bryher, *The Heart to Artemis*, pp. 149–50.

8 *Virginia Woolf: The Critical Heritage*, ed. Robin Majumdar and Allen McLaurin, Routledge, London and Boston, 1975, p. 58. Reprinted by permission of Taylor and Francis Group.

9 Bryher, *The Heart to Artemis*, p. 166.

10 I am grateful to Karen Stockham for drawing my attention to this discrepancy.

11 Muriel Files' obituary of Dorothy appeared in the *Journal of the*

Fell and Rock Climbing Club, no. 71, vol. 24 (III), 1988.

12 Jan Morris, *Spain*, Faber, London, 2008.

13 William S. Rubin, *Miró in the Collection of The Museum of Modern Art*, The Museum of Modern Art, New York, 1973, p. 21. Reprinted by permission of MoMA.

Switzerland

1 *Pennine Alps Central – Weisshorn – Dent Blanche – Monte Rosa – Matterhorn – Italian Valley Ranges – Valpelline South*, compiled and edited by Robin G. Collomb, Alpine Club Guide Books, Alpine Club, London, 1975.

2 Pilley, 'The Misty Isle of Skye', *Climbing Days*, p. 102.

3 Tom Gauld, *You're All Just Jealous of My Jetpack: Cartoons*, Drawn and Quarterly, Montreal, 2013.

4 Hermann Hesse, *Steppenwolf*, S. Fischer Verlag AG, Berlin, 1927.

5 Dorothea and Ivor write about this further in their article 'The North-East Arête of the Jungfrau and Other Traverses', *Alpine Journal*, 35/227 (November 1923), pp. 161–5.

6 Dorothy Richards, Diary, 28 June 1934, RCM.

7 Alan Harris, G. Bell & Sons, draft letter to Mrs I. A. Richards, 27 March 1929, Reading University.

8 Dorothy Richards to Mr Bickers, G. Bell & Sons, written in 57 Chesterton Road, Cambridge, England, 12 January 1932, Reading University.

9 'The friendship was cordial, intellectual, even-tempered, and close,' wrote John Constable, 'but confidences, if there were any, never found their way to paper.' 'I. A. Richards, T. S. Eliot, and the Poetry of Belief', John Constable, *Essays in Criticism*, 40 (3) (1990), p. 222.

10 T. S. Eliot to Eleanor Hinkley, 8 June 1931, *The Letters of T. S. Eliot Volume 5: 1930–1931*, Faber, London, 2015.

11 Events described in Dorothy Richards' diary, 17 July, 12 August and 20 July (on page for 19 July) 1928, and see D. E. Pilley and I. A. Richards, 'The North Ridge of the Dent Blanche', *Alpine Journal*, 43 (1931). Richards, *Selected Works*, *Volume 4. Practical Criticism* (1929). Note how each event is given equal weight!

12 Richards, *Selected Letters*, p. xiv.

13 Pilley, *Climbing Days*, p. 153.

14 *ibid.*, pp. 148–9.

15 *ibid.*, photograph facing p. 110.

16 *ibid.*, pp. 152–3.

17 *ibid.*, p. 159.

18 A nod to the fact that we were walking on the cusp of the French- and German-speaking areas of Switzerland. '283 AROLLA', Carte national de la Suisse 1:50,000, Office fédérale de topographie, 3084 Wabern, 1977.

19 Pilley, *Climbing Days*, pp. 159–60.

20 Collomb, *Pennine Alps Central . . .*, Alpine Club Guide Book.

21 Pilley, *Climbing Days*, p. 162.

22 Although the huts are mentioned in Tim's postcard home from Arolla on 8 July 1981 – see n. 11.

23 Pilley, *Climbing Days*, p. 243.

24 *ibid.*, p. 162.

25 Although the meeting is mentioned in Tim's postcard home from Arolla on 8 July 1981 – see n. 11.

26 Postcard to Mr and Mrs Christopher Richards, Willsbridge, postmarked Boston, Mass., 20 November 1967.

27 Postcard to George E. A. Richards, Willsbridge, postmarked Boston, Mass., 20 November 1967.

28 Pilley, *Climbing* Days, p. 340.

29 Dougal Haston, *Calculated Risk*, Diadem Books, London, 1979.

30 Interview with W. G. Sebald by Toby Green, 'The Questionable Business of Writing', http://www.amazon.co.uk/gp/feature. html?ie=UTF8&docId=21586.

31 Bonington and Clarke, *Everest – The Unclimbed Ridge*, p. 64.

32 *ibid.*, p. 84.

33 Bonington and Clarke, *Everest – The Unclimbed Ridge*, p. 111.

34 André Georges, *Une vie pour la montagne*, Éditions FAVRE S.A., Lausanne, 2010.

35 I. A. Richards, 'Joseph Georges (1892–1960)', *Alpine Journal*, 1961, p. 381; see Appendix I, p. 333.

36 Pilley, *Climbing Days*, p. 316.

37 Richards, 'Joseph Georges (1892–1960)', *Alpine Journal*, 1961, p. 381; see Appendix I, p. 333.

38 As well as climbing in the mountains around la Giette, Rosula and André have climbed together abroad. Their ascent of Nanga Parbat in Pakistan is detailed in Georges, *Une vie pour la montagne*, p. 156.

39 Georges, *Une vie pour la montagne*, p. 192. Ulvetanna (2,930 metres) – 'the Wolf's Tooth' in Norwegian – is located within the Southern Drygalski Mountains of Queen Maud Land, Antarctica and was first climbed by a Norwegian party in 1994.

40 Dorothy Pilley, Diary, 26 July 1976, RCM.

41 Dorothy Pilley, Diary, 24 July–2 August 1976, RCM.

The Lake District

1 Pilley, *Climbing Days*, p. 58.

2 Dorothy Pilley Richards, 'The Good Young Days'.

3 Pilley, *Climbing Days*, p. 77.

4 Dorothy Pilley Richards, 'Agua', *Journal of the Fell and Rock Climbing Club*, no. 56, vol. 19 (III) (1962), p. 250; see Appendix II, p. 362.

5 Pilley Richards, 'The Good Young Days'.

6 Pilley, *Climbing Days*, p. 79.

7 Janet Adam Smith, 'Dorothea Richards (1894–1986)', *Alpine Journal*, 1987; see Appendix I, p. 343.

8 Pilley Richards, 'The Good Young Days'.

9 'The Lake District: South-Western area', Ordnance Survey Explorer Map OL6 – Scale 1:25 000, 2011.

10 Pilley, *Climbing Days*, p. 78.

11 Pilley Richards, 'The Good Young Days'.

12 Pilley, *Climbing Days*, p. 59.

13 Pilley Richards, 'The Good Young Days'.

14 E. E. Cummings, 'when faces called flowers float out of the ground', 1950; *e.e. cummings selected poems 1923–1958*, Penguin/Faber, 1960. Copyright 1950, © 1978, 1991 by the Trustees for the E. E. Cummings Trust. Copyright © 1979 by George James Firmage, from *Complete Poems: 1904–1962* by E. E. Cumming, edited by George J. Firmage. Used by permission of Liveright Publishing Corporation.

The Dent Blanche

1 Jack Underwood, 'Sometimes your sadness is a yacht', *Happiness*, Faber, London, 2015.
2 Postcard to George E. A. Richards, Willsbridge, postmarked Boston, Mass., 20 November 1967.

Epilogue

1 Pilley Richards, 'The Good Young Days'.
2 Richards, 'The Lure of High Mountaineering'; see Appendix II, p. 348.

Appendices

1 I. A. Richards, 'Lighting Fires in Snow', *Goodbye Earth and Other Poems*, Harcourt Brace, New York, 1958; *New and Selected Poems*, Carcanet, Manchester, 1978.

Index

Numbers in *italics* refer to pages with illustrations.